"This excellent collection of essays inspires sustainable digital humanities services in libraries, archives, and museums. Administrators will be convinced of the value of incorporating digital humanities into the core mission of academic libraries."

Corrie Marsh
Scholarly Communications and Collection Development Librarian
Old Dominion University

"Contextualizing with concrete examples and current debate, White and Gilbert's collection of essays surveys and analyzes the role of libraries in digital humanities research. Comprehensive and engaging, these essays present arguments and case studies that are sure to enliven the discussion of the forces that shape and constrain the use of digital collections. As the authors explore the myriad ways in which libraries absolutely must work with digital humanities, they scrupulously confront some of the problems associated with such endeavors. These essays show that in both physical and virtual space, libraries need to be full and essential partners in research in these new fields of inquiry. This original and compelling assessment is essential for those interested in libraries and in digital humanities."

Orville Vernon Burton
Founding Director of the Institute for Computing in Humanities, Arts, and Social Science (ICHASS) at the University of Illinois (emeritus), Associate Director for Social Sciences and Humanities at the National Center for Supercomputing (NCSA) at the University of Illinois (emeritus), and Director of the Clemson University CyberInstitute

Laying the Foundation: Digital Humanities in Academic Libraries is the approachable collection of digital humanities writings we've been waiting for. All types of librarians interacting with the humanities will find this book a practical reference and a step toward the future. Laying the Foundation further introduces digital humanities as a function of all libraries—for the good of our collective future. The experiences and case studies contributed to this book will no doubt become the building blocks of programs in public and academic libraries.

Emma Molls
Scholarly Communication and Social Sciences & Humanities Librarian
Iowa State University Library

Laying the Foundation

Digital Humanities in Academic Libraries

Laying the Foundation

Digital Humanities in Academic Libraries

Edited by John W. White and Heather Gilbert

Charleston Insights in
Library, Archival, and Information Sciences

Purdue University Press
West Lafayette, Indiana

Cataloging-in-Publication data on file at the Library of Congress.

Library of Congress Cataloging-in-Publication Data

Names: White, John W., 1974- editor. | Gilbert, Heather, 1976- editor.
Title: Laying the foundation : digital humanities in academic libraries /
    edited by John W. White and Heather Gilbert.
Description: West Lafayette, Indiana : Purdue University Press, [2016] |
    Series: Charleston insights in library, archival, and information sciences
    | Includes bibliographical references.
Identifiers: LCCN 2015041528| ISBN 9781557537393 (pbk. : alk. paper) | ISBN
    9781612494494 (epub) | ISBN 9781612494487 (epdf) | ISBN 9781557537515
    (open access epdf)
Subjects: LCSH: Academic libraries--Relations with faculty and
    curriculum--United States. | Humanities libraries--United States. |
    Humanities--Digital libraries. | Humanities--Research--Data processing. |
    Humanities--Electronic information resources. | Humanities--Study and
    teaching (Higher)--United States.
Classification: LCC Z675.U5 L36 2016 | DDC 027.70973--dc23 LC record
available at http://lccn.loc.gov/2015041528

Contents

Preface

Laying the Foundation[1]

This volume was inspired by a conference held at the College of Charleston in June 2014. Many of the participants in that conference, "Data Driven: Digital Humanities in the Library," are also contributors to this book; however, it is notable that the book is not the published proceedings of the conference. The essays compiled here are not simply expanded and refined versions of some of the conference presentations. Instead, they are largely a reflection of the informal conversations and serendipitous learning that truly made "Data Driven" a success. Many of the contributors were also presenters at the conference. Some of the volume's authors, such as Stewart Varner, attended the conference, but did not make a formal presentation. Others, such as Sarah Melton, were not in attendance, but were cited as influential in creating digital humanities (DH) scholarship in the library. Rather than attempting to provide little more than a transcript of the conference itself, *Laying the Foundation: Digital Humanities in Academic Libraries* is an expanded discussion of the core themes that emerged *from* the conference—namely, that the ways in which humanists organize and interact with their data is largely dependent on how that data is collected, described, and made available in academic libraries, archives, and museums.

DH practitioners utilize digital tools and innovative pedagogy to more deeply examine cultural, architectural, and historical records. A central theme of this volume is that archives, museums, and libraries provide much of the physical and virtual space where the digital humanities "happen." Therefore, it follows that the institutions that house the artifacts, records, and digital assets that make many DH research projects possible should play a vital role in how that research is created and curated. It is with this in mind that we decided to change the title of the volume to reflect the central theme that emerged from the conference—that, at many institutions, it is libraries and librarians that maintain DH infrastructures and make learning through the digital humanities possible. Even when libraries are not the campus "home" for DH centers, it is clear that their collecting, description, and access policies have a dramatic impact on digital humanists. It is also clear, as demonstrated by several contributions to this book, that librarians can play a significant role in undergraduate instruction in the digital humanities.

Laying the Foundation is not an attempt to define the nebulous boundaries of what does and does not constitute digital humanities. Although its authors address this debate, the volume is instead intended as a conversation starter among rank-and-file librarians about how and why librarians, archivists, and museum professionals should engage with digital humanists as full partners in both research and teaching. The authors of this volume do address the differences between DH and "digital history," as well as many of the other epistemological debates raging at academic conferences, on blogs and other social media, and in the pages of refereed journals dedicated to DH scholarship. However, our primary objective is to encourage librarians to recognize, as Trevor Muñoz so eloquently argues in Chapter 1, that DH scholarship is deeply rooted in and wholly compatible with library and archival science. Collectively, its authors argue that librarians are critical partners in DH instruction and inquiry and that libraries are essential for publishing, preserving, and making accessible digital scholarship.

Laying the Foundation is organized into four sections. The first attempts to address the relationship between DH scholarship and "the library." Muñoz contends that libraries and library administrators should incorporate digital humanities "into the core conceptual equipment and the work practices of librarians." He argues that there are tangible benefits to encouraging academic inquiry among librarians—that librarians should look beyond academic work as an opportunity to provide a service and instead be full and equal partners in all that DH has to offer. Likewise, James Baker determines that the central function of libraries (to collect, catalog, and preserve knowledge) is, for both good and bad, the cornerstone of the digital humanities. He notes that the collection and description of historiography provides source material for new methods of inquiry. Conversely, he also concludes that library practices are also often the cause of frustrating constraints for DH scholars.

The second section examines the practice of DH scholarship in the library. Katherine Rawson's contribution, for example, examines how generations of librarians and their communities have played a valuable role in preserving and making accessible a treasure trove of materials related to the study of foodways in New York. Mary Battle, Tyler Mobley, and Heather Gilbert provide a blueprint for digital libraries seeking to address the issue of silences in their collections through the careful curation of professional digital exhibits that provide a broader context for explaining underrepresented histories in archival collections. Similarly, Seth Kotch explains how the lessons learned through a generation of DH scholarship have helped shape and make more accessible the oral history collection for the Long Women's Movement at the University of North Carolina.

The third section combines the experiences of academic librarians in the development of DH centers at Emory University, the University of Kansas, and the University of Colorado Boulder. The essays by Sarah Melton and by Brian Rosenblum and Arienne Dwyer contend that library administrators can reallocate resources within existing organizations to answer campus demand for digital scholarship/humanities resources. The chapter authored by Rosenblum and Dwyer is especially adept at describing many of the unexpected pitfalls of launching a large DH center in a time of more competition for campus resources. Thea Lindquist, Holley Long, and Alexander Watkins argue that reconstructing existing DH programs within the university can generate broader and more efficient support for digital humanities scholarship in the library.

The final section is focused on pedagogy and instruction. We hope that, for many librarians, this section provides some guidance for integrating DH into library instruction. Benjamin Fraser and Jolanda-Pieta van Arnhem and also Harriet Green describe how they have fit DH instruction into existing bibliographic instruction models. Stewart Varner contends that such a reallocation of resources within the library is not so much a change of direction or consolidation, but part of the larger evolution of "digital pedagogy" in a direction that favors librarians who are well suited to engage students and faculty in discussions focused in the areas of "digital mapping, text analysis, multimedia websites/online exhibits, and Wikipedia editing."

In the introduction to a collection of essays dedicated to DH in the *Journal of Library Administration* in January 2013, Barbara Rockenbach contended that "[l]ibraries are well positioned to support" DH because "[l]ibraries have always been places of interdisciplinary activity; places of neutrality not associated with any particular academic department."[2] As Rockenbach suggests, academic libraries are nexuses of research and technology—resources made available to students and faculty regardless of discipline or departmental affiliation. However, adding digital humanities to the core mission of the academic library requires a clear understanding of the resources and skills required. This knowledge is especially important to library administrators who routinely struggle with resource allocation in times of high demand and shrinking budgets. In our conversations with our counterparts at the "Data Driven" conference and in the pages of *Laying the Foundation*, we were pleased to find a community of librarian scholars who shared our interests and values and addressed these resource requirements head on in their own institutions. We hope that the arguments and case studies presented in the pages that follow will not only enliven the discussion of DH in the library and contribute to a burgeoning field of inquiry, but also assist librarians in their quest to lay a foundation for digital humanities research and pedagogy in their own institutions.

John W. White, PhD

June 2015

NOTES

1   The editors would like to thank Amanda Noll, project coordinator of the Lowcountry Digital History Initiative. This volume would not have come together without her tireless assistance.

2   Barbara Rockenbach, "Introduction," *Journal of Library Administration* 53 (January 2013): 3.

Part 1

WHY DIGITAL HUMANITIES IN THE LIBRARY?

1 | Recovering a Humanist Librarianship through Digital Humanities

Trevor Muñoz

INTRODUCTION

The many discussions—at conferences, on blogs, and in the professional literature—about how librarians can best engage with the digital humanities (DH) reveal a notable absence. The position of digital humanities work in many academic research libraries—as a service point for specialized consulting or training—suggests that DH is widely seen as external to the core functions of research libraries. What this suggests, in the context of librarianship's historical development as a profession, is that the possibilities of digital humanities research in the library have been shaped by the absence of a strong tradition of humanist library theory and practice. Incorporating digital humanities into the conceptual equipment and the work practices of more librarians could help to develop a tradition of humanist librarianship suited to our present technological age.

THE VALUE OF DIGITAL HUMANITIES BEYOND THE TACTICAL

Because of librarianship's history, there is particular risk in treating the digital humanities as "a tactical term."[1] Much of the current debate over the place of digital humanities within librarianship is unsatisfying precisely to the extent that it is occupied with "the reality of circumstances in which ['the digital humanities'] is unabashedly deployed to get things done— 'things' that might include getting a faculty line or funding a staff position, . . . revamping a lab, or launching a center."[2] If, in an academic library context, support for "the digital humanities" can generate support for a new space or a new professional position, why not package the digital humanities with another new activity and refer to the whole as "digital scholarship" and multiply the potential return by appealing to other, wealthier precincts of a campus at the same time? From a tactical, managerial perspective—indeed, why not? This chapter will suggest that it may be possible for librarianship to win a great deal of tactical success but lose out on an intellectual transformation vital to the profession's longevity and impact.

READING "RESEARCH"

Behind and beneath many of the current debates about how to understand and incorporate digital humanities are larger and more long-standing questions about the place of "research" in librarianship. Reflecting, from the perspective of a library administrator, on some of the institutional challenges that often block librarians from doing digital humanities, Mike Furlough concludes: "Is research the library's core business?"[3] This question is only one instance of a concern that repeatedly breaks into the open at the fault line between the tactical and the intellectual considerations of digital humanities. As Furlough again asks: "Research . . . sure, it's a core activity of the faculty, but is it a core business function of the University?" Despite its facetiousness, this response highlights the doubled nature of these and similar objections to the place of research, and by extension the digital humanities, in librarianship. First, there is an "othering" of research as a domain belonging to "the faculty" (regardless of the fact that librarians at many institutions hold some kind of faculty status). Second, the common patterns of professional discourse seem to divide research into two kinds: topics related to the efficient business operations of libraries as institutional structures, and everything else.[4] The former is strongly preferred so that, even when research is admitted as part of librarianship, it seems like an extension of management.

Lest the foregoing critique be mistakenly assumed to apply to one or a few individuals, a close reading of a report/editorial titled "Top Trends in Academic Libraries," authored by no less a professional/institutionalized voice than the Association of College and Research Libraries (ACRL) Research Planning and Review Committee, exhibits many of the same features. This report, published in the June 2014 issue of *College and Research Libraries News*, functions as a kind of prioritized environmental

scan produced by a major professional organization and is meant, one sus-
pects, as less a communication of new findings than as a confirmation—a
mutual signaling that there is sufficient national momentum to consider
this particular evolving area a good bet for some kind of engagement in a
library's local environment. The statement on digital humanities reads, in
its entirety:

> Academic libraries can play a key role in supporting humanities
> faculty in their research by creating partnerships and collabo-
> rations and helping to connect with other campus units needed
> to implement and carry out digital humanities research.[5]

Almost everything about this summary seems, if not wrong as a description
of a certain common attitude, then at least equally revealing of assumptions
about librarianship that transcend the particular issue of digital humanities.

From the first phrase—"Academic libraries can play a key role . . ."
—there are signs of trouble. The substitution of an institution, "academic
libraries," for any specific actors (i.e., the librarians who make an institution what it is) signals that the claims to follow are directed toward the
marketing and perpetuation of a particular organizational structure rather
than anything else.[6] The next phrase identifies a target market segment
("humanities faculty") for this pitch. The assertion that "academic libraries can play a key role in supporting *humanities faculty* in their research"
(emphasis added) again locates "research" somewhere else on campus and
not also within libraries conducted and directed by librarians. The fact
that the members of the ACRL committee who selected digital humanities
meant to highlight opportunities for collaboration but handle the subject
in a way that undermines its possibilities suggests an internal dissonance
worth noting. If digital humanities research belongs to the faculty, what is
the basis for "deeper" collaboration that is not merely instrumental? Noting
that roles for librarians in digital humanities work are often shaped toward
things that librarians are perceived to be good at doing, like project management, Roxanne Shirazi asks: "What does [it] mean for collaborative scholarship between librarians and faculty when project management and other
'major service activit[ies]' [are] so clearly secondary to 'actual research'?"[7]
In the passage by the ACRL committee quoted above, the way in which the
specific language on collaboration is constructed leaves ambiguous whether

librarians are counted in these collaborations and connections or whether librarians are merely facilitating, moving jigsaw pieces around to connect other unrelated parties in a kind of a matchmaking service that leaves the library-as-institution safely funded but ultimately uncommitted.

The language of the last section of the ACRL committee's statement on digital humanities has industrial overtones: libraries "help to connect with other campus *units* needed to *implement* and *carry out* digital humanities research" (emphasis added). This description echoes one of the more stinging caricatures of digital humanities, from Alan Liu's essay "Where Is Cultural Criticism in the Digital Humanities":

> It is as if, when the order comes down from the funding agencies, university administrations, and other bodies mediating today's dominant socioeconomic and political beliefs, digital humanists just concentrate on pushing the "execute" button on projects that amass the most data for the greatest number, process that data most efficiently and flexibly (flexible efficiency being the hallmark of postindustrialism), and manage the whole through ever "smarter" standards, protocols, schema, templates, and databases uplifting Frederick Winslow Taylor's original scientific industrialism into ultraflexible postindustrial content management systems camouflaged as digital editions, libraries, and archives—all without pausing to reflect on the relation of the whole digital juggernaut to the new world order.[8]

Certainly, there are things that need to be implemented and carried out to bring research to fruition. Data needs to be processed, standards do need to be updated and upheld, and faculty need to be supported. Yet, to frame libraries' engagement with the possibilities of digital humanities in ways that draw unreflectively from this Taylorist tradition is to risk falling into the caricature that Liu critiques and to miss the real, transformative value that digital humanities work can offer.

UNCOVERING HISTORIES OF THE LIBRARIAN ROLE

Is it possible to find historical origins for some of these assumptions that seem to shape and condition the possibilities for digital humanities librarianship in unfortunate ways?

Discourses around the issue of "research" lead back to and through a particular set of historical contingencies (in the U.S. context) that have created this current "librarianship" that seems sufficiently incommensurable with the modern humanities to potentially blunt the transformative possibilities of a digital humanities. Library historian Wayne Wiegand traces some of these contingencies back to the "unique professional configuration that librarianship assumed in the last quarter of the nineteenth century."[9] By professional "configuration," Wiegand means the structure of claims librarianship made for unique expertise and authority "in the fast-growing world of new professions."[10] He argues that the socioeconomic class and educational background of most late-nineteenth-century librarians and library administrators was such that these groups shared relatively homogenous ideas about a cultural canon and the relationship between literacy and a certain form of social order.[11] Thus, according to Wiegand, "[T]he library science that emerged . . . generally embraced two practical concerns: the 'science' of administering an institutional bureaucracy and an expertise unique to the institution being administered."[12] Casting this in more general terms, Christine Pawley observed that library and information studies have chiefly operated within discourses of "pluralism" and "managerialism."[13]

The absence of a humanist tradition of library theory and practice cannot be directly connected to the imprint of information-work-as-industrial-labor that Wiegand and Pawley describe. In the late 1920s, a group of researchers and library leaders, which became quite influential due to the crucial aid and funding of the Carnegie Corporation, made a concerted effort to enlarge the definition of what could be meant by librarianship using the ascendant episteme of their day: "science."[14]

The locus for the group's efforts was the newly created Graduate Library School (GLS) at the University of Chicago. Where earlier library schools were largely, even explicitly, vocational by the 1920s, as Harris recounts, "This practical . . . , intuitive, and experiential approach to education began to draw some fire."[15] The GLS was one response to this situation—it represented the culmination of several years of professional debate as well as a stream of funding from the Carnegie Corporation. In the first issue of *The Library Quarterly* (*LQ*), the new professional journal born of the same reform initiatives, Douglas Waples, the acting dean as well as a faculty member in the school, noted mildly that, because much of the editorial work of producing the *LQ* was to be done by GLS staff, "readers of the journal should accordingly have some interest in the School's policies and activities which the journal must in some measure reflect."[16] Waples's article set off a highly visible round of the contentious debate over what the GLS project represented for librarianship. It is worth emphasizing that contemporaries on both sides recognized that plans for the new school represented a site at which the meaning of "librarianship" was being (re)constructed—largely through a debate about the character of "research."

The heart of the contention was Waples's discussion, halfway through his report on "policies and activities" in *LQ*, of "the sort of library science to which research during the next years should contribute." What is crucial to note is that "science" in this context had a historically specific valence. In outlining the program of the GLS, Waples marks his allegiance to a version of "science" created and popularized by the philosopher John Dewey. Dewey gained enormous influence as a popularizer of "science" by promoting a version of the scientific method as a flexible and generalizable approach to problem solving across domains.[17] Dewey's approach differed from an earlier wave of science popularizers in the late nineteenth century who promulgated descriptions of science as an offshoot of rigorous logic and empiricism.[18] Dewey's interest in science was as a model of knowledge construction: "Science signifies . . . the existence of systematic methods of inquiry, which when they are brought to bear on a range of facts, enable us to understand them better and control them more intelligently."[19] Thus, in his article on "What Is a Library Science?," Waples declares that Dewey's book *The Sources of a Science of Education*:

> gives organization and clear perspective to the pros and cons of scientific method as applied to a social enterprise like librarianship. No writing has appeared to date which in short space so helpfully presents a philosophy of research in the social studies.[20]

Waples's chief interlocutor in the pages of *LQ*, C. Seymour Thompson, begins his first reply by noting archly that "It seems we have become pretty well agreed that we have not now a library science, but we are apparently determined that we will have one."[21] Yet Thompson largely accepts Dewey's "science" as the definitional ground upon which the debate over a "library science" will be conducted.

To understand the prospects of digital humanities ideas and approaches in librarianship, the more interesting elements of the debates over "library science" and the GLS are the responses of critics, especially those critics arguing from a humanist tradition. Thompson's critique of Waples and the GLS program is not the defense of a status quo, but is instead an alternate proposal for reform. He accepts the findings (if not the recommendations) of reports, such as that prepared by C. C. Williamson, which described shortcomings in the professional background and training of librarians—the same reports that provided the impetus for the founding of the GLS. "We ourselves have too generally undervalued educational qualifications,"[22] Thompson writes. Thompson rejects the earlier, narrowly vocational managerial vision of librarianship: "In developing a body of administrative methods adequate to meet the needs of the new ideals of service, for a long period we placed an exaggerated emphasis on technique and routine, from which we have not yet entirely recovered."[23] He also critiques the new vision of librarianship as Dewey-ian social research: "Regardless of what may have been accomplished by the new research in other fields . . . our problems, our circumstances, and particularly, our aims and purposes differ so greatly from those of business that the analogy here is not trustworthy."[24] Thompson centers his alternative proposal on a link between libraries and a high-culture Victorian humanism: "In trying to prove that we were of actual dollars and cents value, we lost much of the older admiration for the cultural value of the library."[25] Instead he advocates for "a revival of the *bibliothecal spirit*"[26] (original emphasis) in the training and practices of librarianship. The classical Greek and Latin origins of "bibliothecal," an adjective meaning "belonging to a library" (OED), only emphasize the alignment between Thompson's "good books" and a Western cultural canon—something like Matthew Arnold's "the best that has been thought and said."[27]

John V. Richardson, in his history of the GLS, notes that even though the Carnegie Corporation was the force behind the school, there were some in the corporation who were skeptical of its direction. These included Robert M. Lester, a "policy adviser" who reviewed some of the reports on the school's direction and goals prepared by Waples. Lester worried that the program of research as outlined would "result in dehumanizing the librarian as being a mathematically minded pseudo-educator in place of a man of books to aid those in research of reading material—with and without a purpose."[28]

In the pages of *LQ*, Thompson embraced librarianship as an educational enterprise but in terms that aligned education with an identifiable humanist tradition and against Dewey and Waples. "If librarianship is primarily an educational profession, its fundamental and dominating purpose must be educational; if its principal purpose is educational, the most important qualification for a librarian must be—education."[29] Making reference to a presidential address given by Charles Coffin Jewett, librarian and assistant secretary of the Smithsonian Institution, at the 1853 conventions of librarians that was one of the precursors to the founding of the American Library Association, Thompson goes on to aver that "the most important qualification for librarianship, the qualification that must underlie all others, is 'a knowledge of good books,' with the high standards of education which that presupposes." Lester and Thompson seem to share a concept of "education" that opposes the "science" and "research" concepts of Waples and Dewey.

Lester's "pseudo-educator" who emphasizes "derival and application of formulae" is a figure of the Dewey-ian man. In this Lester seems to share Thompson's ideal of the educator as someone trained in the appreciation of a cultural canon—the "knowledge of good books" to which Jewett referred a half-century earlier. Here then at the beginning of the 1930s are representatives of a recognizable humanist tradition alert to the emergence of a competing episteme and actively engaging with it in debates over the nature of librarianship. What is significant about these debates is that they mark a phasing out of a humanist approach to library theory and practice (such as it was). Since the early twentieth century, the prevailing discourse of librarianship has mixed managerialism and social research approaches largely without admixture of methodological traditions from the humanities.

A NEW HUMANIST LIBRARIANSHIP?

In 2002, Jerome McGann, director of the *Rossetti Archive*, one of the most significant early digital projects to appear on the World Wide Web, used a prominent editorial in *The Chronicle of Higher Education* to urge his fellow literary scholars to engage with what was then called *humanities computing* and is now better known as *digital humanities*.[30] McGann forecast that "in the next 50 years, the entirety of our inherited archive of cultural works will have to be re-edited within a network of digital storage, access, and dissemination"[31] and he observed, with some apparent misgivings, that his humanist colleagues were largely being preceded in this project by librarians. By the date of McGann's editorial, librarians already had a significant history of using computing in their work in a variety of ways—for automation of tasks related to inventory, cataloging, information search and retrieval, and more.[32] Moreover, there was a body of professional library literature related to the creation and operation of digital libraries and a membership organization for libraries invested in such work (the nascent Digital Library Federation).[33] What then was the source of McGann's concern? He explained: "Many, perhaps most, of those people are smart, hardworking, and literate. Their digital skills and scholarship are often outstanding. Few, however, have a strong grasp of the theory of texts."[34] From McGann's perspective, what was missing from the digital work of librarians was a conversance with, if not a mastery of, a body of specialized knowledge—concepts, theory, method—developed in humanities disciplines about the preservation and transmission of recorded culture. "It has been decades since library schools in this country required courses in the history of the book," McGann observed, but, at the same time, English departments have developed their "own ignorance of the history of language or the sociology of texts." McGann attributes this to academic fashion but, at least in librarianship, the roots go deeper—to the occlusion of a larger conceptual space for humanism in the field.

This is a long way from questions that might seem timelier in considering how librarians can engage the digital humanities. However, the supposedly timely questions—like "Should every library have a digital humanities center?"—no matter the seeming exigency of acting decisively in some tactical moment of opportunity—are, especially now, a waste of our collective time. Instead, as Shannon Mattern has argued, "We need to ensure that we have a strong epistemological framework—a narrative that explains how the library promotes learning and stewards knowledge—so that everything hangs together, so there's some institutional coherence."[35]

The goal of this chapter has been to attempt to justify digital humanities research as core to the theory and practice of librarianship in its own intellectual terms rather than as a useful lever in some temporary tactical maneuver. Digital humanities in the library can be more than a service opportunity; it can be more than an occasion to renegotiate professional status and prerogatives: digital humanities in the library can and should be a source of ideas.

NOTES

1   Matthew G. Kirschenbaum, "Digital Humanities As/Is a Tactical Term," in *Debates in the Digital Humanities*, ed. Matthew K. Gold (Minneapolis: University of Minnesota Press, 2013), 415–28; http://dhdebates.gc.cuny.edu/debates/text/48.

2   Ibid., 415.

3   Michael J. Furlough, "Some Institutional Challenges to Supporting DH in the Library," *Mike Furlough* (blog), August 15, 2012, www.mikefurlough.net/?p=51.

4   See, for example, Michael K. Buckland, "Five Grand Challenges for Library Research," *Library Trends* 51, No. 4 (Spring 2003): 675–86.

5   ACRL Research Planning and Review Committee, "Top Trends in Academic Libraries: A Review of the Trends and Issues Affecting Academic Libraries in Higher Education," *College and Research Libraries News* 75, No. 6 (June 1, 2014): 294–302.

6   In direct contrast to this is the concept of "New Librarianship" of which R. David Lankes states that "the mission of librarians is to improve society through facilitating knowledge creation in their communities." R. David Lankes, *The Atlas of New Librarianship* (Cambridge, MA: MIT Press, 2011).

7   Roxanne Shirazi, "Reproducing the Academy: Librarians and the Question of Service in the Digital Humanities" (presentation at American Library Association Conference, Las Vegas, NV, 2014), http://roxanneshirazi.com/2014/07/15/reproducing-the-academy-librarians-and-the-question-of-service-in-the-digital-humanities.

8   Alan Liu, "Where Is Cultural Criticism in the Digital Humanities?," in *Debates in the Digital Humanities*, ed. Matthew K. Gold (Minneapolis: University of Minnesota Press, 2013), http://dhdebates.gc.cuny.edu/debates/text/20.

9   Wayne A. Wiegand, "The Development of Librarianship in the United States," *Libraries & Culture* 24, No. 1 (January 1, 1989): 99–109. See also Wayne A. Wiegand, "Tunnel Vision and Blind Spots: What the Past Tells Us About the Present; Reflections on the Twentieth-Century History of American Librarianship," *The Library Quarterly: Information, Community, Policy* 69, No. 1 (January 1, 1999): 1–32.

10 Wiegand, "The Development of Librarianship in the United States," 102.

11 Ibid., 100–102. See also Thomas Augst, "Faith in Reading: Public Libraries, Liberalism, and the Civil Religion," in *Institutions of Reading: The Social Life of Libraries in the United States*, ed. Thomas Augst and Kenneth E. Carpenter

(Amherst, MA: University of Massachusetts Press, 2007), and Michael H. Harris, "The Role of the Public Library in American Life: A Speculative Essay," in *Occasional Papers*, No. 117 (Urbana-Champaign: University of Illinois, Graduate School of Library Science, 1975).

12 Wiegand, "The Development of Librarianship in the United States," 103.

13 Christine Pawley, "Hegemony's Handmaid? The Library and Information Studies Curriculum from a Class Perspective," *The Library Quarterly: Information, Community, Policy* 68, No. 2 (April 1, 1998): 123–44.

14 Michael H. Harris, "The Dialectic of Defeat: Antimonies in Research in Library and Information Science," *Library Trends* 34, No. 3 (Winter 1986): 515–31. Also Pawley, "Hegemony's Handmaid?," 135–36.

15 Harris, "The Dialectic of Defeat," 516.

16 Douglas Waples, "The Graduate Library School at Chicago," *The Library Quarterly: Information, Community, Policy* 1, No. 1 (January 1, 1931): 26–36.

17 J. L. Rudolph, "Epistemology for the Masses: The Origins of 'The Scientific Method' in American Schools," *History of Education Quarterly* 45, No. 3 (2005): 341–76.

18 Ibid., 344–47.

19 John Dewey, *The Sources of a Science of Education* (New York: H. Liveright, 1929).

20 Waples, "The Graduate Library School at Chicago," 30.

21 C. Seymour Thompson, "Do We Want a Library Science?," *Library Journal* 56, No. 13 (July 1931): 581–87.

22 Ibid., 582.

23 Ibid.

24 Ibid., 583.

25 Ibid,. 582.

26 Ibid., 583.

27 Matthew Arnold and Stefan Collini, *Culture and Anarchy and Other Writings* (Cambridge; New York: Cambridge University Press, 1993).

28 John V. Richardson, *The Spirit of Inquiry: The Graduate Library School at Chicago, 1921–51* (Chicago: American Library Association, 1982): 90.

29 Thompson, "Do We Want a Library Science?," 582.

30 Jerome J. McGann, "Literary Scholarship in the Digital Future," *Chronicle of Higher Education* 49, No. 16 (December 13, 2002): B7.

31 Ibid.

32   W. Boyd Rayward, "A History of Computer Applications in Libraries: Prolegomena," *IEEE Annals of the History of Computing, 24(2)* (2002): 4–15.

33   For one example of the literature on this topic, see Ross Atkinson, "Library Functions, Scholarly Communication, and the Foundation of the Digital Library: Laying Claim to the Control Zone," *The Library Quarterly: Information, Community, Policy* 66, No. 3 (July 1, 1996): 239–65.

34   McGann, "Literary Scholarship in the Digital Future."

35   Shannon Mattern, "Library as Infrastructure," *Places Journal* (June 2014), https://placesjournal.org/article/library-as-infrastructure.

2 | A History of History through the Lens of Our Digital Present, the Traditions That Shape and Constrain Data-Driven Historical Research, and What Librarians Can Do About It[1]

James Baker

INTRODUCTION

Historians have a long and often fraught relationship with numbers. None other than the great French Annalist historian Fernand Braudel acknowledged in 1967 that his methods—temporal and spatial extrapolation of demographic data that enabled him to estimate undocumented population sizes, to grapple with history in the *longue durée*—were controversial. "Historians accustomed to accept only things proved by irrefutable documentation," he wrote, "quite justifiably find these uncertain methods disturbing. Statisticians share neither their misgivings nor their timidity."[2] For although Braudel's historian peers were adept at telling stories across broad sweeps of history, not all were comfortable with statistical representations of past phenomena that seemed divorced from primary sources, that seemed incompatible with the narratives of great men and their institutions whose histories remained in vogue.

Braudel was no prophet, and yet his observations do extrapolate beyond his own temporal surroundings, his very own *histoire événementielle*. Historians today have the opportunity to use long runs of messy textual data, reconstructed models of places and spaces, and tools repurposed from computational and engineering environments to explore past phenomena. For example, by using a process called optical character recognition (OCR), heritage institutions and commercial publishers alike have made millions of pages and billions of words searchable in ways hitherto impossible and unthinkable. This has been an extraordinary boon for scholars. And yet the files created during this process, typically in Extensible Markup

Language (XML) and archival image formats, are never facsimiles of the original source material. Rather their verisimilitude to the traces of the past they seek to capture—the text on a page, the form of that page—can vary wildly depending on a variety of sociotechnological factors. So for all that we librarians do to promote their use and their potential to make a radical intervention in the narratives humanists tell, historians might well find disturbing—and with some justification—the use of these files at scale as a means of exploring past phenomena, just as—by Braudel's reckoning—historians did five decades ago with respect to statistical analysis.

To these concerns we shall return, for simultaneously and largely unperturbed an efflorescence of digital history has taken place. A decade of pioneering work by Tim Hitchcock and Bob Shoemaker on *Old Bailey Online*, *London Lives*, *Connected Histories*, and *Locating London's Past* has brought structured and unstructured humanities data to new audiences, and new audiences to data-driven and computational approaches to historical problems.[3] In turn, this has driven unprecedented and unexpected use of the accounts of trials at the Old Bailey criminal court, source material hitherto appreciated primarily by a small group of social historians working on early-modern crime and punishment in the London and its environs. In areas where data is harder to capture or is less voluminous, historians have undertaken their own data generative work. Here the *Dirty Books* project stands out—research that used a densitometer to study traces of human interaction with the bottom right-hand corners of medieval prayer books and by doing so approach an understanding of the use of those prayer books.[4] People, things, and experiences are also at the heart of the *Virtual Paul's Cross Project*.[5] Here modeling of sound and space re-creates a lost past experience—the experience of hearing an early modern sermon at St. Paul's Cross, an outdoor space beside medieval St. Paul's Cathedral that was lost during the Great Fire of London in 1666. The model has empowered historians to infer fresh insights about how sermons would have been delivered in the unamplified and noisy environment: the imposing aural impact on the model of the bell at St. Paul's that tolled at fifteen-minute intervals suggests that preachers such as John Donne timed their sermons around the bell, perhaps reaching climatic moments just as the bell was set to chime. Historians of the contemporary world, by contrast, have no shortage of data, and those historians whose research has addressed periods after 1996, after the public deployment of the World Wide Web, are confronted with vast amounts of web data that are almost too large, too complex, and too unstructured to handle. And yet historians have persevered. Ian Milligan has demonstrated how blending traditional elements of the historian's toolkit—sampling, source analysis, close reading—with computational clustering and networking of data can bring the World Wide Web within the purview of historical research.[6] This work is imperative to the future of historical research (discussed later).

Complementing all this digital history has been no lack of theory. Bob Nicholson has called for wider acceptance of methods that blend close and distance reading. "Faced with this mountain of print," Nicholson writes, "we have two choices: to continue subjecting tiny fragments of Victorian culture to close reading, or to supplement this approach by exploring a much larger proportion of the archive through 'distant reading.'"[7] Of course, millions of digitized pages scratch only the surface of our physical archives, so historians have been at the forefront of stressing the cultural and political biases of mass digitization[8] and the need to construct rigorous models for sampling digital collections that shift bias away from the digitization process and back to the bias in the chosen category of source material.[9] For all the utopian rhetoric around the democratization of historical research in a digital age, research today remains as littered with barriers as in the predigital age, with novel hierarchies often causing research to be bounded by what is permissible rather than by what is possible.[10] And even where permissions are attained, digital historians have been keen to stress the limitations of what is possible with digital platforms, texts, and tools. Digital scholars have emphasized the need to constantly press colleagues and students to consider what is inside the black boxes of interfaces, data, and software.[11]

These critiques are not, however, the same as warning historians away from the use of digital data derived from past traces. For, as historians trained in source analysis, digital historians know the strengths and weaknesses of their sources. In the case of OCR-derived text whose "accuracy" is questionable, this data is not a poor facsimile of traces of the past, but—like a photograph, illustration, or oral history of a past event[12]—is instead a new category of source with its own affordances, limitations, and relationships to those past traces. Seen is this way, digitization is not routine and mechanized, but creative and performative, a transformation of a physical thing into a new research object, into derived data, into a data form that can enrich, connect, and reconfigure the original data point, the physical thing itself, the stuff of history all historians seek to explore.[13]

This digital history is gathering critical histories.[14] One recent telling of that history argues for digital history to take better account of the history of computing.[15] Such histories are a sign of maturity, and as practitioners broaden their gaze they see that an urge to historicize their practice chimes with a wave of histories of the digital humanities, computing, and libraries. Notable work ranges from Trevor Muñoz's plea in the present volume for librarians to shape the future of the digital humanities through a grounded reinvestigation of the history of librarianship, to Rens Bod's *A New History of the Humanities*, a text that emphasizes with astonishing breadth a deep history of pattern matching in the humanistic method.[16] Elsewhere, Stéfan Sinclair and Geoffrey Rockwell have emphasized the human contingency and materiality of early work in humanities computing as a provocation for reflecting on the human contingency and materiality of current digital humanities project.[17] In a similar vein, both Melissa Terras and Julianne Nyhan, Andrew Flinn, and Anne Welsh have called for greater understanding of the prehistories and histories of the DH movement.[18] Indeed as Willard McCarty has argued, the digital humanities needs "to begin remembering what our predecessors did and did not do, and the conditions under which they worked, so as to fashion stories for our future."[19] And he has a point, because evidence of forgetting to remember and its consequences abound. For example, in June 2014 the newly formed Cambridge Centre for Digital Knowledge (CCDK) published a mission statement whose ahistorical phasing of digital humanities work, a phasing detached from the rich, diverse roots of DH, provoked the not unreasonable ire of McCarty.[20] Bethany Nowviskie would no doubt see CCDK's statement as evidence that there is little end in sight for the eternal September of the Digital Humanities, especially as the field spreads, institutionalizes, and atomizes.[21]

Taken together this body of reflective work constitutes a growing recognition that histories are vital tools for grappling with the future of digital research in the humanities. The remainder of the present chapter takes this history building a step further, concurring with Bod that histories of the humanities from *the vantage point of digital research* are crucial for future cross-fertilization between the two. I take as my example the discipline of history, a discipline whose source material—as I have described—is now available through network technology and digital libraries at a previously incomparable scale. At the same time this discipline has failed to reap the full rewards of digital transformations in society and culture. For this situation to change, I suggest that librarians armed with knowledge of how and why this failure has manifested itself, of the historiographical traditions that shape and constrain the ability of historians to undertake and assimilate data-driven approaches to the past, are valuable collaborators in digital history projects, research, and pedagogy.

Of course, it is neither wise nor possible to approach as a whole a discipline as wide ranging in geographical focus, exhaustive in chronological scope, and varied in method as the discipline of history. Instead, this chapter restricts itself to exploring the discipline through those introductory texts many historians will be familiar with from the undergraduate classroom. For doing so through the lens of digital history reveals patterns worthy of close attention by all invested in the present and future of both digital history and digital research in the arts and humanities, not least librarians, in whose domain the stewardship and description of digital resources largely fall.

◆ ◆ ◆

John Tosh's *The Pursuit of History* is a classic introductory text in the discipline of history. First published in 1984, it has been substantially revised since and is now in its fifth edition. Together with these periodic revisions, Tosh's clarity, concision, and measured evaluation of scholarly trends have contributed to his volume becoming a favorite in the classroom. The history of these multiple editions offers a valuable perspective on the discipline they serve. For even if an analysis of their differences cannot hope to track changes over time in the research trends of all historians, the editions do represent a significant discursive contribution to the evolving process of self-definition and self-identification within the profession.

Of course "digital history" was unknown when Tosh originally wrote *The Pursuit of History*. "History and computing" on the other hand was an established, if minor, subfield and both Tosh's first and second editions reflect this in the index. Published in 1984 and 1991 respectively, these editions include three entries for "computers," all of which correspond to a chapter on quantitative methods entitled "History by Numbers." Here Tosh argues that the growth of computing in the discipline of history prior to the 1980s can be attributed to two factors: a desire to study more than histories of great men that turned historians to different sources, many of which needed counting;

and the relative affordability from the 1960s onward of computers, which experienced cost reductions that may have kept computers out of reach of individuals but not of research-focused history departments, many of which were able to afford computers, justify their purchase, and acquire prestige from investment in them. This interplay between computing and historical research meant that "both the kind of data it [the computer] could handle and the operations it could carry out were rapidly diversified."[22] Though unattributed, Tosh may well have been referring here to early concordance work with historical texts, the history and significance of which is currently enjoying a renaissance.[23] Nevertheless, the prevailing context for computation in both editions of *The Pursuit of History* is numerical work and statistical analysis, with the computer being a labor-saving, operational, and research management device yoked to numbers. Thus, Tosh sees fit to both emphasize the importance of statistical work to the profession—whether enabled by computational resources or not—and to add a considered note of caution. "Statistics," he writes, "may serve to reveal or clarify a particular tendency; but how we interpret that tendency—the significance we attach to it and the causes we adduce for it—is a matter for seasoned historical judgement, in which the historian trained exclusively in quantitative methods would be woefully deficient."[24] Familiar as it should sound, the argument is worth stressing: past phenomena are not revealed by numbers or by computation, but by the historian's interpretation of those numbers and that computation.

By the fifth edition of *The Pursuit of History* (published in 2010, over a decade after the fourth), the historical profession had changed profoundly. Comparative, postcolonial, and global history had emerged out of the ashes of conflict between macroanalytical social historians and microanalytical cultural historians and the rebuttal of postmodernist critique became a keen focus for work on the historical method.[25] In response to these changes, a range of novel approaches to historical phenomena featured prominently in the fifth edition of *The Pursuit of History*. Whole chapters discussed historian's qualitative research into gender, race, and colonialism. By contrast, a mere two and a half pages were reserved for discussion of quantitative history, statistics, computation, and the implications of macroanalytical work.

Seen from the vantage point of digital history, this is a striking and troubling transformation. For just as historians began to harness the infinite archive, just as digital history was gaining momentum, just as the digital object libraries that had spent over a decade creating and collecting were beginning to be more widely used by humanities researchers as more than finding aids, just as interfaces—scholarly or otherwise—revealed the unimaginable breadth and volume of sources at the historian's disposal, and just a year before the Alliance of Digital Humanities Organisations invited all on the fringes into its "Big Tent," a key textbook in the discipline of history relegated quantitative history and the skills associated with it—both mathematical and conceptual—to marginal status.[26] In doing so and at a time when computational devices of various forms had become ubiquitous tools in the creation of the historian's work, *The Pursuit of History* removed from its index all references to "computers."

Whether he saw their causes as intellectual or social, there were good reasons for Tosh to shift the emphasis of *The Pursuit of History* in the direction he did. Though the 1960s and 1970s had been a fertile, confident, and critical period for quantitative work in history,[27] big picture, quantitative history began to decline in the 1980s when microhistorical, qualitative history began its ascendancy. In an Anglophonic context at least, the "fear of the mathematical" that Willard McCarthy characterizes as a defining feature of late-twentieth-century humanist scholarship was reflected in historians distancing themselves—and by extension their students—from numerical work.[28] That fear coalesced with a fear of scale, of appearing insufficiently close to the archive, of accusations of abstraction, and of lacking specialism and focus.[29]

It is curious that Tosh fails to note the implications for the historical profession of these shifts away from research with numbers and at scale. For extending his logic that "the historian trained exclusively in quantitative methods would be woefully deficient," an historian trained exclusively in qualitative methods, with no grounding in numbers, in computation, would be also "woefully deficient." And this scenario is not hypothetical. It is now a reality born out of the apotheosis of the very approaches given prominence in the fifth edition of *The Pursuit of History*. Given the technology and data historians now have at their disposal, the sort of measured discussions in Tosh's first edition around how to do history at scale and by numbers and around how that work fits into the task of historians at large should be a standard part of the historian's craft, of their training, of their conceptual universe.[30] In the fifth edition of *The Pursuit of History* and in the picture of the profession it paints, they are neither present nor required.[31]

An absence of respect for computational analysis can be observed in other comparable texts. In her robust counter to both naive empiricism and postmodernism, Mary Fulbrook's *Historical Theory* lingers on the intersection between traces of the past and historical narratives but not on the varied character of those traces or the skills needed to handle them (except to say that all traces are valid depending on the question at hand).[32] Another popular textbook, *History: An Introduction to Theory, Method and Practice* by John Marriott and Peter Claus, aims to bridge the gap in praxis and epistemology between studying history at school and in higher education.[33] It demystifies concepts and surveys the field circa 2010, but quantitative approaches and methods do not feature. In *Historiography in the Twentieth Century: From Scientific Objectivity to the Postmodern Challenge*, George Iggers traces the discipline of history's gradual abandonment of macrohistory, grand narratives, and its postwar roots in sociological theory. First published in 1997, his epilogue for the 2005 reprint stresses the need for global history to build on the gains it made in the late 1990s and for a program of synthesis. But Iggers doubts that need will translate into reality—for doing global history requires teams of authors to grapple with problems of global scale and for those authors to willingly "operate on a speculative plane of global history alien to historians who avoid empirical work." The implication is that historians who avoid empirical work are in the majority. [34]

In sum, these textbooks—and many more like them—fail to address the loss of quantitative methods from the historian's toolkit and the implications of this for the profession at large. Only Iggers—in language reminiscent of Braudel—notes the potential adverse consequences of that loss with respect to the strength of the global history project. But even he seems curiously nonplussed—*Historiography in the Twentieth Century* contains no call for action and is far from a manifesto for change.[35]

History in Practice by Ludmilla Jordanova is perhaps singular in the genre for arguing at length in favor of rehabilitating quantitative analysis as a core component of the historian's craft. Published in 2000, her first volume argued that the development of undergraduate curricula by the profession should weigh a fashion for certain approaches—for example, microhistorical, cultural approaches—against an overall sense of the skills historians should have. "Economic history," she wrote, "is particularly vulnerable in this respect."[36] Continuing, she said:

> Economic history (like some other fields) is a fundamental part
> of the discipline, of which every student *ought* to have some
> understanding [. . .] Faced with the choice between courses
> on the history of sport or the history of animals and those on
> economic, political, social or intellectual history, I would hope
> students would be able to see that the latter are likely to be of
> more general use than the former.[37]

Central to the historian's craft here is the understanding of how to negotiate the relationship between big and small history, between macro and micro, between "scientific" and humanistic methods.

In the second edition of *History in Practice*, published in 2006, Jordanova extended this discussion of core skills and tools further, to address how historians could and should respond to novelty in the digital age in light of the professional attributes they wish to preserve. A section entitled "Webs of Affinity" begins by setting the scene: websites offer access to "unimaginable" volumes of historical information; the links between them and the portals that allow researchers to discover them are increasing in sophistication; and many hitherto difficult-to-obtain sources are now at the fingertips of the historian. These factors by themselves, Jordanova argues, "hardly possess the capacity to change radically the ways in which professional historians work."[38] What does possess that power is the manipulation of those websites and the data they contain, and the imagination to see that "unforeseen patterns may emerge which could not have been detected without information technology."[39] Such power requires judicious use and the ability for researchers to utilize these technologies. She concludes that scholars will have to reflect with care on their practice, on how working with data may encourage "fantasies of being able to do truly exhaustive research" or of how our present concerns and uses of technology—say, social networks—may cause an unintended vogue for certain approaches—say, network analysis—in the methods historian use to underpin their explorations of historical phenomenon.[40] Once historians have negotiated the potential and pitfalls of digital technologies, Jordanova continues, they will need both new skills and old skills reapplied. And yet the ability of historians to deliver this is at risk in the siloed and fractured professional landscape that emerged from the cultural turn for, as Jordanova notes: "It is to be regretted that, like economic history and demographic, history and computing is often seen as a specialist domain dominated by enthusiasts."[41]

History in Practice stands out among history textbooks as the sole voice that identified and lamented a decline of quantitative skills, latterly computationally enriched, in both the training offered to historians and the historian's craft, a decline this chapter has observed in the publication history of Tosh's *The Pursuit of History.* In the context of the present volume, it seems to me that we—the library community—must both share and expand upon Jordanova's lament. For to do aspects of digital history well, to take full advantage of those sources—be they ledgers, ephemera, books, newspapers, sound recordings, videos, web pages, or personal digital media—that libraries make available to historians as data, as source material that can be manipulated, counted, and prodded by machines working at their behest, that can be queried at scale rather than merely presented in digital forms yoked to print paradigms, the historical profession needs quantitative skills and a critical understanding of the profession's deep and contested relationship with quantitative research. Librarians can be key collaborators who ensure that historians and other humanistic scholars have the ability to do rigorous quantitative research, but, in order for these partnerships to work, it is clear from the before-mentioned textbooks that there is much work to be done.[42] Emerging historians in particular need to know how to count as historians and how to be critical of the role of data and computation in that counting, for should they go on to attempt digital research of a data-driven variety, the quality of their work may depend on their possession—or otherwise—of these once core skills.

If the future of the historical profession itself is not at stake here, then its health as judged by its ability to explore historical phenomena using the best tools and methods for the job certainly is. Dan Cohen and Roy Rosenzweig identified this nearly a decade ago when they called for historians to wake up to the loss taking place of *the* primary historical record of our time—the website.[43] The salience of their concern that historians were not taking the digital age seriously and were ill prepared for research using this category of source has only amplified since. Librarians need to ask urgently whether the historians they work with, many of whom were trained during the apotheosis of cultural microhistorical research, are equipped to deal with categories of sources such as the archived web. Librarians need to be mindful of whether historians entering undergraduate study in 2016 and graduate programs in 2020 are likely to be capable of exploring the born-digital, data-rich post-1996 world. Librarians also need to understand whether, without major intervention, future historians will be equipped with the skills to tackle vast, technically complex, and enormously rich archives of websites, email, social media traffic, and personal digital media. Slowly we observe that the profession is waking up to this imperative, to the reality of its present, and to how the debates of the past can be of service to its future.[44] In the United Kingdom, nonprint legal deposit powers granted to the British Library have empowered the UK Web Archive to move from selective capture of web publications to annual domain crawls of all ".uk" websites and associated publications.[45] The Institute of Historical Research has taken a leading role in exposing the historical community to this source material, to its affordances, its limitations, its demands of researchers, and its vital role in future historical research. Nonetheless more work remains to be done. For as stewards of digital resources know, a tidal wave of data is not coming—it is here.[46]

Of course it is quite possible the wave might pass by the historical community altogether. Most professional historians living today will never use web archives or personal digital media as research objects. More, but likely far less than a majority, will during their career use digital collections outside of print paradigms and use software tools and algorithms to manipulate data at scale.[47] For these reasons Braudel's struggles may well continue to resonate—many historians may indeed continue to find unpalatable the uncertain methods of a quantitative, at scale, or knowingly imperfect variety. But we should all be concerned if a detachment from data-driven methods crystallizes into uncritical oppositional dogma, not least the many librarians who grapple daily with how to ingest, catalog, describe, and explore such data and how to scale those processes in anticipation of a coming uplift and change in researcher demand. These same librarians are conversant in the challenges of size, technical complexity, and legalities associated with doing research with this data. They have both the will and the skills to effect change, and by complementing these attributes with a perspective on the historical profession as seen through the lens of digital history, of the historiographical traditions that shape and constrain the ability of historians at large to undertake and assimilate data-driven approaches to the past, these librarians can be valuable collaborators in digital history projects, research, and pedagogy. They can use their contextual knowledge to make the uncertain certain, the unpalatable palatable, and they can work with historians to overcome the profession's timidity toward mathematics, scale, and distance from the archive. Together with historians, these librarians can begin in earnest to exploit in novel and unexpected ways the digital collections that libraries, archives, and museums have spent over two decades managing, securing, and promoting.

◆ ◆ ◆

As libraries explore the complex forces that shape and constrain the use by historians of their digital collections as data, context—as with all things history touches—will remain king. For seen in the context this chapter discusses, digital transformations in society and culture offer the historical profession as many continuities as discontinuities—in short, the profession has had these discussions, or at least a version of these discussions, before and outcomes of a tone and character satisfactory to the profession at large were reached. Among these were the reflections advanced by the French Annales School. In 1973 Emmanuel Le Roy Ladurie wrote:

> In history, as elsewhere, what counts is not the machine, but the problem. The machine is only interesting insofar as it allows us to tackle new questions that are original because of their methods, content and especially scale.[48]

His "machine" was the computer, the role of which in historical research was—as his fellow Annalist Braudel had observed less than a decade earlier—under scrutiny. But as Ladurie knew full well, that machine could equally be a map, a calculator, a square ruled notebook, a library catalog, a filing cabinet, or indeed any tool historians have profitably used to undertake their craft and to deepen their understanding of past phenomena. As reflexive scholars steeped in these traditions, in a rich and critical continuum of historical research and method, digital historians know that better history results from methods that see not the novelty of a tool, but the new questions that can be asked of sources with the tool in their hands. When that reflexivity is mainstreamed, the digital resources libraries steward and curate will be best exploited. To achieve that mainstreaming and for the current efflorescence of digital history to be sustained, an efflorescence library professionals are—as the present volume demonstrates—benefiting from and are collaborating in, the historiographical traditions that shape and constrain data-driven historical research should be emphasized, disseminated, and fostered. By taking into account not only the traditions and perspectives but also the histories and controversies of humanities disciplines, while laying the foundations for digital humanities work, library professionals can, I argue, play a crucial role in making this happen.

NOTES

1   I thank Thomas Padilla for his generous comments on an early draft of this chapter.

2   Fernand Braudel, *Capitalism and Material Life, 1400-1800*, trans. Miriam Kochan (London: Weidenfeld and Nicholson, 1973), 6–7.

3   Tim Hitchcock et al., *The Old Bailey Proceedings Online, 1674–1913* 7.0 (March 2012), www.oldbaileyonline.org; Tim Hitchcock et al., *London Lives, 1690–1800* 1.1 (April 24, 2012), www.londonlives.org; Tim Hitchcock et al., *Connected Histories* (2013), www.connectedhistories.org; and Tim Hitchcock et al., *Locating London's Past* 1.0 (December 17, 2011), www.locatinglondon.org.

4   Kathryn Rudy, "Dirty Books: Quantifying Patterns of Use in Medieval Manuscripts Using a Densitometer," *Journal of Historians of Netherlandish Art* 2, No. 1–2 (2010).

5   John Wall et al., *Virtual Paul's Cross Project* (2013), https://vpcp.chass.ncsu.edu.

6   Ian Milligan, "Clustering Search to Navigate a Case Study of the Canadian World Wide Web as a Historical Resource," in *Digital Humanities 2014* (2014), http://dharchive.org/paper/DH2014/Paper-83.xml.

7   Bob Nicholson, "Counting Culture; or, How to Read Victorian Newspapers from a Distance," *Journal of Victorian Culture* 17, No. 2 (2012). By using the phrase "distant reading," Nicholson invokes and reimagines a phrase coined by Franco Moretti to argue for literary analysis using digital tools. See Franco Moretti, *Distant Reading* (London: Verso, 2013).

8   David Armitage and Jo Guldi, "The Return of the Longue Durée: An Anglo-American Perspective," *Annales: Histoire, Sciences Sociales* 69 (2014): 44.

9   Pieter Francois and Ben O'Steen, *The Sample Generator* (2013), http://sample generator.cloudapp.net.

10   Andrew Prescott, "Dennis the Paywall Menace Stalks the Archives," *Digital Riffs* (February 2, 2014), http://digitalriffs.blogspot.co.uk/2014/02/dennis-paywall-menace-stalks-archives.html.

11   Melodee Beals, "Record How You Search, Not Just What You Find: Thoughtfully Constructed Search Terms Greatly Enhance the Reliability of Digital Research," *LSE Impact of Social Sciences* (June 10, 2013); Andrew Hobbs, "The Deleterious Dominance of the Times in Nineteenth-Century Scholarship," *Journal of Victorian Culture* 18, No. 4 (2013); Daniel J. Cohen and Roy Rosenzweig, *Digital History: A Guide to Gathering, Preserving, and Presenting the Past on the Web* (Philadelphia: University of Pennsylvania Press, 2006). See also the decision of *Connected Histories* and *Welsh Newspapers Online* (2013), welshnewspapers.llgc.org.uk, to expose the OCR text within their interfaces.

12   See Peter Burke, *Eyewitnessing: The Uses of Images as Historical Evidence* (Ithaca, NY: Cornell University Press, 2001).

13   Steven E. Jones, *The Emergence of the Digital Humanities* (New York: Routledge, 2014).

14   The most significant of these remains Cohen and Rosenzweig, *Digital History*.

15   William J. Turkel, Shezan Muhammedi, and Mary Beth Start, "Grounding Digital History in the History of Computing," *IEEE Annals of the History of Computing* (2014): 72.

16   Rens Bod, *A New History of the Humanities: The Search for Principles and Patterns from Antiquity to the Present* (Oxford, UK: Oxford University Press, 2013).

17   Stéfan Sinclair and Geoffrey Rockwell, "Towards an Archaeology of Text Analysis Tools," *Digital Humanities 2014* (2014), http://dharchive.org/paper/DH2014/Paper-778.xml.

18   Melissa Terras, "A Decade in Digital Humanities," *Melissa Terras' Blog*, May 27, 2014, www.melissaterras.blogspot.co.uk/2014/05/inaugural-lecture-decade-in-digital.html; Julianne Nyhan, Andrew Flinn, and Anne Welsh, "Oral History and the Hidden Histories Project: Towards Histories of Computing in the Humanities," *Literary and Linguistic Computing* 30, No. 1 (2013): 71–85. http://dx.doi.org/10.1093/llc/fqt044.

19   Willard McCarty, "Getting There from Here. Remembering the Future of Digital Humanities (Roberto Busa Award Lecture 2013)," *Literary and Linguistic Computing* 29, No. 3 (2014): 283–306. http://dx.doi.org/10.1093/llc/fqu022.

20 Willard McCarty, "Digital Knowing, Not Digital Knowledge," *Humanist* 28, No. 140 (June 23, 2014), lists.digitalhumanities.org/pipermail/humanist/2014 -June/012095.html.

21 Bethany Nowviskie, "Eternal September of the Digital Humanities," *Bethany Nowviskie* (blog), October 15, 2010, www.nowviskie.org/2010/eternal -september-of-the-digital-humanities.

22 John Tosh, *The Pursuit of History: Aims, Methods and New Directions in the Study of Modern History*, 2nd ed. (London; New York: Longman, 1991): 153.

23 Sinclair and Rockwell, "Towards an Archaeology of Text Analysis Tools."

24 John Tosh, *The Pursuit of History: Aims, Methods and New Directions in the Study of Modern History*, 1st ed. (London; New York: Longman, 1984): 197.

25 For the emergence of microhistory, see David Armitage and Jo Guldi, "The Return of the Longue Durée" and *The History Manifesto* (Cambridge, UK: Cambridge University Press, 2014). For the preoccupation with rebuttals of postmodern critique, see Richard Evans, *In Defence of History* (London: Granta, 1997) and Mary Fulbrook, *Historical Theory* (London; New York: Routledge, 2002).

26 "Big Tent Digital Humanities" was the theme of *Digital Humanities 2011*, held in Stanford, California.

27 Jacob M. Price, "Recent Quantitative Work in History: A Survey of the Main Trends," *History and Theory* 9 (1969): 11, 13.

28 McCarty, "Getting There from Here," 7. Criticism of cliometrics (the application of econometric models to past phenomena) was another influential force that contributed to the distancing of historical practice from numerical work. Lawrence Stone's emphasis on the narrative and particular (as opposed to analytical and statistical) nature of historical research in "The Revival of Narrative: Reflections on a New Old History," *Past & Present* 85 (1979): 3–24, is a classic essay in the genre.

29 As David Armitage and Jo Guldi argue, these fears were not driven by intellectual rationale but by the job market; Armitage and Guldi, "The Return of the Longue Durée," 10–15. Tosh is silent on this subject, though of course a textbook aimed at undergraduates is perhaps not the venue for ruminations on administration in higher education.

30 A comparable argument is made in Armitage and Guldi, "The Return of the Longue Durée," 21, 39, and *The History Manifesto*.

31 In February 2015, as this manuscript was in the final stages of preparation for publication, a sixth edition of *The Pursuit of History* was published. The

edition includes small sections on the place of digital sources in historical research. These overview passages contain reflections that range from astute criticisms of the digital archives historians now have at their disposal, such as the poor coverage of the digitized record in relation to both the size and thematic coverage of the total historical record, to unfortunate lapses of reason: Tosh's comment that "nothing on the Internet is wholly original, though it is often treated as though it was" is not only nonsense, but also takes no account of the wholly born digital materials that citizens, organizations, and governments create every day and that historians will rely on to re-create our present and our recent past. Crucially, no mention is made of computational approaches to historical research using these sources or of combining the digital with the quantitative methodologies that were dropped by the fifth edition. So, although the coverage of digital sources in the sixth edition is a welcome development, the coverage of digital history remains far from satisfactory.

32 Fulbrook, *Historical Theory*.

33 John Marriott and Peter Claus, *History: An Introduction to Theory, Method, and Practice* (London; New York: Longman, 2011).

34 George Iggers, *Historiography in the Twentieth Century: From Scientific Objectivity to the Postmodern Challenge* (Middletown, CT: Wesleyan University Press, 2005; first published 1997): 155. Price ("Recent Quantitative Work in History," 13) has similar qualms about the preparedness of historians for cooperative working.

35 Note that although Pat Hudson's *History by Numbers: An Introduction to Quantitative Approaches* (New York: Bloomsbury Academic, 2000) provides an excellent introduction to counting as a historian, it is not a generic history textbook and falls outside the remit of this study.

36 Ludmilla Jordanova, *History in Practice*, 1st ed. (London: Arnold, 2000), 202.

37 Ibid., 203.

38 Ludmilla Jordanova, *History in Practice*, 2nd ed. (London: Arnold, 2006): 187.

39 Ibid., 188.

40 For the application of network analysis to historical research, see Claire Lemercier, "Formal Network Methods in History: Why and How?," *HAL Sciences de l'Hamme et de la Société* 2 (August 12, 2011), halshs.archives-ouvertes.fr /halshs-00521527.

41 Jordanova, *History in Practice*, 2nd ed., 188.

42 A useful example of how these approaches can complement one another appears in Jordanova, *History in Practice*, 1st ed., 49–55.

43 Cohen and Rosenzweig, *Digital History*.

44 See, for example, T. M. Kelly, *Teaching History in the Digital Age* (Ann Arbor: University of Michigan Press, 2013); Turkel, Muhammedi, and Start, "Grounding Digital History," 74, and Armitage and Guldi, *The History Manifesto*.

45 See "Non-Print Legal Deposit: FAQs," *The British Library.uk* (2013), www.bl.uk/catalogues/search/non-print_legal_deposit.html.

46 For further examples of the research community responding to this challenge, see the Social Sciences and Humanities Research Council (Canada)–funded "Postwar English-Canadian Youth Cultures: A Digital History, 1945–1990" project led by Ian Milligan (ianmilligan.ca/the-next-project/project-proposal-sshrc, 2013) and the National Endowment of Humanities (United States of America)–funded "Archive What I See Now" project led by Michele C. Weigle (secure grants.neh.gov/publicquery/main.aspx?f=1&gn=HD-51670-13, 2013–2014).

47 Historians do of course use search engines, largely uncritically, to manipulate data at scale every day; see Ted Underwood, "Theorizing Research Practices We Forgot to Theorize Twenty Years Ago," *Representations* 127, No. 1 (2014): 2, 9.

48 Emmanuel Le Roy Ladurie, "L'historien et l'ordinateur," *Le territoire de l'historien* (Paris: Gallimard, 1973): 11.

Part 2

THE PRACTICE OF DIGITAL HUMANITIES IN THE LIBRARY

3 | Digital Public History in the Library: Developing the Lowcountry Digital History Initiative at the College of Charleston

Mary Battle, Tyler Mobley, and Heather Gilbert

INTRODUCTION

In recent years, the growing availability of user-friendly, open-source digital tools has generated unprecedented opportunities for a range of cultural heritage institutions and scholars to participate in developing online exhibition projects. For many library, archival, museum, and academic institutions, digital exhibitions built through open-source tools have the ability to significantly enhance public engagement with scholarly information and multimedia resources at relatively minimal costs in contrast to physical exhibitions. Virtual outreach strategies are particularly crucial for these institutions at a time when operating budgets are often stagnant or shrinking, despite increasing demands for accessing greater and more diverse audiences. Still, the staff time, project management skills, and resources for sustainability that are required for effectively developing and promoting digital projects for the public can be daunting, particularly at smaller institutions with limited staff availability and funding.

In this chapter, the founding developers of the Lowcountry Digital History Initiative (LDHI) describe how they customized open-source digital tools, organized a network of multi-institutional collaborators, and implemented a replicable project workflow and open peer review editorial process to establish an innovative digital public history project at a medium-sized academic library.[1] As a relatively new project that launched in March 2014, LDHI introduces strategies for sustainably and efficiently developing high-quality online exhibitions that could benefit a range of scholars and

35

cultural heritage institutions. Hosted by the Lowcountry Digital Library at the College of Charleston in Charleston, South Carolina, LDHI serves as a site for contributors to translate archival materials, historic landscapes and structures, and scholarly research into widely accessible digital exhibitions.[2] Rather than develop one isolated exhibition, LDHI features numerous online exhibitions, and will continue to produce new projects over time. In partnership with the College of Charleston's Avery Research Center for African American History and Culture and the Program in the Carolina Lowcountry and Atlantic World (CLAW), each LDHI exhibition also connects to the project's overall mission to highlight underrepresented race, class, gender, and labor histories within Charleston, the surrounding Lowcountry region, and the historically interconnected Atlantic World.[3] Finally, each LDHI exhibition reflects a collaborative network of scholars, librarians, and museum professionals from various local, national, and international institutions who support LDHI's inclusive public history mission, and who collectively benefit from the online promotion of their institutional resources and scholarship. LDHI will undoubtedly grow and change significantly in the future, but this overview of its early development provides insights into the project's initial challenges and opportunities, which could benefit various scholars and institutions seeking to expand their public impact through online exhibitions.

DEVELOPING A COLLABORATIVE ONLINE EXHIBITIONS PLATFORM

The concept for LDHI grew out of the mission of the Lowcountry Digital Library (LCDL) at the College of Charleston. LCDL first launched in 2009 through funding support from the Gaylord and Dorothy Donnelley Foundation (the same organization that would later fund LDHI in 2013).[4] LCDL's mission is to make the Lowcountry region's unique cultural heritage materials from a range of large and small institutional partners more accessible to the public through digitization and the construction of a regional digital archives repository.[5] LCDL soon became part of the statewide South Carolina Digital Library, which was selected as one of the first service hubs of the Digital Public Library of America that launched in 2013.[6] As of 2015, the Lowcountry Digital Library hosted over 65,000 digitized archival records, and featured digitized archival collections from over seventeen partner institutions.

Although LCDL's digital collections offer wide access to numerous archival collections, in 2011, LCDL staff determined that online exhibitions could enhance this access by promoting public awareness of the historic contexts and significance of these archival materials and the Lowcountry region more broadly. These staff members, which included digital librarians and humanities scholars, began exploring strategies for developing online exhibitions that could be supported within the context of a medium-sized academic library. Rather than start from scratch, the staff initially tested these strategies by updating an existing digital project, entitled *African Passages*, which was developed by the College of Charleston's CLAW Program in partnership with UNESCO in the early 2000s.[7] The original version of this online exhibition features engaging visual materials and historic information about the history of slavery on rice plantations along the Ashley River Corridor in Charleston, but the site was built using HTML and Javascript, which is difficult to maintain and update over time. In 2012, the Lowcountry Digital Library successfully obtained a grant from the Humanities Council[SC] to support updating this site and expanding its historic focus and exhibition materials.[8]

LCDL staff began the exhibition update by changing the scope of *African Passages* to address the history of slavery and the trans-Atlantic slave trade from the Atlantic World to Charleston and the South Carolina Lowcountry. The staff also changed the title of the exhibition to *African Passages, Lowcountry Adaptations*, to emphasize how slavery and the experiences of Africans and African Americans in the Carolina Lowcountry evolved over time from the colonial to the antebellum periods. They also explored various digital tools for rebuilding the site and eventually chose Omeka and Omeka's *Exhibit Builder* plug-in.[9] Omeka is an open-source digital publishing platform that was released in 2008 by the Roy Rosenzweig Center for History and New Media at George Mason University. As described later in this chapter, this platform features numerous plug-ins that are strikingly user-friendly for contributors with a range of digital skills. Building the new *African Passages, Lowcountry Adaptations* site in Omeka ultimately made this online exhibition more stable and adaptable, as well as visually engaging and accessible.[10] While LCDL's digital librarians implemented Omeka, the humanities scholars developed new exhibition text and acquired archival materials from various institutions to feature in the project. These items included digitized materials from LCDL's partner institutions, as well as various national and international archival repositories. Through extensive links within the text, *African Passages, Lowcountry Adaptations* became both a more expansive online exhibition and a gateway to various digital history resources on the subject of slavery and the slave trade in the South Carolina Lowcountry, North America, and the Atlantic World.

Once the *African Passages, Lowcountry Adaptations* exhibition update was under way, the LCDL staff decided to maintain this regional and interconnected Atlantic World theme as they searched for new digital projects. One challenge, however, was that the project workflow for *African Passages, Lowcountry Adaptations* was time consuming. It was a slow process for individual staff members to write and edit the exhibition text, acquire exhibition materials, and lay out the exhibition in Omeka. They needed more help. LCDL staff initially addressed this issue by recruiting various scholars to serve as editorial contributors for the exhibition text of *African Passages, Lowcountry Adaptations*. For new projects, they began considering ways to expand on this collaborative approach. Rather than relying on curators from their staff, they determined that a network of project authors, editorial contributors, and archivists could help strengthen the research, writing, editorial review, and digitized materials featured in their exhibitions. Significantly, this collaborative approach also made the workflow faster.

Graduate student assistants played a key role in making LCDL's online exhibition-building workflow more efficient and sustainable. The College of Charleston does not currently include humanities PhD programs, but it does feature a Master of Arts (MA) degree in the Department of History, in partnership with The Citadel, The Military College of South Carolina.[11] This two-year program offers paid graduate assistantships to a select number of its students to work in various campus positions.[12] Starting in 2012, the College of Charleston's Department of History generously began funding graduate assistantships to work part-time (ten to twenty hours a week) on LCDL digital projects. This support proved crucial to establishing a feasible project workflow for building online exhibitions. Though MA students at the College of Charleston are only available to hone their digital humanities skills for one to two years before they graduate, due to the ease of learning how to use Omeka's *Exhibit Builder*, the time constraints for these students are not prohibitive. Students can learn to lay out an exhibition project in Omeka with only a few days of training, and can use other similarly user-friendly open-source tools such as Timeline JS and Neatline to develop additional exhibition features such as interactive maps and timelines.[13] These tools require minimal technological expertise, so students are able to dedicate significant time during their work hours to acquiring multimedia exhibition materials from various archives and assisting with text edits, as well as leading exhibition layout tasks.

To enable long-term viability and audience interest in their online exhibitions, LCDL staff also decided that they would focus on creating a single, unified online exhibitions platform hosted by the Lowcountry Digital Library, rather than build multiple, stand-alone exhibitions. This platform would feature exhibition content created by multiple project authors and collaborators, which then underwent outside editorial review to ensure high-quality scholarship. LCDL staff wanted this exhibitions platform to sustainably grow and change over time, much like an academic journal or dynamic virtual museum space. This required significant project management support. Even with the help of graduate student assistants, LCDL still needed a full-time digital exhibitions coordinator to not only train and manage students, but also to develop lasting relationships with scholars, archivists, and museum professionals to recruit online exhibition projects and facilitate editorial review.

In 2012, LCDL staff translated these goals into a successful grant application for a major award from the Gaylord and Dorothy Donnelley Foundation to fund a full-time project coordinator for the newly designated Lowcountry Digital History Initiative, hosted by the Lowcountry Digital Library. They filled this position starting in January 2013, and in addition to *African Passages, Lowcountry Adaptations*, the project coordinator began working with graduate student assistants to update other existing digital projects hosted by the College of Charleston, such as *After Slavery: Race, Labor, and Politics in the Post-Emancipation Carolinas* (originally published in 2006 and redesigned for LDHI in 2013) and *Voyage of the Echo: The Trials of an Illegal Trans-Atlantic Slave Ship* (originally published in 2010 and redesigned and expanded for LDHI in 2014).[14] In partnership with CLAW and the Avery Research Center, LCDL staff also began recruiting new exhibition projects. Meanwhile, LCDL's digital librarians began customizing Omeka for the purpose of developing LDHI as a permanent online exhibitions platform that would be featured on the home page of the Lowcountry Digital Library.

PROMOTING INCLUSIVE PUBLIC HISTORY

To effectively launch LDHI, LCDL staff had to shift from developing or upgrading individual digital projects in the short term to conceptualizing a large-scale, long-term digital initiative. Ultimately, the founding developers of LDHI required five key components to sustainably implement a project of this scale: (1) dedicated institutional support for hosting and preserving digital exhibition projects; (2) access to open-source, user-friendly digital project building software; (3) a network of collaborative partners with a range of humanities and technological skill sets; (4) funding support for a project coordinator; and (5) a mission that addresses local, but also wide-reaching public history needs. For the first four components, the LDHI project team relied on preservation support from the Lowcountry Digital Library and the College of Charleston, generous collaborators, fortunate timing with open-source software developments, and start-up funding support from the Humanities Council of South Carolina and the Gaylord and Dorothy Donnelley Foundation.[15] The last component—LDHI's mission to focus on underrepresented histories—grew from long-term issues with public history narratives in Charleston and the surrounding Lowcountry region. Although marginalized histories are not unique to this area, they stand out in an influential historic tourism destination like Charleston that attracts millions of visitors each year. In recent years, numerous historic sites and tours in Charleston and the surrounding Lowcountry region have begun to develop more inclusive interpretation strategies, particularly connected to the historic experiences of African Americans and the history of slavery and its race and class legacies in the area. LDHI sought to contribute to these efforts through a cost-effective, widely accessible online exhibitions platform.

Charleston first emerged as a major tourism destination in the late nineteenth and early twentieth centuries. As historian Stephanie Yuhl explains, popular narratives about the history of this city and the surrounding Lowcountry region developed through a locally crafted "golden haze of memory," where white elites "translated their personal and small group memories into easily consumable forms that fixed a public idea of

Charleston—genteel, ordered, historic, romantic—in the American imagi-nation."[16] White elite nostalgia for the region's colonial and antebellum past ultimately became the overarching theme for Charleston's burgeoning tour-ism industry. Throughout the twentieth and into the twenty-first centuries, these narrow representations persisted and specifically served to minimize or romanticize the significance of African Americans, the institution of slav-ery, and the race and class legacies of slavery in the Lowcountry area.[17]

For this reason, although LDHI seeks to address a range of historic topics, in partnership with the Avery Research Center, the project team particularly encourages exhibitions that highlight African American his-tory and culture. Despite a long history of marginalization, Africans and their descendants played a central role in Lowcountry history. From the seventeenth to the nineteenth centuries, more enslaved Africans arrived in Charleston through the trans-Atlantic slave trade than any other North American port.[18] Many were then transported to other towns, colonies, and later states through the domestic slave trade, but a significant number were sold as chattel property to nearby plantations in the surrounding Lowcoun-try region, particularly to work in rice agriculture.[19] This resulted in the Carolina colony and later state of South Carolina featuring a black popula-tion majority that lasted, with some temporary fluctuations, from the early eighteenth century into the mid-twentieth century.[20] Both during and after slavery, large black populations in urban contexts such as Charleston, and in surrounding rural areas, carved out social structures, resistance strate-gies, and cultural identities that still resonate in the present. Major black political activists and community leaders emerged from both the rural and urban areas of this region, and they proved influential in local and national struggles for social and political equality during and after slavery, the twen-tieth-century civil rights movement, and into the present.[21]

By the twenty-first century, Charleston's public history narratives had the potential to influence vast numbers of local, national, and international visitors.[22] The downtown peninsula of *Historic Charleston* particularly overflows with museums, mansion tours, and guided walking, driving, and carriage tours, while surrounding suburban areas feature numerous former forts and plantations that now function as tourist sites. Until recently, how-ever, few of these historic attractions addressed the significance of Africans and their African American descendants, or the central role of slavery and its race, class, and labor legacies in the history of the area.[23] In this setting, the benefits of digital public history interpretation are numerous. Collaborative online exhibitions can expand public awareness and appreciation for the diverse complexity of Charleston and the Lowcountry's history at relatively minimal costs, and within a fuller range of the region's historic structures and landscapes. Digital tools offer dynamic interpretation of historic sites without requiring the costs of a new physical exhibition or museum building, or facilities to accommodate significant visitor traffic. Existing historic sites and guided tours, as well as school programs, can enhance or transform their current interpretation or teaching strategies by presenting archival images, oral history recordings, interactive maps and timelines, or video clips organized through online exhibitions to help users visualize and connect to more diverse histories. In addition, online exhibitions can offer site-specific interpretation with minimal impacts on the communities or natural environments currently living within these spaces. Digital projects also offer distinct opportunities for multi-institutional collaboration across academic, archival, library, and museum contexts to organize rich historic information and multimedia materials from shared resources. In a destination city like Charleston with a long history of race, class, and labor struggles, these collaborative, cost-effective, and widely accessible strategies for generating inclusive interpretation have the potential to be transformative.

Digital public history projects also offer opportunities for multi-institutional collaborations across international as well as regional contexts. Fully comprehending Charleston's history requires looking beyond the city, region, and even North America, to include the trans-Atlantic exchanges and influences of a complex multicultural and multinational network.[24] For these reasons, LDHI's mission goes beyond Charleston and the Lowcountry to engage the interconnected histories of the Atlantic World. Through this approach, Charleston and the surrounding Lowcountry can be understood as one of many historic areas in the Atlantic World where African, Native American, and European populations encountered one another in colonial contexts of oppression, resistance, and conflict, as well as creative adaptation, influence, and exchange.[25] These populations ultimately generated new multicultural societies that often grew to include populations from around the world. Like Charleston, many Atlantic World societies reflect this complex web of cultural influences today—and still struggle with legacies of social, political, and economic inequalities that began with this early history. To include these international connections, the LDHI project team established a mission to recruit exhibitions that address underrepresented histories throughout Charleston and the interconnected Atlantic World.[26]

DIGITAL PUBLIC HISTORY TOOLS

While digital public history offers many benefits for highlighting underrepresented histories, until recently, the tools needed to build visually engaging and content-rich online exhibitions often required significant technological and graphic design experience. Many museums, archives, and academic institutions with constrained budgets and limited staff time could not afford to dedicate a significant amount of resources to building a digital project, much less multiple projects at a time. These limitations began to change as new open-source, user-friendly resources started to become available, particularly the Omeka digital publishing platform, and significantly for LDHI, the Omeka *Exhibit Builder* plug-in. In addition, the Scholars' Lab at the University of Virginia released Neatline in 2010, which offers open-source tools for building interactive maps and timelines that are compatible with Omeka exhibitions.[27] Once these tools are installed, humanities scholars with minimal technological training can use Omeka and Neatline to conceptualize and build online exhibition projects.[28] In particular, humanities students can learn to use these tools in a short period of time, so that they can effectively contribute to the often time-consuming effort of developing digital projects. LDHI ultimately would not have been feasible without user-friendly, open-source tools that allow individuals with a range of skill sets to become digital content builders.

Still, when LDHI officially received grant funding and began development in 2013, the site's function as an online exhibitions platform, rather than an archival repository for individual digital items, meant that it required significant customization beyond an out-of-the-box installation of Omeka. For this reason, the project team customized Omeka to focus on enhancing the presentation of digital exhibitions for LDHI, while hiding other core components like individual item records and digital collections. This type of customization required a self-hosted instance of Omeka, which the team installed on one of the library's internal Ubuntu Linux virtual machines.[29] A basic installation of Omeka is simple to run thanks to well-maintained documentation and an intuitive initial configuration. Like many web-publishing platforms, Omeka relies on PHP and MySQL, so for a digital librarian, the application's structure follows familiar design conventions. This familiarity in an already flexible, open-source platform makes Omeka inherently friendly to an intermediate developer. For the customization that came next, the project team did not have to spend significant time learning application-specific quirks and conventions, and instead could focus directly on the necessary code adjustments.

Omeka, like other content management systems such as WordPress and Drupal, allows developers to compartmentalize and package certain functions into plug-ins (or modules with Drupal). The plug-ins expand on the core functionality of the system, allowing Omeka developers and site administrators to tailor an Omeka installation to their specific needs through individual plug-in selection. In this case, LDHI would serve as a digital exhibitions platform, and many of these exhibitions would feature specific items held in the Lowcountry Digital Library's Fedora Commons repository. The Omeka development community had already created both an *Exhibit Builder* and *FedoraConnector* plug-in, which LDHI could then rely on for its distinct focus on exhibitions.[30]

Exhibit Builder is a core plug-in included with every installation of Omeka, while the *FedoraConnector* plug-in for Omeka was created by the Scholars' Lab at the University of Virginia and requires separate installation. The LDHI project team modified both of these plug-ins for LDHI's Omeka installation so it would connect efficiently with LCDL collections, while hiding certain Omeka elements from the public that are unnecessary for LDHI. Specifically, the LDHI team modified the *Exhibit Builder* plug-in to allow the selection and presentation of Fedora Commons objects, as well as other exhibition materials uploaded into Omeka, within exhibition layout pages. They also modified the *FedoraConnector* plug-in to add theme-specific code for *jQuery* lightbox functionality that would override item page links. As a result, when users click on images of exhibition materials in LDHI, they open into a larger lightbox, rather than a separate item page. Other plug-ins have been added or created over time as needed for the project. For example, for LDHI's front page and exhibition browse pages, LDHI's digital librarians drafted an *Exhibit Grid* shortcode plug-in to allow a shortcode on an Omeka Simple Page that generates a grid of exhibit thumbnails and titles to enable visually engaging search options for the exhibitions.[31] The ease of Omeka plug-in development and modification also allows the LDHI project to effectively and sustainably grow and change over time.

Theme customization began once the project team determined the core structure of LDHI and selected or modified all necessary plug-ins. The *Exhibit Builder* plug-in allows users to select different themes for each exhibition within one installation, which means administrators can give individual themes their own unique identities. However, all exhibitions in this installation fell under the umbrella of the LDHI project, so the project team decided to develop custom theme options that were visually cohesive while also remaining flexible enough to allow for interchangeable logo and thumbnail images. They also ensured that the final theme tied in cohesively with Lowcountry Digital Library branding efforts. The resulting theme provided a distinct visual identity for all LDHI exhibits while retaining flexibility for exhibit-specific needs like custom logos and thumbnails. To expedite the development process, the web developer used the *Foundation* front-end framework by ZURB.[32] *Foundation* and similar frameworks, like the *Bootstrap* package core layout and component code, work across a variety of devices.[33] For the LDHI theme, *Foundation CSS* provided the logic for the site's overall grid structure.[34] In *Exhibit Builder*'s digital exhibitions, for example, the project team could use *Foundation*'s row and column classes to manage the alternating text and image layouts on exhibition pages without having to manually write CSS each time that would account for available viewport space as the site scaled between mobile devices and desktops. Additionally, *Foundation Panels* added convenient styling for exhibition and home page navigation.[35] By relying on a framework rather than entirely custom code, the project team was able to rapidly develop LDHI's base theme and respond to changing needs for exhibitions as LDHI grew over time. Development on the LDHI Omeka site continued through the summer of 2013, and LDHI's project team continues to provide updates as needed.

In March 2014, LDHI publicly launched with nine online exhibitions. Many of these exhibitions feature materials or collections that are digitized in the Lowcountry Digital Library, but they also feature archival materials that have not yet been formally digitized or that are from a range of local, national, and international archives. For many exhibitions, graduate student assistants also developed maps and timelines, so that users can explore historic information and materials on LDHI through a range of interactive features. Currently, academic scholars interested in increasing public engagement with their work have authored most of LDHI's exhibitions. Their contributions are significant and in many ways generous, considering that the professional or publication credit for digital public history work is still unclear in terms of the academic job market and academic tenure and promotion.[36] But the LDHI team also recognizes that various large and small museum institutions in the Lowcountry, as well as Atlantic World partners, include physical exhibitions with rich historic information and materials that could greatly benefit from greater public access through an online platform. Although many of these institutions feature websites, they do not necessarily have the staff or editorial resources for developing in-depth online exhibitions. LDHI currently features one adaptation of a physical exhibition from a museum institution, *Keeper of the Gate: Philip Simmons Ironwork in Charleston, South Carolina* developed with the Philip Simmons Foundation.[37] The site also hosts a few exhibitions, such as *The James Poyas Daybook: An Account of a Charles Town Merchant, 1760–1765* by Neal Polhemus, that focus primarily on one major collection from an archival repository or museum partner.[38] Currently, LDHI is in the process of expanding its partnerships with a range of cultural heritage institutions that could benefit from increasing digital access to their institutional resources.

LDHI PROJECT WORKFLOW

This section outlines LDHI's general project workflow for recruiting, developing, reviewing, and publishing LDHI exhibitions. As noted, establishing this collaborative, multi-institutional exhibition development process with scholars, graduate students, archivists, librarians, and museum professionals has been crucial to making LDHI feasible at a medium-sized academic institution like the College of Charleston. This overview also demonstrates how LDHI's workflow can be adapted to a range of project collaborations as the LDHI team expands its institutional and scholarly partnerships in the future.

Step One: Project Planning Meeting

The first step to developing an LDHI online exhibition is an initial planning meeting. LDHI team members will meet with an interested project author or institutional partner to discuss ways to develop a project based on a specific topic that fits LDHI's inclusive public history mission. In some cases, a scholar has academic research that he or she would like to make more accessible through digital public history tools. In other cases, a cultural heritage institution such as a museum or library has a physical exhibition that it would like to adapt to an online context. At the meeting, participants will consult with the LDHI team to discuss ways to organize their research or project for a digital public history context. They will also identify potential archival materials and multimedia resources to feature with the exhibition, and consider possibilities for developing features such as interactive maps and timelines to accompany the text and exhibition materials.

Step Two: Internal Editorial Review

Once the project author or institutional partner submits an exhibition text draft, LDHI team members will begin an internal editorial review. Their goal in the first round of editorial input is to make sure that the exhibition text is well organized and features clear, accessible writing for a public history context. The standards for accessible public history writing can range widely, but LDHI generally requires exhibition texts that are more concise than academic articles, but not as brief as physical exhibition texts. In a physical exhibition, visitors are temporarily walking through an exhibition space and their attention span is often short. In contrast, online exhibition viewers are generally exploring the project while sitting with a laptop or mobile device, and they can return multiple times to continue reading the text. For this reason, LDHI regularly offers more in-depth exhibition narratives, though the project team is also exploring options for more concise mobile-friendly features in the future. To prevent overly dense academic discussions, the LDHI review process specifically limits any scholarly jargon and features a list of sources at the end of each project rather than footnotes within the exhibition text. Once the author completes this first round of edits, LDHI staff send the text to outside editorial contributors who provide input on the text based on their relevant expertise.

Step Three: External Open Peer Review

In the early stages of developing LDHI, the project team decided to implement an open peer review editorial process, rather than use the closed review approach typically found with academic journals. More than anything, this was a practical choice. As a new digital project with temporary grant funding, establishing a formal editorial board for closed review did not seem feasible. LDHI also does not have enough staff to guarantee a regular publication schedule like an academic journal. For these reasons, the project team decided to implement an open review editorial process, where project authors work with LDHI staff to recruit editorial contributors to review individual projects, rather than making a commitment to an editorial board. Through this approach, LDHI can reach out to editorial contributors who offer specialized expertise on individual exhibition topics, either as scholars, archivists, museum professionals, or in some cases, as first-hand witnesses.[39] Each editorial contributor then receives credit in the Sources section of that exhibition for his or her input.

Step Four: Acquiring Exhibition Materials

Throughout the development of the exhibition text, LDHI graduate student assistants work on acquiring digitized materials to feature with the exhibition, and create interactive maps and timelines using open-source tools. Visual materials can range from images of archival materials such as historic documents, photographs, and artifacts, to present-day images of historic landscapes. The LDHI team is also currently working to include more multimedia materials such as audio and video oral histories in the exhibitions.[40] Graduate assistants often begin by targeting specific archival materials requested by the project author, which may be located in a range of local, national, or international archival repositories. If the materials are not yet digitized, students will work with archivists to locate them in different repositories and request scans and caption information. If collections are already digitized, students will search for exhibition materials in the Lowcountry Digital Library (if they are from an LCDL partner institution) or in other online repositories with credible rights and permissions information, such as the Library of Congress or the Digital Public Library of America.[41] Though the Lowcountry Digital Library hosts LDHI, exhibition items often come from a range of archival repositories. Still, LDHI exhibitions regularly prioritize materials from LCDL partners and link to their institutional websites and collections. Students and LDHI staff also work with project authors to negotiate rights and permissions with different institutions for featuring their materials in an online context. With a limited budget, LDHI staff often target materials that are in the public domain, or in archival institutions that are willing to waive the rights and permission fees because the exhibitions are intended for educational use and are made freely available to the public through a Creative Commons license.[42]

In some cases, LDHI graduate assistants also help with digitizing and providing preliminary metadata for archival materials that are eligible for inclusion in the Lowcountry Digital Library. For example, students may identify items for an LDHI exhibition from a relevant collection that belongs to one of the Lowcountry Digital Library's partner institutions. Rather than just scan those materials for the LDHI exhibition, the students may formally digitize a representative sample from the collection to expand LCDL's holdings. The exhibition can then link to further collection examples beyond the featured exhibition item.[43] For this reason, all LDHI graduate assistants undergo digitization and metadata creation training through sessions hosted by LCDL's project director. As a result, the digitization, description, and ingestion of collections that include items featured in LDHI exhibitions are often fast-tracked for completion in LCDL. Prior to engaging LDHI graduate assistants in the digitization process, much like exhibitions, these select digitization projects were often overly time consuming for LCDL staff. By making digitization and description part of the project workflow, LDHI graduate assistants can also contribute to LCDL and receive a more cohesive digital library training experience.

Step Five: Online Exhibition Layout

Once the exhibition text has been vetted through an internal and external review process, the final draft is ready for layout in Omeka. The project coordinator assigns one of the graduate assistants to take the lead, and that student will upload all of the acquired exhibition materials (with approved rights and permissions) into Omeka with the correct caption information, and then begin selecting images to accompany different sections of the reviewed exhibition text. If the exhibition features items from LCDL, students can use the *FedoraConnector* plug-in for a more efficient uploading process. In some cases, authors provide guidance on which materials they would like to feature in each exhibition section. Otherwise, under the supervision of the LDHI project coordinator, graduate assistants guide the layout process and insert relevant hyperlinks throughout the text. Once a layout draft is ready, other graduate assistants will provide editorial input on the exhibition before they send it to the LDHI project coordinator and codirector for review. Once approved internally, the project coordinator sends a password-protected link to the project author or partner institution to review the exhibition and provide final editorial input. After final approval, the online exhibition is ready to publish.

Step Six: Publication and Promotion

After publication, the LDHI staff promotes the exhibition through social media outlets, as well as presentations at conferences and public venues. They also encourage educators to use the exhibitions in the classroom, and encourage project authors and partners to promote their projects through presentations, workshops, and institutional or academic websites. In the future, the LDHI team will explore further institutional collaborations to expand LDHI's promotional outreach.

CONCLUSION

As of 2015, LDHI had published fifteen online exhibitions (with many more in progress), and experienced strong user interest based on Google Analytics.[44] Though the LDHI team has not conducted a formal assessment of the project's audiences, they have received informal positive feedback from educators who use LDHI projects in their teaching as well as cultural heritage professionals, and the project has received recognition from professional organizations such as the American Library Association and the Organization of American Historians.[45] In addition, LDHI staff members have presented on the project at numerous regional, national, and international academic, library, and museum conferences, as well as to local community groups and educators. Graduate student assistants have also increased LDHI's social media presence through LCDL's Twitter and Facebook accounts. Although the project team is pleased with LDHI's outreach and engagement, they hope that the initiative will continue to grow in the future, both in overall site organization and by developing new projects with a greater range of scholarly and institutional partners. They also hope to engage a wider range of users by providing mobile-friendly features as well as in-depth online exhibitions, and by developing more accessible educational resources and activities targeting a range of grade levels. Finally, the LDHI team will continue to develop strategies for cost effectively sustaining the LDHI platform within the resources currently available at the College of Charleston and also through additional grant funding.

The LDHI team ultimately believes that innovative and rapidly increasing digital public history tools can significantly help expand, redefine, and greatly enrich how individuals engage with historic and cultural information and sites in landscapes and communities throughout Charleston, the Lowcountry region, and beyond. Libraries in small to medium-sized academic institutions like the College of Charleston often have limited resources, but through multi-institutional collaboration they can still develop sustainable strategies for engaging digital resources, while also connecting to the public history needs of their partners and stakeholder communities. As LDHI continues to grow in the future, the project team hopes that this initiative will prove to be an engaging and sustainable example of innovative and inclusive digital public history work in academic libraries.

NOTES

1   Lowcountry Digital History Initiative, http://ldhi.library.cofc.edu.

2   Lowcountry Digital Library, http://lcdl.library.cofc.edu.

3   Avery Research Center for African American History and Culture, http://avery.cofc.edu; Program in the Carolina Lowcountry and Atlantic World, http://claw.cofc.edu/about.html.

4   Gaylord and Dorothy Donnelley Foundation, http://gddf.org.

5   "About," Lowcountry Digital Library, http://lcdl.library.cofc.edu/about; "Contributing Institutions," Lowcountry Digital Library, http://lcdl.library.cofc.edu/institutions.

6   South Carolina Digital Library, http://scmemory.org; Digital Public Library of America, http://dp.la.

7   For more information about the original *African Passages* online exhibition and this update, see "Project History" in "African Passages, Lowcountry Adaptations," *Lowcountry Digital History Initiative* (March 25, 2015), http://ldhi.library.cofc.edu/exhibits/show/africanpassageslowcountryadapt/overview/projecthistory; also "Education: Sites of Memory," United Nations Educational, Scientific, and Cultural Organization, www.unesco.org/new/en/education/networks/global-networks/aspnet/flagship-projects/transatlantic-slave-trade/activity-proposals/sites-of-memory.

8   Humanities Council[SC], http://schumanities.org.

9   Omeka, http://omeka.org/; Omeka, "Exhibit Builder," http://omeka.org/add -ons/plugins/exhibit-builder.

10 Mary Battle, lead curator, "African Passages, Lowcountry Adaptations," *Lowcountry Digital History Initiative* (2013), http://ldhi.library.cofc.edu/exhibits /show/africanpassageslowcountryadapt.

11 "Graduate Program: Master of Arts in History," College of Charleston, http:// history.cofc.edu/graduate-program/index.php.

12 As an academic institution with typically small class sizes, the College of Charleston generally does not have humanities graduate students work as teaching assistants, which means their assistantships can be located in a range of academic contexts, including libraries. This point is crucial, because graduate assistants at many larger academic institutions often focus on teaching, so they are not as available to assist with library projects.

13 Timeline JS, http://timeline.knightlab.com; Neatline, http://neatline.org.

14 Brian Kelly et al., "After Slavery: Race, Labor, and Citizenship in the Post-Emancipation Carolinas," *Lowcountry Digital History Initiative* (2014), http://ldhi.library.cofc.edu/exhibits/show/after_slavery; John Harris, "Voyage of the *Echo*: The Trials of an Illegal Trans-Atlantic Slave Ship," *Lowcountry Digital History Initiative* (2014), http://ldhi.library.cofc.edu/exhibits /show/voyage-of-the-echo-the-trials.

15 Digital collections and digital projects that promote scholarship are explicitly identified as a key priority in the College of Charleston Libraries' strategic plan, which indicates that the college will continue to offer resources for long-term digital preservation and maintenance for LDHI.

16 Stephanie Yuhl, *A Golden Haze of Memory: The Making of Historic Charleston* (Chapel Hill; London: University of North Carolina Press, 2005): 187–88.

17 Yuhl, *A Golden Haze of Memory*, 11.

18 "Estimates," *Voyages: The Trans-Atlantic Slave Trade Database*, www.slavevoyages.org/tast/database/search.faces; Ira Berlin, *Many Thousands Gone: The First Two Centuries of Slavery in North America* (Cambridge, MA; London: Harvard University Press, 1998); James McMillin, *The Final Victims: The Foreign Slave Trade to North America, 1783–1810* (Columbia: University of South Carolina Press, 2004).

19 Steven Deyle, *Carry Me Back: The Domestic Slave Trade in American Life* (Oxford: Oxford University Press, 2006); William Dusinberre, *Them Dark*

Days: Slavery in the American Rice Swamps (New York and Oxford: Oxford University Press, 1996); Daniel Littlefield, *Rice and Slaves: Ethnicity and the Slave Trade in Colonial South Carolina* (Chicago: University of Illinois Press, 1991); Philip Morgan, *Slave Counterpoint: Black Culture in the Eighteenth-Century Chesapeake and Lowcountry* (Chapel Hill: University of North Carolina Press, 1998); Judith Carney, *Black Rice: The African Origins of Rice Cultivation in the Americas* (Cambridge, MA; London: Harvard University Press, 2001); Max S. Edelson, *Plantation Enterprise in Colonial South Carolina* (Cambridge, MA: Harvard University Press, 2011).

20   Peter Wood, *Black Majority: Negroes in Colonial South Carolina from 1670 through the Stono Rebellion* (New York: Alfred Knopf, 1974); Walter Edgar, *South Carolina: A History* (Columbia: University of South Carolina Press, 1998): 64–81, 485–87. Today, African Americans continue to be a significant minority in South Carolina. As of the 2010 census, African Americans made up nearly 28 percent of South Carolina's overall population. "State and County Quick Facts: South Carolina," U.S. Census Bureau.

21   Bernard E. Powers, Jr., *Black Charlestonians: A Social History, 1822–1885* (Fayetteville: University of Arkansas Press, 1994); Charles Joyner, *Down by the Riverside: A South Carolina Slave Community* (Champaign: University of Illinois Press, 1984); Mark M. Smith, *Stono: Documenting and Interpreting a Southern Slave Revolt* (Columbia: University of South Carolina Press, 2005); Douglas R. Egerton, *He Shall Go Out Free: The Lives of Denmark Vesey* (Madison, WI: Madison House, 1999); Katherine Mellen Charron, *Freedom's Teacher: The Life of Septima Clark* (Chapel Hill: University of North Carolina Press, 2009); Peter F. Lau, *Democracy Rising: South Carolina and the Fight for Black Equality since 1865* (Columbia: University of South Carolina Press, 2006); Edward A. Miller, Jr., *Gullah Statesman: Robert Smalls from Slavery to Congress, 1839–1915* (Columbia: University of South Carolina Press, 2008); *Toward the Meeting of the Waters: Currents in the Civil Rights Movement of South Carolina during the Twentieth Century*, ed. Winfred B. Moore and Orville Vernon Burton (Columbia: University of South Carolina Press, 2008).

22   In 2014 alone, the South Carolina Department of Parks, Recreation, and Tourism estimates that 5,600,000 visitors came to Charleston County, with the city of Charleston serving as the central attraction. "Estimated Visitation to South Carolina by County," South Carolina Department of Parks, Recreation, and Tourism.

23 Ethan J. Kytle and Blain Roberts, "'Is It Okay to Talk about Slaves?' Segregating the Past in Historic Charleston," *Destination Dixie: Tourism & Southern History*, ed., Karen L. Cox (Gainesville: University Press of Florida, 2012). Notably, a few independent guides, exhibitions, organizations, and sites stand as exceptions to Charleston's traditionally exclusive interpretive focus. For example, institutions such as the College of Charleston's Avery Research Center for African American History and Culture and the City of Charleston's Old Slave Mart Museum both explicitly focus on black history and culture and the Lowcountry region's history of slavery. In the future, the developing Gullah Geechee Cultural Heritage Corridor and International African American Museum in Charleston will also greatly expand public awareness of these histories. In addition, long-standing historic institutions in the area are beginning to demonstrate new interpretive priorities. For example, the Preservation Society of Charleston recently launched a campaign to erect a series of markers dedicated to Charleston's twentieth-century civil rights history, and various historic plantation sites now feature tours that address African American experiences during and after slavery. Despite these promising developments, however, inclusive change continues to be a challenge. Even when they are willing to reconsider traditional tourism narratives, many of the city's public history producers face limited institutional budgets and staff time to research and develop new historic resources, interpretation strategies, or physical exhibitions.

24 Carney, *Black Rice*; Edelson, *Plantation Enterprise*; Littlefield, *Rice and Slaves*; Wood, *Black Majority*; *South Carolina and Barbados Connections: Selections from South Carolina Historical Magazine*, ed. Stephen Hoffius, (Charleston, SC: Home House Press, 2011).

25 Thomas Benjamin, *The Atlantic World: Europeans, Africans, Indians and Their Shared History, 1400–1900* (Cambridge, UK: Cambridge University Press, 2009); David Eltis, *The Rise of African Slavery in the Atlantic World* (Cambridge, UK: Cambridge University Press, 2000); David Brion Davis, *Inhuman Bondage: The Rise and Fall of Slavery in the New World* (Oxford, UK; New York: Oxford University Press, 2006).

26 Current examples of LDHI exhibitions that highlight Atlantic World connections include Mary Battle, lead curator, "African Passages, Lowcountry Adaptations," *Lowcountry Digital History Initiative* (2013), http://ldhi .library.cofc.edu/exhibits/show/africanpassageslowcountryadapt; Carl Wise

and David Wheat, "African Laborers for a New Empire: Iberia, Slavery, and the Atlantic World," *Lowcountry Digital History Initiative* (2014), http://ldhi.library.cofc.edu/exhibits/show/african_laborers_for_a_new_emp; and John Harris, "Voyage of the Echo: The Trails of an Illegal Trans-Atlantic Slave Ship," *Lowcountry Digital History Initiative* (2014), http://ldhi.library.cofc .edu/exhibits/show/voyage-of-the-echo-the-trials.

27 The partnership between the Center for History and New Media (CHNM) and the Scholars' Lab launched in 2011. Their goal was to "enable scholars, students, and library and museum professionals to create geospatial and temporal visualizations of archival collections using a Neatline toolset within CHNM's popular, open source Omeka exhibition platform." For more information see Tom Scheinfeldt, "CHNM and Scholars' Lab Partner on 'Omeka + Neatline,'" *Omeka* (blog), http://omeka.org/blog/2011/02/15 /chnm-and-scholars-lab-partner-on-omeka-neatline.

28 LDHI's project team considered several other free and/or open-source options for building online exhibitions before they decided on Omeka. They determined that Omeka offered the most user-friendly interface for humanities scholars with minimal technical training. Other options included WordPress, www.wordpress.org; Drupal, www.drupal.org; and Simile Exhibit, www.simile -widgets.org/exhibit.

29 Virtualmachines, https://help.ubuntu.com/community/VirtualMachines.

30 "Exhibit Builder," *Omeka*; "FedoraConnector by Scholars' Lab," *Omeka*, http://omeka.org/add-ons/plugins/fedoraconnector.

31 "Exhibitions," *Lowcountry Digital History Initiative*, http://ldhi.library.cofc .edu/allexhibits.

32 Foundation, http://foundation.zurb.com.

33 Bootstrap, http://getbootstrap.com.

34 Grid, http://foundation.zurb.com/docs/components/grid.html.

35 Panels, http://foundation.zurb.com/docs/components/panels.html.

36 Fortunately, major academic organizations such as the American Historical Association are beginning to propose strategies for evaluating digital humanities projects as credible scholarly work for consideration in hiring, tenure, and promotion in academic institutions. For more information, see Seth Denbo, "Draft Guidelines on the Evaluation of Digital Scholarship," *AHA Today: A Blog of the American Historical Association*, http://blog.historians .org/2015/04/draft-guidelines-evaluation-digital-scholarship.

37 Philip Simmons Foundation, "Keeper of the Gate: Philip Simmons Ironwork in Charleston, South Carolina," *Lowcountry Digital History Initiative* (2014), http://ldhi.library.cofc.edu/exhibits/show/philip_simmons.

38 Polhemus's exhibition revolves around the James Poyas Daybook, which is held in the archives of the Charleston Museum and digitized through LCDL. Neal D. Polhemus, "The James Poyas Daybook: An Account of a Charles Town Merchant," *Lowcountry Digital History Initiative* (2014), http://ldhi.library.cofc.edu/exhibits/show/james_poyas_daybook_eighteenth. Other LDHI exhibitions that highlight specific archival collections from a LCDL partner institution include "Keeper of the Gate: Philip Simmons Ironwork in Charleston, South Carolina" (Avery Research Center's Philip Simmons Collection) and "The Pollitzer Family of South Carolina" (South Carolina Historical Society's Pollitzer Family Papers). Philip Simmons Foundation, "Keeper of the Gate"; Jessica Short and Katherine Purcell, "The Pollitzer Family of South Carolina," *Lowcountry Digital History Initiative* (2013), http://ldhi.library.cofc.edu/exhibits/show/pollitzer_family_sc.

39 For example, for Kerry Taylor's *The Charleston Hospital Workers' Movement, 1968–1969*, one of the strike leaders, Mary Moultrie, served as an editorial contributor. Kerry Taylor, "Sources: The Charleston Hospital Workers' Movement, 1968–1969," *Lowcountry Digital History Initiative* (2013), http://ldhi.library.cofc.edu/exhibits/show/charleston_hospital_workers_mo/sources_3.

40 For examples, see Millicent Brown, Jon Hale, and Clerc Cooper, "Somebody Had to Do It: First Children in School Desegregation," *Lowcountry Digital History Initiative* (2015), http://ldhi.library.cofc.edu/exhibits/show/somebody_had_to_do_it; and Taylor, "The Charleston Hospital Workers' Movement, 1968–1969."

41 Digital Public Library of America, http://dp.la. Library of Congress: American Memory.

42 "Contribute," *Lowcountry Digital History Initiative*, http://ldhi.library.cofc.edu/contribute.

43 For example, in 2013, LDHI graduate assistant Beth Gniewek was in charge of acquiring exhibition materials for "The Orangeburg Massacre" by Jack Schuler. In the process, Gniewek identified numerous materials from the Cleveland L. Sellers Papers at the Avery Research Center for the exhibition, and worked with Avery Research Center archivist Aaron Spelbring and digital scholarship librarian Heather Gilbert to digitize a sampling from this collection to go in

LCDL. While only a few collection items appear in the exhibition, through Gniewek's digitization work, users can follow links to see the digitized materials from this collection in LCDL. Jack Shuler, "The Orangeburg Massacre," *Lowcountry Digital History Initiative* (2013), http://ldhi.library.cofc.edu /exhibits/show/orangeburg-massacre.

44 According to Google Analytics, as of December 2015, nearly two years since the project's initial launch in February 2014, LDHI has received over 82,000 individual users, over 103,000 sessions, and over 252,000 page views. Google Analytics (December 2, 2015), http://www.google.com/analytics.

45 "Annual List of Best Historical Materials Selected by RUSA's History Section," *American Library Association*, www.ala.org/news/press-releases/2015/02 /annual-list-best-historical-materials-selected-rusa-s-history-section; Bradford J. Wood, "Lowcountry Digital Library; and Lowcountry Digital History Initiative," *Digital History Review in The Journal of American History* 102, No. 1 (June 2015): 330.

4 | *Curating Menus:* Digesting Data for Critical Humanistic Inquiry

Katherine Rawson

INTRODUCTION

Beginning in 2011, people across the United States came to the *What's On the Menu?* website and typed in snippets of text—names of dishes and prices on menus that ranged from the 1850s to the 2000s. They were working from images of menus digitized and held by the New York Public Library (NYPL). Out of curiosity, interest, or school assignment, these people were building a data set of over one million points of information about American dining.

This data set, which continues to grow, is a treasure trove for researchers, particularly those interested in twentieth-century America and its food culture. Anyone can easily download the data set from NYPL's website; however, the data is not easy to use: though the set is structured, the information in it is messy. Because untrained volunteers typed the menu item data in a free-text field, it contains an array of orthographic variations. The menu data, much of which was created by an earlier team of volunteer transcribers working from handwritten catalog cards, is also highly irregular.

Propelled by the promise of the data despite its messy state and by the investments of the many people who created it, *Curating Menus,* the project that is the focus of this chapter, aims to make the data more usable for researchers. It does so by beginning with a framework of critical inquiry about the data.

Curating Menus is an ongoing research and data curation project that relies on the New York Public Library's *What's On the Menu?* data. Its goal is to produce and foster scholarship about food and foodways in the twentieth-century United States by cleaning, indexing, and presenting the *What's*

On the Menu? data for analysis by scholars (including ourselves). The project consists of two key parts: humanities research and data curation. However, these parts are not completely distinctive. They are recursive, shaping and informing each other, and most often, they are integrated. *Curating Menus* is as much about fashioning structures of knowledge as it is about the many technical pieces that we will use in the process.

Curating Menus uses a recursive and integrated structure of knowledge that acknowledges the many people involved in creating the data set. It aims to maintain the information that these different people produced—from the process of collecting the menus in the early twentieth century to the structure of the downloadable files from the NYPL Labs. *Curating Menus'* approach to data curation, then, is deeply informed by humanities methods and theories. In particular, feminist practices and feminist theories of the archive shape our project.

This chapter will explore three interrelated projects, all based in libraries. From 1899 to 1923, volunteer librarian Frank E. Buttolph collected thousand of menus for the New York Public Library. These menus were eventually digitized and became the corpus for *What's On the Menu?*, a crowdsourced transcription project developed by NYPL Labs. This chapter will describe the stakeholders for these projects and reveal the individual contributions to generating and curating the projects' data. This case study in data curation as cultural construction begins with two claims: there are traces of many contributors in our data sets, and a critical engagement requires us to see them. Ultimately, this chapter argues that scholars and librarians can and should structure digital projects in a way that reveals explicit engagement with these traces.

DIGITAL PRODUCTION, FEMINISM, AND CRITICAL HUMANISTIC INQUIRY

Despite its goal of cleaning and using a data set, the first product of *Curating Menus* was an archive-based research essay. The essay examined the life and work of Frank E. Buttolph. Because she collected and curated most of the menus, understanding her positionality and the culture she worked in is important to using data in ways that are rigorous. Beginning with cultural context—and believing that it is central to how we can use data to answer humanities questions—shaped how the *Curating Menus* team approached curating the data as well.

The work of feminist scholars not only framed our understanding of the history of Frank E. Buttolph, but it also provided ways of approaching digital data curation. In "Whence Feminism? Assessing Feminist Interventions in Digital Literary Archives," Jacqueline Wernimont explores how the development and format of two well-known literary digital projects, the Orlando Project and the Women Writers Project, constitutes a "feminist archive" beyond collecting women's writing. She considers the ways that the digital archive facilitates feminist structures. By providing documentation that makes editorial decisions and power visible, these projects push against a single authority in the archive and allow for the imagining of alternative interventions. Further, by presenting the technosocial scene in which these projects developed, Wernimont illuminates the feminist work that collaboration can do, transforming and distributing authority in the archive.[1]

In "Feminist HCI: Taking Stock and Outlining an Agenda for Design," Shaowen Bardzell presents similar structural understandings of how feminist frameworks can shape design in human–computer interactions. Three of the elements that she focuses on—pluralism, participation, and self-disclosure—align with those Wernimont identifies.[2] These principles influenced the approach of *Curating Menus*. Instead of "correcting" data or developing an authoritative data set, the project aims to maintain the contribution of multiple participants and to make those contributions clear—not simply as an acknowledgment of their work, but as a pluralistic and transparent approach to knowledge-making.

HANDS

As the product of 115 years of work and not one but two (maybe three) crowdsourcing projects, the *What's On the Menu?* and *Curating Menus* data is the cumulative work of many people.

Trevor Muñoz and I began *Curating Menus* in 2014. As we began to formulate questions that we could answer using the *What's On the Menu?* data, we wanted to answer the question "What does this data represent?" Armed with years of humanities training, we turned not to the cells in our spreadsheet, but to the people who made this data. Defined both as the origin and the record of origin, provenance is central to using humanities data in ways that are rigorous—to see the ways that it is situated historically, shaped by the people and societies that formed it.

When discussing our project's provenance, I sometimes say that Muñoz was looking for a food scholar to work on the data he'd been curating and that I was lucky to be that person. But our origin story is slightly more complicated. We are not actually filling in gaps for each other: we are both humanities scholars and librarians, with backgrounds in food culture. Despite our different educational credentials, we have worked on a range of digital humanities projects, hold less traditional library positions, and are fairly knowledgeable of and invested in food. I say this because our positionality—who we are professionally and culturally (and even what seem like trivial biographical notes: we were born three months apart)—impacts our research and the ways we clean and sort data for future use. Just as the lives of the other people who are part of this long story of food information shape what we are working with and how it can best be used, so do we.

Muñoz and I also understand that the way we choose to categorize and normalize data for search and analysis will shape what we and other scholars ask and see. Where will we decide to make distinctions? Are Chicken Marsala and Coq au Vin and Chicken with Wine Sauce a collection of related dishes? Or maybe thornier because of what seems—on both sides—so apparent: is a half of a chicken, a quarter of a chicken, and a chicken the same thing?[3] And what are the implications of us deciding so?

As the scholarship of food makes quite clear, our dishes and our meals are intimately tied to how we define ourselves and each other. *Curating Menus* will draw on the knowledge and perspectives of the people working in the many fields our data has implications for: food studies, history, cultural studies, environmental studies, and anthropology.

Before this project, Muñoz had already been working with the data, using it to train colleagues and graduate students in the humanities and in library and information sciences to curate data. After an initial data curation seminar, Muñoz and MLIS student Lydia Zvyagintseva developed a precursor project to *Curating Menus*, in which they began exploring ways to clean the data and categorize it for future researchers.[4] The project was framed as a prototype *for* content-interested researchers; our current work shifts the focus—we are simultaneously researchers using the content and developers of improved data resources.

Curating Menus also collaborates with a set of public librarians from the digital humanities-focused NYPL Labs, who developed and worked on the *What's On the Menu?* project. Over a dozen people at NYPL Labs and other departments produced the infrastructure for this large-scale crowd-sourcing transcription project of the library's menus. Since the project's launch, thousands of volunteers have transcribed and reviewed over 17,500 digitized menus.

A decade before *What's On the Menu?*, twenty-first-century librarians digitized the menus, and another set of volunteers transformed the paper records of the menus into a database. This earlier project understood the immense usefulness of being able to explore the menus by a variety of categories. By transcribing the collection's records from print catalog cards into a database, researchers could search by restaurant, location, and other metadata previously buried in the records.[5]

Both of these digital projects at the New York Public Library, as well as *Curating Menus*, relied on decades of work by librarians who acted as stewards of the collection. These librarians worked with scholars as they sifted through the thousands of sorted-by-date boxes of menus. They accessioned Buttolph's personal papers in the 1980s, including correspondences that trace the development of the collection and include information about the meals they represent.

Each of these digital projects was born from the work of Buttolph and the many individuals who donated the menus, in what was (if one forgives the anachronism) an early twentieth-century crowdsourced project. Buttolph was a teacher and translator from a small town in Pennsylvania who had a deep engagement with how to make and preserve history, particularly social history in the United States. Although she collected a range of materials in the twenty years she volunteered at the New York Public Library, her longest and most significant project was her collection of menus, which she believed, was for "future students of history." To obtain the materials, she corresponded with hundreds of people, placed ads in trade magazines, and worked with newspaper and journal editors to publish stories about the collection that encouraged readers to contribute their menus to grow it even further. She then cataloged and prepared the menus for preservation and access.[6]

These letters, articles, and catalogs are artifacts of the people who made the menus. They are the historical record of the restaurant managers, the cooks, the printers, the people who we are trying to get to, across a hundred years and a passel of formats, with our million points of data. The history of the collection matters because it reflects the ways that the data was shaped and what it can tell us. For a large data set like this, it is important to understand how it was created and parsed over time. In this case, diving into the provenance provides detailed texture and insights into knowledge organization.

FINGERPRINTS

What traces are left on the data? How do we maintain meaningful traces while making messy data easier to use? It is no surprise that the data based on eight decades of individuals typing and retyping information is full of variation. In fact, the accuracy of the NYPL data is perhaps more impressive. The NYPL's downloadable data set includes information from three places: NYPL's metadata, the menu collection database, and the *What's On the Menu?* transcriptions.

The two key moments that introduced inconsistency in the data points were the earlier volunteer-made menu metadata database and the crowd-sourced menu transcription project.

In the menu file of the *What's On the Menu?* data set, for example, researchers might encounter "Waldorf Astoria," "Waldorf-Astoria," "WAL-DORF ASTORIA," "waldorf astoria," "Waldorf Astoria Hotel," "Hotel Waldorf Astoria," "The Waldorf Astoria," "Waldorf," or simply, "Astoria."[7] Having standardized data that conforms to a controlled vocabulary would allow researchers eventually to run analyses about who used the Waldorf Astoria for their events, what the restaurant served, whether that changed over time or between groups, and how it compared to other similar establishments or to its sister establishment in Philadelphia. The material could also be combined with manuscript materials from the hotel, such as ledgers and recipes.

Collating the data by normalizing to a single name can be a problem. Not all similarly named places signify the same place. Though they stood on the three hundred block of Park Avenue in New York City, the Waldorf, the Astoria, the Waldorf-Astoria, and the Waldorf Astoria are different historical (though interconnected) establishments. Our goal then was to smooth out orthographic inconsistencies while maintaining meaningful variations in the data. This is at the heart of making good humanities data sets that can be machine queried: how do we keep the texture while smoothing out the inconsistencies?

We take two approaches. First, we maintain the original data point, and simply add more information to the data set. Second, for the new, normalized data, we decide what variation was significant. When are transcribers maintaining information that is meaningful, and when are the differences just manifesting differences in transcription methods—keeping capitalization or not, for example?

Curating Menus' solution to normalizing relies on a technical method and a research method. The data set has identifiable features that, almost certainly, do not signify difference. For example, in this set, variation in capitalization is almost never meaningful. These can be removed en masse, computationally. Second, we identify entities we would need to research. Given a list of similar place names, we study historical records—often beginning with the images of the menus themselves—to see if places or organizations are the same.

A similar issue happens with the food items. How do we deal with thirteen ways to describe a half chicken? Again, we can identify the things we are almost certain do not signify difference: "chicken (half)," "half chicken," "half of a chicken," "1/2 chicken," "Half chicken," and "HALF CHICKEN" are probably similar enough to smooth out their differences.[8] However, our data structure also keeps a record of the orthographic differences, in case they are of value to Buttolph's "future historians," who may be invested in representations of fractions or the economic status of word order or preposition use. We are also aware of how different the actual half chickens might have been. We or other scholars may be able to make judgments about the chicken's preparation based on other aspects of the menu, further historical research, or perhaps even an analysis of the other items on the menu.

While tools like Google's *Refine*, now *OpenRefine*, offer solutions for smoothing out these kinds of variation through pattern-based clustering, they can have scale limitations and don't provide a simple way to keep the original orthography and have a clean collection.[9] To find the matching selections of dishes across the data computationally, we built a small piece of software, which relies on *Elasticsearch*, and wrote a query that finds what we call "fingerprints."[10] These are words in a dish, without care to order, capitalization, punctuation, or some prepositions and articles. The name signifies a unique characteristic that identifies a dish (like a human fingerprint). While in the project's software code, these fingerprints allow us to create more uniform data, they are also reminiscent of the smudges that let us know this data was crafted and shaped by people who had a stake in it being useful, people who believed in its worth.

DUSTING FOR FINGERPRINTS

While Frank E. Buttolph made sure that there were no fingerprints on the menus she collected, often returning submissions that had traces of food or dirt on them, we can still see all sorts of hands in her work. In handwritten and typed letters, in articles from the early twentieth century, and even in which menus are in the collection, we see the people who fashioned it. Our goal is to find ways to add these traces to the data set, while increasing the usefulness of the information in the transcriptions as well.

Curating Menus aims to reveal strata of meaning. Each layer in the data set shapes the experiences of another and provides the kind of rich resource that humanities scholars seek in their research. In addition to adding information, the many people who worked on this data set across the twentieth and twenty-first centuries also structured their data in ways that are significant, not only because they influence the validity of the evidence, but also because they suggest different kinds of questions. Being aware of those implicit structures of knowledge allows scholars to see the landscape of information and knowledge differently. Two of those organizational structures—Buttolph's catalog cards and the "What's On the Menu?" interface—demonstrate different kinds of readings of their objects.

When we started the *Curating Menus* project, the plan was to briefly discuss the contours of the data on our website, a precursor to digging into the data itself. Nonetheless, as Muñoz and I discuss in "When a Woman Collects," we found ourselves digging much deeper into the initial development of the collection, in part because we wanted answers to *why* the collection looked like it did. Given what we learned about the development of this research collection, we have a much clearer idea of the kinds of cultural questions Buttolph would have been interested in.

For example, understanding Buttolph's catalog cards is critical to understanding the overall project. Knowledge is structured in many ways, but metadata is integral to how people research in the digital humanities. Metadata makes it possible to make claims about the data or to perform comparative or other pattern-seeking analytical processes, be they computational or not. A long intellectual and practical history with metadata is part of why digital humanities make sense in libraries, why librarians are DH scholars, and why DH scholars collaborate with librarians.

The *What's On the Menu?* data comes in four connected CSVs, structured around the menus, menu items (a transcribed dish), menu pages, and "dishes." Each of these has data from multiple sources, including the transcription data, metadata about the transcription and the menu created by the computer application, and bibliographic metadata from the cataloging and database of the menu collection.

In the file for the menus, there are columns for "place," "event," "occasion," "venue," and "notes." The separate category for sponsor and location reflects an important element of the original print collection on which the data set is based, and its origins can be found in Buttolph's catalog collection.

The Frank E. Buttolph menu collection includes eighteen boxes of menus and boxes of catalog cards that match each menu. Buttolph categorized and organized the cards by type of group that was organizing the meal or the occasion for the meal. Then each category (Masonic orders, for example) was organized by place (states, New York City). On each card is the sponsoring organization (the cards are further ordered alphabetically by this piece of information), the date she accessioned the menu, and the date and location of the meal (i.e., June 1, 1918; Bellevue Hotel). If Buttolph had more than one menu from the sponsor, those menus were also listed on the same card, with locations and dates.

In Buttolph's organization, it is more significant that both meals are from the Masons than that the meals occurred next to each other in New York City. The date of a meal is important enough to record, but not an element of organization at all. Although one does not need an explicit understanding of Buttolph's categorization in order to use the *What's On the Menu?* data set, knowing about her organization system may suggest more useful questions for research.

Her schema is simply *recorded* by the catalog cards, but her collecting practices are embedded in the very structure of the collection. This means two things: First, it exposes that there *are* questions that are appropriately answered by the collection at scale, and it gives a sense of what some of those questions could be. Second, it necessitates paying attention to subsetting the data in ways that are not encumbered by (or conversely could focus on) her interests in social structures and particularly celebration, the nation-state, and civic organizations.

Buttolph's schema is embedded in the data, a featured demonstrated by my own experience with it. Before looking at Buttolph's catalog cards (which are held at the New York Public Library), I began organizing the menu data myself. It was apparent that there were two basic types of menus: (1) menus for ordering and (2) set menus for events. These different constructions of menus—a space for choice and availability versus a description of what would or did take place—reflect different food practices. Food events would often have been confined to particular invited guests who would be eating the same meal at the same time. Conversely, ordering menus are often from public establishments, where people eating together may have different meals and people in different parties would eat at different times. The information the menus include is also dissimilar (prices or not, for example) and signifies differently (event menus reflect decisions about structuring taste and theme, for example).

However, there were numerous menus that fit into a middle space: menus from steamships and railroads, for example. These menus had characteristics of each descriptive type. They were often without prices, and they were sometimes singular in what they offered. The experience of people eating and making food in these places was key to why they didn't seem to fit into my categories. The people on trains and steamships were not invited, like at an event; however, they also did not have access to an array of options, as one does in a cityscape of restaurants. We framed five basic types: restaurant, association/group, person, transit, and hotel. While these categories did not cover all the menus, they seemed to reflect the menus.[11] Buttolph's categories recorded in her catalog cards mapped on to these categories, and her metadata system also encoded the significance of event and daily menus, through both categories of organization and recording location and sponsor. Moreover, she considered the sponsor to be the more significant part of the menu, an organizational structure that suggests a set of questions quite different from those about restaurant development.[12]

Just as Buttolph's collecting and categorization practices shape our data set, so do the decisions of the NYPL librarians and developers as they created the framework and tools for the *What's On the Menu?* project. The group decided that users would transcribe dishes and prices—the names of food and how much they cost. This information could be cross-referenced with metadata included in the digitization process to learn something about food history in the United States. The information that the NYPL staff decided users would record might seem self-evident for a menu transcription project; however, it reflects decisions to not include other types of information, which may also be important to researchers. There is no way of recording non-dish–related textual content—the taglines of restaurants, phone numbers and addresses, food categories, information about staff and management, any origin stories, pithy phrases, or citations of Bible verses. This kind of text can reveal a great deal about the kind of establishment the food was served at. The group decided not to include this information because it was much less uniform and because they were aiming to collect a volume of information with as little burden on the users who would transcribe the information as possible.[13]

In the *What's On the Menu?* data set, visual information, or design, is also omitted. In fact, many of the twentieth-century discussions of the Buttolph menu collection are about design. Buttolph herself was interested in the menus' pictures and materials: watercolors of airplanes, sketches of literary figures, silk pages, ribbons to bind, a range of handwriting styles and handmade fonts.

The data set omits information about the framing and layout of the menu where the dishes occur: are they listed as desserts, as appetizers, as roasts, as entrees? How do different menus divide their contents? Not having a space for this data in the set is part of the nature of shaping a project: resources are finite; to attend to one part, we jettison another. It also means that the data does not accommodate some kinds of work. However, this kind of information can still be tied to the data. The *What's On the Menu?* data set does this in two ways: it includes a link to the digitized menu page, providing relatively easy access to the image (which could be analyzed by humans or perhaps computer vision), and it includes information about the position of each dish on the page, making it possible to aggregate dishes based on where they are placed on a menu.

CONCLUSION

The decisions data creators and curators make shape what scholars can say and unmasks how digital humanities is formed by human frameworks as much as technological possibility and limitation. *Curating Menus* contends with and makes accessible the structures of knowledge that we have found within the data set and that we are making. This part of the process of humanities data curation has several features.

First, *Curating Menus* adds information rather than correcting or overwriting it. In this way, it disperses authority and maintains plural notions of knowledge. Second, it aggregates materials that may be able to be added to the data set later, or may be in forms that cannot be added to the data set. This includes things like biographical information about Buttolph, which may ultimately be another feature or classification in the data set, but is currently a narrative. In addition to the images of the menus themselves, *Curating Menus* aims to digitize the letters from the Buttolph collection—mostly written to her, including contextual information about the establishments, menus, and sometimes even the meals they accompanied. Our goal is to link these letters to the menus, just as the dish data is linked to the images of the menus. We also want to include sample images of Buttolph's cards as well as annotated photographs of the catalog card collection in its boxes.

We are aiming to create a different kind of documentation for digital humanities projects. This documentation draws on the characteristics of both technical documentation and archival practices. Like the programming languages and tools we use, it includes documentation that tells about how to use the data and how it was prepared; however, we are also documenting in ways that reflect what the librarians, including Buttolph, have done: including biographical and historical information and analysis of the many people who made this data through essays and bibliographies.

The construction of the project acknowledges and connects knowledge structures. A simple version of this is the data dictionary we wrote in order to clearly identify the materials in the NYPL CSVs, which gives information about each of the categories of the data and where that information comes from. A more complex version of this is indexing that includes and allows for multiple information structures, with information about the provenance of those structures. This allows us to include things from Buttolph's categorization as well as NYPL's, to add our own, and to leave space for future scholars who may want to connect a wealth of other information including dictionaries of organizations, food sources, or environmental data.

NOTES

1   Jacqueline Wernimont, "Whence Feminism? Assessing Feminist Interventions in Digital Literary Archives," *Digital Humanities Quarterly* 7, No. 1 (2013).

2   Shaowen Bardzell, "Feminist HCI: Taking Stock and Outlining an Agenda for Design," in *Proceedings of the SIGCHI Conference on Human Factors in Computing Systems* (2010):1301–310.

3   For the record, our current answer is "no."

4   Lydia Zvyagintseva, "Organizing Historical Menus: A Data Curation Experiment," *MITH* (blog), June 31, 2013, http://mith.umd.edu/taxonomizing -historical-menus-a-data-curation-project.

5   Michael Lascarides and Ben Vershbow, "What's On the Menu?: Crowdsourcing at the New York Public Library," *Crowdsourcing our Cultural Heritage,* ed. Mia Ridge (Surrey, UK: Ashgate, 2014).

6   Trevor Muñoz and Katie Rawson, "When a Woman Collects Menus: Sifting Stories and Histories of Frank E. Buttolph's Research Collection," *Curating Menus* (April 2014), http://www.curatingmenus.org/articles/when-a-woman -collects-menus.

7   According to NPYL Labs's Ben Vershbow, 157 variations were encountered.

8   In the NYPL data, each spelling or form constitutes a dish, which leads to overlaps.

9   Trevor Muñoz, "Borrow a Cup of Sugar? Or Your Data Analysis Tools?—More Work with NYPL's Open Data, Part Three," *Trevor Muñoz* (blog), January 2014, http://trevormunoz.com/notebook/2014/01/10/borrowing-data-science-tools -more-work-with-nypl-open-data-part-three.html.

10   The normalization is being done with a small piece of *JavaScript* software we developed. This chapter does not cover the technical aspects of *Curating Menus*.

11   For names of sponsors that were ambiguous, we looked on the menus and Googled the name. This produced some surprises: What appear to be men's names are often department stores; "house" is more likely a hotel than a restaurant. It also presented a few conundrums, including this one: in what category is a casino?

12   Two of the most significant scholarly contributions using the Buttolph menu collection, before *What's On the Menu?*, focus on restaurant culture: Andrew P. Haley, *Turning the Tables: The Aristocratic Restaurant and the Rise of the American Middle Class, 1880–1920* (Chapel Hill: University of North Carolina Press, 2011), and a suite of essays by historian Paul Freedman.

13   Lascarides and Vershbow; Trevor Owens, "Digital Cultural Heritage and the Crowd," *Curator: The Museum Journal* 56, No. 1 (2013): 121–30.

5 | Many Voices, One Experiment: Building Toward Generous Interfaces for Oral History Collections with *Mapping the Long Women's Movement*

Seth Kotch[1]

INTRODUCTION

This chapter will address one approach to extending the archival model outside the library, as represented by the library's online catalog, and into the more flexible and experimental space of digital humanities. Therefore, it is less digital humanities *in* the library, than digital humanities *inspired by* the library and done with the strengths and habits of the library in mind. It addresses *Mapping the Long Women's Movement*,[2] a project that reimagines the oral history collection as a dynamic digital space that illuminates connections between materials and invites browsing among them. The project team's experience with this work pointed to ways in which traditional and nontraditional archival processes can inspire and support DH projects, and the way in which DH projects can nudge and challenge archives to create more responsive interfaces and useful presentations.

Mapping the Long Women's Movement represents fifty oral histories with people in the Appalachian South that address the strikingly understudied story of second-wave feminism in the region.[3] These interviews situate southern women's activism in the context of the women's movement of the 1970s, not only by adding new perspectives to a critical conversation dominated by studies of coastal cities but also by understanding the role of space and place in the creation and development of feminist consciousnesses, institutions, networks, and activisms in places like rural Bumpass Cove, Tennessee, and urban Knoxville. This project focused on the grassroots women's movement that developed in eastern Tennessee; women-led unionization drives; antipoverty campaigns; environmental justice campaigns; reproductive rights and women's health; and women's fight for access to and equity in public education and in the workplace. The research was grounded in an extensive, deeply theoretical body of scholarship, perhaps most notably works by Doreen Massey, Anne Enke, and Nancy Fraser that explore how women and their allies use public and private spaces to build movements,[4] but ultimately it rested on the lived experiences of the interviewees.

The interviews trace feminist activism in rural and urban areas and showcase how widespread the women's movement was, the pathways leading in and out of the movement, and the routes movement activists—not all of whom self-identify as activists, as participants in a movement, or as feminists—used to pursue their own civic, personal, and professional growth. Interviewees ranged from labor, civil rights, and environmental activists to artists, attorneys, clergy, and community and church activists. Their testimonials to the role of space in shaping their lives and identity suggested the utility of a digital project that could visualize those spaces and their connections to one another.

The goal of *Mapping the Long Women's Movement (MLWM)* was to visually represent not just feminist use of space in Appalachia, but also connections between people, places (like towns and cities, not to mention the American South as a whole), and spaces (like universities, health clinics, homes, and other commercial and public spaces). The interviews themselves yielded not only stories of personal transformation and productive activism on reproductive services and domestic violence, among other issues, but also revealed a network of activism that extended beyond the southeastern United States and into urban centers in the Northeast and the West and even to international sites. By situating the interviews on a Cartesian map, the project team hoped to add "showing" to the interviewees' "telling" about their lives.

Doing this showing required something of an epistemological shift away from the standard model in place at the Southern Oral History Program and many other oral history programs, major and minor, wherein the creation of research matter exists separately from its preservation, archiving, and dissemination and toward a model where the presentation of the material flows out of its intellectual underpinnings. This new model would not only present oral histories in response to a keyword search or browsing prompt, but would also allow users to explore results in ways that could be suggestive, provocative, and revealing. This project would visualize an archival collection while allowing users to manipulate that visualization.

Our approach to this collaborative work—which engaged staff historians and field scholars at the Southern Oral History Program[5] in the Center for the Study of the American South[6] at the University of North Carolina at Chapel Hill (UNC), archivists at Carolina's Southern Historical Collection,[7] and staff and students at the newly organized Digital Innovation Lab[8] in the UNC's Department of American Studies—draws on Mitchell Whitelaw's concept of a "generous interface." Whitelaw posits interfaces that "offer rich, browsable views; provide evocative samples of primary content; and support an understanding of context and relationships."[9]

The inspiration behind our understanding of Whitelaw's ideal is the fact that in many archives, and certainly in the expectations of the users of those archives, the digital has replaced the corporeal. To paraphrase David Weinberger's three orders of order[10]: In the first order, we organize things. In the second, we organize partial information about those things, such as cards in a card catalog, which exist nearby in a discernible order. The third order, though, is "dynamic and miscellaneous,"[11] casting aside the limitations of organizing physical objects in physical spaces and allowing both archivists and users to dynamically organize and reorganize archives every time they use them without interfering with other users' interventions.

For library users, gone is the expectation of a rich visual and physical experience that follows a fairly bare-bones textual search; it seems increasingly true that users want the experience of searching *itself* to offer them something. And even if there is a fascinating and thought-provoking object awaiting them on a shelf in a library, it is less and less likely researchers will pursue it if they can see a suitable representation of it online. In short, the archive's representation of the object has subsumed the object. The work of archiving can no longer be understood as separate from the work of disseminating. At Carolina, that dissemination is done through the Southern Historical Collection (SHC).

One of the great strengths of the Southern Oral History Program (SOHP) is that its interviews are archived in the University of North Carolina's Southern Historical Collection. It is easier than ever for individuals and small organizations to responsibly and effectively archive and make available oral histories, but the advantages that affiliation with UNC Libraries gives the SOHP are undeniable. That our interviews are archived and preserved at a major research university library means that they are available to scores of students, teachers, and researchers around the world; that they will be preserved as long as possible as physical objects (cassettes, papers) and in perpetuity as digital objects (MP3s, WAVs, documents) even as file formats change; and that they are likely to benefit from the technical and access innovations taking place in the library, whether or not the SOHP is aware of them. And, maybe most important to the staff historians and student-historians at the SOHP, the arrangement frees them to research and conduct more interviews.

The arrangement is mutually beneficial. Under the shared supervision of SHC and SOHP staff, student archivists at "the Southern," as it is known, catalog and maintain the SOHP's thousands of oral histories, including preservation and web audio and text records such as transcripts, tape logs, and field notes. Those texts are scanned with optical character recognition software to make them keyword searchable, and each is assigned a number of Library of Congress keywords, which are more or less useful for bounded browsing within the collection.

But like any happy marriage, this partnership is not without its problems. And like in any happy marriage, these problems are best addressed through communication and experimentation. The issues discussed below are common to any curated collections of research objects (i.e., "libraries"), but to oral historians they seem especially troubling for oral histories, which are complex, compound sources similar to but not identical to the books and articles with which they share virtual shelf space.[12] It is important to emphasize that these thorny issues do not bother many trained academic scholars, some of whom reject curation as interference, mistrust transcripts produced by third parties, and have a more specific sense of their research needs than undergraduate students or so-called "laypersons." Trained historians are not the audience for this project. Our audience is the undergraduate student, the public outside of academia, and those more interested in serendipitous discovery than targeted research, though we hope as we continue to develop it, the project will have broad application for scholars, particularly in their teaching.

Before laying out the problems mentioned above, it may be useful to briefly define terms. *Mapping the Long Women's Movement* is at its heart an oral history visualization project. But what is an oral history? This is not the space to explore this deceptively complex question at length. Scholars have written at length on the discipline, which, emerging in the 1940s and reforming itself in the crucible of the 1960s and with precursors stretching back at least to the 1930s, sought to include yet unheard voices in historic scholarship: those of African Americans, Latin@s, women, the working class and others whose lives, seeming smaller to many working historians, were ignored.[13] Its advocates fought for its recognition as a legitimate discipline and they seem to have succeeded, as measured by the wide adoption of oral history methodology across disciplines not only as a core research tool but also as an essential complement to traditional archival research. Practitioners continue to think on the page about oral history's past and future, which has become deeply entangled with digital practices and dissemination due to its reliance on technology for production and consumption.

ORAL HISTORY PROBLEMS IN A DIGITAL PRESENT

The question here, though, is not "What is oral history?"; it is "What is *an* oral history?" And, more specifically, "What is an oral history for the purposes of this digital project?" There are many answers, among them that oral history is triumvirate of word and deed: a methodology, the application of that methodology in a structured interview, and the result of that application in a representation of the interview.[14] In the archive, the oral history exists as the latter: a series of integrated audio and textual records that model but are not constrained by the narrator-driven sequential telling of a life history. This definition, such as it is, leads us to the first and perhaps most insidious of oral history's problems: silence.

Silence. Oral historians like to talk about the power of the human voice, channeling Bakhtin's celebration of the power of personal narratives to illuminate unseen aspects of the human experience. But as many oral historians have pointed out—Jacquelyn Hall citing the field's central irony and Michael Frisch hauling up its "deep, dark secret"[15]—very few people actually listen to oral history, and by and large, once the interviewer stops the recording, the interviewee is never heard from again. This silence is important for at least two reasons. First, among oral history's strengths is its ability to connect people with the human power to create and interpret history. The core driver of that connection is the sound of the human voice. Its richness, its tone, its inflection, its starts and stops—all these qualities carry meaning that lends itself to interpretation.

There is wide consensus in the oral history community about the limits of just reading oral history as text.[16] When an oral history is transcribed, it undergoes what Frisch calls a "flattening of meaning." Frisch writes,

> Meaning inheres in context and setting, in gesture, in tone, in body language, in expression, in pauses, in performed skills and movements. To the extent we are restricted to text and transcription, we will never locate such moments and meaning, much less have the chance to study, reflect on, learn from, and share them.[17]

Sadly, oral historians and their allies have been complicit in this flattening, creating reams and reams of transcripts and thus offering researchers an easy way to avoid listening and, indeed, to avoid engaging in depth with interviews at all, "CNTRL-F-ing" their way through narrators' life stories.

Furthermore, silence diminishes the power of the interviewee in telling and retelling, even if only by use of the rewind function, their own story. Oral history scholarship is rooted in the noble if not always realized concept of shared authority[18]: the oral historian brings his or her expertise about the context of the interviewee's life, and the interviewee brings her or his expertise about its specifics, and of course those areas of expertise overlap and influence one another. By silencing the interview audio, even in a responsibly described collection, the oral historian impedes the field's mission to increase the humanity in the study of history. In other words, using text records of interviews alone scuttles the core mission and values of oral history scholarship.

This is a persuasive point, and was never truer than today, when widely available technology means listening is more possible and likely than ever. Such technology also opens the interpretive doors to scores of students and scholars, who might in the not-too-distant past have been restricted to reading transcripts for their own research projects. Yet oral historians and listening advocates must also acknowledge that even skimming text is preferable to avoiding engagement altogether. An undergraduate with three overlapping paper deadlines will never choose a two-hour audio file over a transcript as a resource; it is important to recognize that ease of use is a virtue, even for powerfully human sources. *MLWM* aims to combine the deep engagement engendered by listening with the utility of skimming, meeting somewhere in the middle between the deep engagement lauded by academic oral historians and complete and utter silence.

Invisibility. For people, invisibility is a superpower. For oral histories, it is a severe hindrance. It can be frustrating and difficult to find oral histories that will help you write a course paper, put together a presentation, create a teaching unit, or write a scholarly book or article. In major collections such as those at UNC, the University of Kentucky, and Berkeley's Regional Oral History Office, to name a few, users need to search across thousands of oral histories, and that is assuming the user knows that there is a body of materials to search and how to search it. Many library users at the University of North Carolina, for instance, will not drive down to the SOHP Collection to search for oral histories. They will search from the Google-esque search bar on the library's home page, and oral histories will appear as digital objects hidden among articles, books, manuscript collections, and more.[19]

If users do attempt a more constrained search among oral histories alone, they often browse under broad subject headings (such as "civil rights," which will yield thousands of results in this and other oral history collections) or type in keywords (again, such as "civil rights"). They sift through voluminous results without much sense for why they are getting the results they're getting, without much sense for why one item appears at the top of the list and another at the bottom, and without much sense for what might actually be useful to them. Oral histories are buried among other resources and assumed to be like those resources, and this invisibility translates to underuse.

Opacity. The invisibility problem stems in part from the unknowability of online searching, but also because the nature of an oral history intertwines itself with another problem: opacity. It is very difficult to gauge the contents of an oral history on first encounter, a problem exacerbated by the absence of a metadata standard for oral histories.[20] Oral history suffers from an "aboutness"[21] problem: to say an interview is about just one thing or one other thing is hopelessly imprecise. Oral histories share a lot with books and articles in that they are complex, varied, interpretive research products built collaboratively on a foundation of life experience, archival research, and secondary research. Like a multi-author volume, they may feature contributions from a variety of participants with a variety of perspectives. But even solo life histories, by far the most common form of oral history, can vary widely, shifting from, for instance, the life history of a child growing up in the rural South to the philosophy of a queer feminist activist, that child grown up. And here is where an oral history diverges from the book, because even a book with an inapt title often features an index, which can not only point the researcher to the precise information he or she may need, but also in summary presents a general sense for what the text is about. Oral histories generally lack indices, and of course their opacity is even murkier if the oral history has not been transcribed, as oral historians and their allies have only just begun experimentation with making legible the contents of digital audio files.

There is one obvious solution to the opacity problem. As one interviewee wrote in a metadata form that accompanied the individual's interview, when asked what the interview was about, "Read the damned thing." Or even better, listen to the oral history! That's research. But that could take hours, and if oral historians and archivists want to encourage students and other untrained researchers to use oral history in teaching, research, community events, and more, they have to compete with the vast stores of easily accessible information out there. Therefore, they must provide some new paths of access. Ideally, in an archive or through an interface on top of an archive, they can provide multiple paths of access to oral histories that are understandable to users.

Moreover, unlike books and articles, oral histories rarely attain surface-level descriptive metadata, otherwise known as titles, during their creation. That oral histories are most often named after the interviewees, such as "Oral History with Jane Doe," means that the grassroots philosophy of oral history plays against its discoverability as an archival object: Jane Doe is unlikely to be recognized by a researcher. For the general researcher, the one who needs the most guidance finding research material, that oral history may as well be titled, "Oral History with Person." Once again, the researcher leaves the oral history behind in favor of a more obviously legible source.

Disconnection. Anyone who has located and retrieved a specific book from a library shelf and then also grabbed the books to the right and left of it, knows how useful a well-crafted title can be for the research process, and how curated—or even just organized—collections can lead to serendipitous discovery. When we buy shoes at Zappos or music at Amazon, these retailers are always prepared to show us more items we might like to purchase through the use of recommendation systems (yes, this is also true at our beloved independent booksellers). These recommendation systems, which are integral to this online retail model of browsing, do not appear to exist in a useful way as part of academic research. Indeed, it is difficult to suggest employing a "retail model" in academia without one's gorge rising just a bit. But one of the premises or promises of digital humanities is applying new skills and intelligences to humanities practice, and retailers have been cleverly applying many of these new skills for years. Oral historians and librarians may not be able to create algorithms to help researchers "shop" for archival material, but it would be useful to find ways to suggest connections between oral histories and perhaps, eventually, empower researchers to suggest and strengthen or question those connections themselves. This requires identifying those connections; however, archivists are already doing that work by assigning basic metadata, such as Library of Congress subject headings, to oral histories that digital humanities practitioners could leverage to work toward a solution to this problem of disconnection.

MAPPING THE LONG WOMEN'S MOVEMENT

Mapping the Long Women's Movement is the straightforwardly if inelegantly titled project that emerged in order to suggest one way to address these problems. *MLWM* envisions the archive as a space that can nurture creativity and even playfulness while maintaining appropriate scholarly rigor and immersion and honoring the human subjects of research. Our basic question: can we visualize these oral histories in a way that encourages discovery, visualizes connectivity, and maintains humanity?

Years ago, someone joked that digital humanities mainly entailed creating bad maps. It is not hard to demonstrate that at the very least, this is no longer entirely true.[22] This comment reflects the way in which early digital humanities work revealed a lowering of technical barriers to innovation before the development of a cross-field theoretical skill set. So while today many digital humanities practitioners would push back against this wry generalization, they would probably recognize that the increasing sophistication and variation among mapping projects in the digital humanities represents a maturation of the field. This comment also serves as a warning against enthusiasts blundering into an unknown discipline, which can only be successfully navigated following thorough training. At the same time, bad maps find their home in the space created by Jesse Stommel's claim that "digital humanities is about breaking stuff."[23] If so, the idea of creating bad maps with good intentions is a liberating concept that should encourage tentative DH practitioners to dive joyfully into their projects, worrying less about whether they are bad than about whether they are so bad as to be useless.

Of course, there are a variety of different ways to map a set of materials, but the *MLWM* project team decided to use a standard Cartesian map because while many of the oral histories poised to contribute to the project described the growth of networks, it was important to represent the physical spaces that influenced and were influenced by social and environmental activism.

Before executing the project, the team had to confront two significant obstacles. The first was the size of the digital audio files and how to get this audio content playing on users' computers. The interviews were recorded as CD-quality WAV files, which tend to create approximately 1 gigabyte of data per hour of audio recording, but the library retains those files for preservation only. The public-facing MP3s are substantially smaller, only creating approximately 100 megabytes of data per hour of audio recording, or averaging one-tenth the size of the WAV file. Still, creating a project that involved loading audio onto users' computers would be disastrous: even a progressive download would be too weighty for most mobile devices and would likely crash browsers on even the more robust machines. We needed *MLWM* to be as lightweight as possible.

A second problem was delivering the audio. At the time of this writing, UNC Libraries is experimenting with deploying a streaming system for its audio collections. When we were developing *MLWM*, we had heard rumors of such a service but were concerned that it would not be able to be implemented by the time we wanted to launch. So we decided to upload the files to SoundCloud. This was something of a leap of faith for oral historians used to the security of a university library, but its benefits were obvious. With a SoundCloud Pro Unlimited account for just $135 a year, we could upload as much audio as we wished to the service, which also offered the possibility of users building playlists, commenting on, and "liking" the audio. This solution is substantially less expensive than building a streaming service on campus; one administrator suggested yearly costs for physical space, server space, maintenance, environmental controls, and more could reach six figures. For the first time the SOHP enjoyed the promise of dynamic interaction with the researchers who use its collections.

PROJECT EXECUTION

Not unlike conducting an oral history, the origination of the *MLWM* project was an act of joint creation that involved considerable shared authority. The idea emerged around the same time that UNC's Digital Innovation Lab (DIL) was being organized. Not yet a true lab, the DIL in 2011 was a group of credentialed scholars, graduate students, and undergraduate students who met in a coffee shop until eventually finding some shared space on Carolina's main campus. The DIL's flagship digital publication platform, DH Press (then known as diPH), evolved in response to its creators' dedication to open-source, open-access, publicly engaged digital scholarship as well as the needs of *MLWM* (bearing in mind that those needs could and would be echoed by projects that followed). DH Press grew into a WordPress plug-in that, in the words of its creators, "enables administrative users to mashup and visualize a variety of digitized humanities-related material, including historical maps, images, manuscripts, and multimedia content."[24] The manuscripts and multimedia in question were oral history transcripts and audio, which *MLWM* sought to describe, connect, and visualize on a map and in other ways.

Creating data for the project began with reading and marking up paper transcripts by hand, a decidedly analog act of data production. Readers read through a body of over fifty oral history interviews, identifying passages of particular relevance and resonance with an eye toward those passages with some kind of spatial identity. After all, in order to be placed on a Cartesian map, oral history material needed some kind of geographic anchor. That anchor was dropped with varying precision: sometimes, by using Google Maps, the project team could determine the (fairly) precise location of a cemetery, for instance, or the site of a significant event. Other locations were less precise: a march that took place in Atlanta, near Emory

University, or a river that was the site of PCB pollution. In these instances, the project team agreed to take a best-guess approach, defaulting to town and city centers when necessary, but always relying on the interviewee to provide essential context for the location assigned to their recollection. The precision of the latitude–longitude pair produced by a Google Maps inquiry and the more subjective recollection provided by the interviewee make for a nice contrast. In the future, we hope to integrate polygon locations into the map so we can describe areas, not just points.

As project historians moved through the interviews, they kept a running list of keywords that slowly began to take shape as a controlled vocabulary. After the number of keywords ballooned to well over one hundred, ranging from "reproductive health" to "education" to "consciousness-raising," the newly formed controlled vocabulary had to be culled down to a limited, understandable list of parent–child categories. In the end, the list featured just twelve parent categories, each of which owned about three child categories.

Each keyword or set of keywords described a portion of an oral history interview. The question of "aboutness," as described above, meant that seeking to assign a set of keywords to an oral history in its entirety would be counterproductive: At what point is an interview about so many things that it may as well be about nothing? And what use is the text itself as far as representing true meanings? Even the most eloquent and well-prepared interviewees rarely say precisely what they mean in an interview, and humans use all kinds of shorthand that can be perfectly clear to the listener or reader but completely opaque to the optical character recognition a library search engine might rely on. Take, for instance, an interview with the daughter of a hugely influential civil rights activist who refers to her father only as "Daddy" and never as "Martin Luther King." Would OCR help direct a King biographer to that interview?

Passages, on the other hand, can be more easily and accurately described, and in describing them, the project team could describe the interview in which they are contained as well. The goal of directing researchers to passages rather than the oral histories as complete products risked elevating the part over the whole, but we believed that if we still provided easy access to the whole, the passage could become a doorway into the complete interview rather than a disincentive to engagement. We assigned no more than three of these pairs to each interview passage, and each interview contained approximately ten passages, with the sections in between acting as accessible but not described research matter. In the final product, we made sure that each excerpt included pathways to the interview as a whole and to the library record for the interview as it exists in the archive.

In an order of operations that will be reversed in future projects, after reading through the interviews, identifying passages, and assigning categories, we used software called *DocSoft AV*, licensed on a temporary basis through UNC, to insert timestamps into the transcripts. First, we stripped the transcripts of everything beyond the text representation of the spoken interview: formatting, transcriptionist notes, page numbers, interruptions, and more. Then, we saved the Word documents as UTF-8 encoded text files and batch uploaded them, along with their corresponding MP3s, to *DocSoft*. *DocSoft*, which uses *Dragon* speech recognition software, inserted shockingly accurate bracketed timestamps into the transcript every few moments. We now had a text transcript that could be aligned closely with its audio partner.

To complete this alignment, we needed to develop a way for our interface to read the transcript. Fairly quickly, our programmer developed a custom script in WordPress that synced the audio and the transcript. The result was a scrolling text transcript that scrolls as the audio progresses as well as the capacity to jump to any point in the audio with a click of the mouse on the transcript. I will let him explain what he did in his own words:

> The player has built in functions and events that are used with custom code that I wrote to sync with the transcript. 1. The transcript has the timestamps coded into each line so when the media player's PROGRESS event reaches a certain position in seconds, it highlights the respective line. 2. Vice versa: when a line is clicked on, it passes the coded timestamp into seconds, which uses the media player's SeekTo function to update the player position.

> I pull the SoundCloud API into the DH Press plug-in code where the custom script handles the "sync." The timestamps are hidden in the transcript html as data attributes on each line (generated dynamically by the DH Press plug-in).

This process addresses the problems of silence and opacity in oral history interviews because, first, it transforms the transcript from a disincentive to listening into a tool that encourages listening, and second, it makes the audio quickly accessible and visible. Listening is no longer a chore; instead, it is something that can occur throughout the research process, and even if that listening is fairly passive, it puts the researcher into contact with the interviewee in a way that could produce deeper understandings of the historic record.

As this and other tasks were under way, researchers contacted every interviewee whose interview we wanted to use in *MLWM* in order to describe the project and be sure they were comfortable with their interview being a part of it. To be sure, each interviewee had freely given permission for virtually anyone encountering their interview in the SOHP collection to make use of it in a variety of not-for-profit ways, but we wanted our first step into full-blown experimentation with interviewees' life histories to take place with their blessing. We found it gratifying that only one interviewee declined to join the project.

As this process drew to a close, the project team had in hand a dense spreadsheet that broke each interview down into passages described with terms from our controlled vocabulary as well as with time codes, so the interview's chapters would be legible both to human users and the custom script that would allow these users to navigate it. The data was cleaned and entered as a batch into DH Press.

The published product, which is not final but is ready for robust use, features a map populated by color-coded markers, each of which represents an interview passage. Users can navigate the site by selecting "legends," which include primary concepts (the parent categories we developed—visible child categories are in the works), spaces (e.g., religious spaces, educational spaces), and interviewees. Users can select and deselect between these options, creating custom maps that might show clusters of educational spaces identified by interviewees, or simply one interviewee's personal narrative as laid out against a Cartesian backdrop. Once we develop the functionality to combine legends, such as overlaying a handful of interviewees with certain kinds of spaces, complex narratives can emerge. But for the time being, we can see the overlap between "Education" and "Civil Rights Movement" as primary concepts, suggesting a relationship between campuses and the movement and inviting students, for instance, to explore that connection.

RISKS

This approach is not without its risks, but for the most part these risks are generalizable to online oral history dissemination. At the root of these risks is the fact that "public" is a much more powerful word than it was twenty years ago. In the pre- and protodigital past, an interviewee might sign a standard interview release form, giving over rights and title to an interviewer or a university and making provision for the free, not-for-profit, public use of their interview. They could do so with the comforting confidence—if not the disappointing certainty—that few people if any would ever read, much less listen to, their interview. Today, a Google search can lead anyone directly to the text and audio, so while the strict meaning of "public" here has not changed, access has exploded. Archives have moved from their strange position as secret-keepers to the sources of rivers of information.

The first and most pressing risk is the potential harm to humans. For years, oral historians have worried what the digital turn means for the privacy of their narrators. For all the commitment of oral historians toward democratizing history, they remain acutely aware that the stories they were seeking to bring into the public understanding of history might be used against their tellers. Although the recent case of the police subpoenas of interviews about Ireland's Troubles[25] has dramatized the ways in which telling stories can harm the teller, it is rare that an oral history can be used to defame an interviewee. Indeed, the interviewee is generally much more likely to inflict harm; after all, it is they who can speak freely about their neighbors and then happily giving the interviewer permission to share their damaging stories widely. But however small the risk, it cannot be overlooked.

Oral historians also worry about decontextualization. Since the oral history engages in a kind of conversation with itself, and a spoken or written passage late in the interview might correct or qualify a passage from earlier in the interview, it is possible that by isolating and describing interview segments rather than the interview itself, researchers could find and make use of bad information. Leaving the interview in its entirety at least puts the onus on the researcher to use the material responsibly; that is, a researcher publishing a false claim drawn from an oral history segment could more readily claim he or she used what was available, whereas someone taking a similar passage from a complete oral history record would have less claim to that excuse. To address this risk, *MLWM* connects each segment to its complete record, both within the project and in the archive, at the least removing deniability and ensuring the part is indeed represented as a portion of a larger whole.

This kind of a project also risks a tottering step toward diminished humanity, as opposed to ascending toward the lofty but attainable goal of the field: to enhance the humanity of history scholarship. The presence of voices reveals humanity, but cramming them into a clump of colored dots on a screen may reduce them into a kind of graphical anonymity, in which they become part of the kaleidoscopic visual clutter of the Internet. The problem we continue to confront is if by claiming to reintroduce the human voice to the study of history through this project, we raise the bar past the point of reaching, and the glaring non-humanness of these clustered dots on the screen exacts a greater toll on meaning. This potential downside raises a larger issue for oral history representation online: How do digital humanities practitioners pick icons to represent people? Or should they?

Since oral histories deal with living human subjects, and often with subjects who do not hold traditional forms of power, oral historians are cautious about these risks and others. But that caution must not prevent joyful experimentation with freely given interviews. In considering their responsibility to the interviewee, oral historians working in digital environments must acknowledge risk without allowing that risk to stifle speech. If the oral historian is confident an interviewee understands the boundaries, or lack thereof, in the digital public space, they must not play gatekeeper unless asked; by doing so they assert ownership they do not have over a story that is not theirs.

Although it is not a risk, there is a practical consideration to add here. While the basic tasks—reading, data creation—of this project are doable without robust infrastructure, this chapter does not pretend it was created without substantial resources not available to most oral history practitioners. As one of just two full-time employees at the SOHP at the time I worked on this project (and as a grant-funded, temporary employee), I was always surprised to hear the program described as a "big dog," as one familiar name in the field did at an Oral History Association conference. But, returning to the institutional relationship laid out at the beginning of this piece, it was the SOHP's relationship with a major research university library that made this project possible, and that means this project is not likely to die out if I move to a new position or forget to renew its web hosting.

CONCLUSION

I am not an archivist. Therefore, it will not surprise me if archivists reading this piece roll their eyes as they observe me fumbling core concepts of the field. But while I am not capable of understanding the archive, I may be capable of breaking it and playing with the pieces in such a way that something useful results. George E. P. Box stated that "all models are wrong; the practical question is how wrong do they have to be to not be useful."[26] I agree with Box that one need not be right to make something useful, and I embrace the idea of being productively wrong. Yet if one thinks about a curated collection such as this one as provocative, manipulable, subjective, and even surprising, such a collection starts to seem like a fairly faithful representation of the voices in it. If the line between the digital representation and the archival object has been blurred if not erased, this outcome does not seem unwelcome.

This project hasn't replaced the Southern Oral History Program's oral history archive. For one thing, it's too small to be useful to a wide array of researchers. But this kind of project, especially at a greater scale, may in the future at least substantially complement the archive as the public-facing element of a digital library. In other words, rather than drawing on material from an archive to make an interesting presentation or visualization, it draws on that material to represent the archive itself. That representation will allow content creators, archivists, students, and other researchers to see into the archive in ways that have heretofore not been possible and to listen to the voices of the past speaking up after decades of unwilling silence.

NOTES

1   Assistant Professor of Digital Humanities, Department of American Studies, University of North Carolina at Chapel Hill. Thank you to Jessica Wilkerson and Liz Lundeen for their insightful comments on this piece.

2   *Mapping the Long Women's Movement*, DH Press (http://projects.dhpress .org/lwm) was funded by a grant reallocation from the Andrew W. Mellon Foundation. It was conceived by Seth Kotch and developed and executed at the Southern Oral History Program by Kotch, Elizabeth Lundeen, and Jessica Wilkerson, with contributions from Hudson Vaughan. The Digital Innovation Lab team was led by Pamella Lach, with programming work by Joe Hope of the Renaissance Computing Institute, Bryan Gaston, and Chien-Yi Hou, and

design work by Jade Davis. Christopher Breedlove, Beth Carter, Charlotte Fryar, and Lauren Stutts assisted with data collection. The project uses oral history interviews researched and conducted by David Cline, Jennifer Donnally, Joey Ann Fink, and Jessica Wilkerson during fieldwork supported by the Southern Oral History Program. Sally Council transcribed the interviews. Jaycie Vos, Jackie Dean, and the interviewers accessioned the interviews into the Southern Historical Collection. The idea of a long women's movement grew out of Jacquelyn D. Hall's conception of a long civil rights movement.

3   For a complete listing of the interviews and links to audio and transcripts, see http://www2.lib.unc.edu/mss/inv/s/Southern_Oral_History_Program _Collection.html#d1e54968.

4   Anne Enke, *Finding the Movement: Sexuality, Contested Space, and Feminist Activism* (Durham, NC: Duke University Press, 2007); Nancy Fraser, *Scales of Justice: Reimagining Political Space in a Globalizing World* (New York: Columbia University Press, 2008); Doreen B. Massey, *Space, Place, and Gender* (Minneapolis: University of Minnesota Press, 1994).

5   Southern Oral History Program, http://sohp.org.

6   Center for the Study of the American South, http://south.unc.edu.

7   UNC's Southern Historical Collection, http://library.unc.edu/wilson/shc.

8   UNC's Digital Innovation Lab, http://digitalinnovation.unc.edu.

9   Mitchell Whitelaw, "Towards Generous Interfaces for Archival Collections," http://mtchl.net/towards-generous-interfaces-for-archival-collections.

10   David Weinberger, *Everything Is Miscellaneous: The Power of the New Digital Disorder* (New York: Times Books, 2007): 17–20.

11   Georgina Hibberd, "Metaphors for Discovery: How Interfaces Shape Our Relationship with Library Collections," http://searchisover.org/papers/hibberd.pdf.

12   Reagan L. Grimsley and Susan C. Wynne, "Creating Access to Oral History in Academic Libraries," *College and Undergraduate Libraries* 16, No. 4 (2009): 278–99.

13   Linda Shopes offers a brief but thoughtful explication of the origins of the field in "What Is Oral History?," posted on *History Matters*, http://historymatters .gmu.edu/mse/oral/oral.pdf.

14   This definition riffs on that offer in Lynn Abrams, *Oral History Theory* (New York: Routledge, 2010): 2.

15   Michael Frisch, "Three Dimensions and More: Oral History Beyond the Paradoxes of Method," in *Handbook of Emergent Methods*, ed. Sharlene Nagy Hess-Biber and Patricia Leavy (New York: Guilford Press, 2008): 223.

16   See Alessandro Portelli, "Oral History as a Genre," in *The Oral History Reader*, ed. Robert Perks and Alastair Thompson (New York: Routledge, 2006).

17   Michael Frisch, "Oral History and the Digital Revolution: Toward a Post-Documentary Sensibility," for publication in *The Oral History Reader*, 2nd ed., ed. Robert Perks and Alastair Thompson (London: Routledge), www .randforce.com/media/frisch--ioha%20revised%20and%20edited%20for% 20oral%20history%20reader.pdf.

18   See, for instance, Michael Frisch, *A Shared Authority: Essays on the Craft and Meaning of Oral and Public History* (Albany: SUNY Press, 1990); Bill Adair, Benjamin Filene, and Laura Koloski, *Letting Go: Sharing Historical Authority in a User-Generated World* (Philadelphia, PA: Pew Center for Arts and Heritage, 2011).

19   Advanced researchers, at least in one study, tended to use broad searching as well. See Max Kemman, Martijn Kleppe, and Stef Scagolia, "Just Google It—Digital Research Practices of Humanities Scholars," in *Proceedings of the Digital Humanities Congress 2012*, in *Studies in the Digital Humanities*, ed. Clare Mills, Michael Pidd, and Esther Ward (Sheffield, UK: HRI Online Publications, 2014), http://arxiv.org/abs/1309.2434.

20   Jaycie Vos, "The Development of a Shared Metadata Standard for Use in Oral History Collections" (MA Thesis, University of North Carolina at Chapel Hill, 2010), https://cdr.lib.unc.edu/record/uuid:882f1c1f -95fb-4d98-a655-2288433f5788.

21   For more on aboutness, see Jonathan Furner, "FRSAD and the Ontology of Subjects of Works," *Cataloging and Classification Quarterly* 50 (2012); 494–516, www.jonathanfurner.info/docs/furner2012.pdf.

22   Stanford's Spatial History Project alone provides an able riposte: http://web .stanford.edu/group/spatialhistory/cgi-bin/site/index.php.

23   Jesse Stommel, "Digital Humanities Is About Breaking Stuff," *Hybrid Pedagogy* (2013), www.hybridpedagogy.com/Journal/the-digital-humanities-is-about-breaking-stuff.

24   *DH Press, a Digital Humanities Toolkit*, http://dhpress.org.

25   Kevin Cullen, "BC Exercise in Idealism Opened Old Wounds," *Boston Globe* (July 6, 2014), www.bostonglobe.com/news/world/2014/07/05/belfast-the -shadows-and-gunmen/D5yv4DdNIxaBXMl2Tlr6PL/story.html.

26   G. E. P. Box and N. R. Draper, "Empirical Model Building and Response Surfaces" (New York: John R. Wiley and Sons, 1987): 424.

Part 3

**BUILDING DIGITAL HUMANITIES
INFRASTRUCTURE AND PARTNERSHIPS**

6 | The Center That Holds: Developing Digital Publishing Initiatives at the Emory Center for Digital Scholarship[1]

Sarah Melton

INTRODUCTION

The Emory Center for Digital Scholarship (ECDS), formed in 2013, brought together several existing library units and programs: the Digital Scholarship Commons (DiSC), the Electronic Data Center, the Lewis H. Beck Center for Electronic Collections, and the Emory Center for Interactive Teaching (ECIT). ECDS is tasked with "break[ing] down barriers" between these preexisting units and "simplify[ing] the process of establishing partnerships with scholars."[1] The center's creation brought these preexisting units, which were previously housed in separate areas of the library, into one space. Positioned in Emory's Libraries and IT Division, the center is able to draw on the resources of both sectors to create and disseminate its work. As of 2015, ECDS had a staff of twelve full-time employees, five graduate research fellows, one postdoctoral fellow, and twenty-eight graduate students.

ECDS provides tiered levels of support in the areas of data management, digital pedagogy, digital publication, archiving, and digital exhibitions. Faculty, students, and staff may walk into the center for help with projects like finding data sources, creating a website, or editing videos. The center's graduate student employees do much of the hands-on work with walk-in requests.[2] Staff may also provide short-term consultations on projects that require more in-depth support, such as creating course content or developing digital pedagogical skills. For longer-term work, patrons may submit proposals for projects that require dedicated staff time. At the time of writing, ECDS was supporting over eighty projects in various stages of development.

95

Many of these projects incorporate publishing, whether through scholarly blogs, journals, or digital scholarship platforms. The center's publication program is part of a larger movement toward publishing in academic libraries. In their study of library publishing activities, Katherine Skinner, Sarah Lippincott, Julie Speer, and Tyler Walters sketch the current landscape of the subfield:

> [Library publishing] has been defined (broadly) as the set of activities led by college and university libraries to support the creation, dissemination, and curation of scholarly, creative, and/or educational works. Using formal production processes, more than 100 North American libraries currently publish original works by scholars, researchers, and students. These publications include journals, monographs, Electronic Theses and Dissertations (ETDs), gray literature, conference proceedings, data, textbooks, and websites.
>
> Library publishing is differentiated from the work of other publishers—including commercial, society, academic, and trade—in large part by its business model, which often relies heavily on being subsidized through the library budget, rather than operating primarily as a cost-recovery or profit-driven activity. Libraries are relative newcomers to the field, largely beginning this work in a digital environment over the last 20 years.[3]

In January 2013, the Library Publishing Coalition (LPC) was launched to support libraries that were engaged in or wanted to build library publishing programs. Over sixty academic libraries—including Emory—joined the organization, whose mission is to foster "collaboration, knowledge-sharing, and the development of common practices for library publishers."[4] Indeed, library publishing is becoming increasingly common in academic libraries. A 2010 Institute of Museum and Library Services (IMLS)-funded survey found that 55 percent of respondents were either offering or interested in starting publishing services.[5] The LPC's 2015 *Library Publishing Directory* highlights the library publishing activities of 124 academic libraries from around the world. Additionally, the *Publishing Directory*'s survey illustrates a strong preference for open access, with 97 percent of campus-based journals being freely available.[6]

The center's publication program reflects these trends. ECDS primarily publishes journals, websites, and other digital initiatives, including digital exhibits and interactive GIS projects. In its work, ECDS places particular emphasis on open-access publication and open-source software. All of the projects highlighted are freely available online, and the code for Emory-developed software platforms is open source. The center is largely funded through the institutional support of Emory's Libraries and IT Division but has also received external funding from the Mellon Foundation. ECDS also receives support from software engineers in the library in developing and designing in-house software platforms.

In this chapter, I will focus on the digital scholarship projects and publication program of ECDS—though it should be noted that other units of the Emory Library also undertake publishing activities. (The Scholarly Communications office, for example, oversees the management of the university repository, including Emory's electronic theses and dissertations.) I argue that collaboration—across the university and other institutions—is central to the center's success. In addition to building partnerships, this work also requires significant institutional support to create scalable, replicable work. As Jennifer Vinopal and Monica McCormick note, digital projects run the risk of turning to "one-off" solutions that are not replicable. Digital scholarship needs are diverse, contend Vinopal and McCormick, and "in attempting to meet them without considering scale and sustainability, we risk developing narrowly focused or short-lived solutions that are difficult to maintain over time and with infrastructure that cannot be repurposed to benefit other projects."[7] I will illustrate how ECDS's philosophical commitment to open-source software and open-access publishing attempts to address some commonly encountered challenges in digital projects, and how each project has required specific kinds of institutional collaboration and assistance.

PROJECTS

Since ECDS's inception, the center has provided support for a host of digital publishing projects. In addition to the four preexisting units, the open-access journal *Southern Spaces* came under the center's purview as a project and serves as a model for faculty, staff, and students who are interested in starting their own publications.[8] But ECDS also supports a wide variety of projects that we define as publishing, even if they do not resemble "traditional" publications like monographs or journals. Given the center's place in the library, we embrace "traditional library values and skills," like preservation, "expertise in the organization of information, and a commitment to widening access," while also advocating for an expanded definition of publishing that incorporates new platforms, methods of disseminating scholarship, and modes of creating knowledge.[9]

Here, I highlight several initiatives that represent our approach to publishing. Many of these projects are related to the study of Atlanta, while others draw on the strengths of Emory's special collections and faculty expertise. I then turn to the support required to create and sustain a publishing program.

SOUTHERN SPACES

Started in 2004, *Southern Spaces* (https://southernspaces.org) is an open-access, peer-reviewed, interdisciplinary journal about the "regions, places, and cultures of the US South and their global connections."[10] Graduate student editorial associates and managing editors staff the journal, with senior scholars and practitioners as editorial reviewers. *Southern Spaces* uses Drupal as its content management system.

As senior editor Dr. Allen Tullos noted in his talk at the 2014 Digital Humanities meeting, it is still relatively rare to find open-access, peer-reviewed journals that support multimedia content.[11] Although a number of platforms are available for open-access publications, many of these only support text-based scholarship or allow for minimal integration of other kinds of media.

In the spring of 2015, *Southern Spaces* launched a redesigned site. As part of this redesign, the journal worked with Drupal consultants to create a series of modules as a "journal in a box." These pieces include *Southern Spaces*'s backend workflow management module, developed to aid in the process of evaluating submissions and communicating with authors, editorial staff, and peer reviewers. During the next year, *Southern Spaces* plans to work within existing networks like the Library Publishing Coalition to promote and disseminate the Drupal distribution, which will be available on GitHub and on Drupal.org.

Southern Spaces also takes graduate student training seriously as part of its work. The staff consists of six to eight graduate students, depending on the semester, and they perform the bulk of the day-to-day editorial work and site maintenance. The editorial staff conducts an initial review of submitted pieces, finds appropriate peer reviewers, helps authors procure media (and often rights to use images, audio, or text), edits video and audio, lays out and copyedits articles, and promotes published pieces on social media. Staff members train each other in these activities and receive technical support from library systems administrators, metadata analysts, scholarly communications specialists, and others. This cross training allows students to become familiar with editorial work, web design and markup, intellectual property issues, and media editing. Using these skills, editorial staff members from *Southern Spaces* have gone on to do digital scholarship work at institutions like the College of Charleston, the University of Pennsylvania, and the Digital Public Library of America.

ATLANTA STUDIES

Atlanta Studies (http://atlantastudies.org) is a multi-institutional collaborative publication that aims to both produce original research on the Atlanta region and provide a platform for data sets and other resources for studying the area (Figure 1). The site endeavors to reach a broad audience, with the editorial and advisory boards consisting of scholars, researchers, public intellectuals, archivists, and librarians from across the southeast.

Projects & Resources
—

We here at Atlanta Studies want to highlight the great projects going on around town. We've also included some resources to make it even easier to learn more about Atlanta.

PROJECTS

Figure 1. *Atlanta Studies* screenshot, showing highlighted projects and resources.

Atlanta Studies developed from a series of informal meet-ups for anyone interested in the study of Atlanta—inside or outside the academy. These meetings grew into an annual symposium that has been hosted by different Atlanta-area institutions each year. Many of the papers from the symposia were fascinating and timely—and came from outside the academy or were aimed at a more general audience. *Atlanta Studies* arose from a desire to see this work published in an accessible venue. ECDS designed the site and agreed to host the long-term project.

The site features articles, longer-form pieces that explore historical and contemporary issues in the Atlanta region. *Atlanta Studies* also provides a place for curated blog posts, often highlighting projects or offering shorter examinations of Atlanta's history and culture. While articles and blog posts are not double-blind peer reviewed, each piece is read and reviewed by two members of the editorial staff. Authors are encouraged to write pieces for a broad public. There is also a projects and resources section that features other work in the region, part of *Atlanta Studies'* commitment to building a network of scholars, activists, and an interested public.

ATLMAPS

ATLMaps (http://atlmaps.com) is a mapping initiative that invites users to contribute to the project. Initially developed at Georgia State University (GSU), *ATLMaps* is a collaboration between ECDS and GSU.[12] The project "combines archival maps, geospatial data visualization, and user contributed multimedia location pinpoints to promote investigation into any number of issues about Atlanta."[13] *ATLMaps* aims to "offer a framework that incorporates storytelling reliant on geospatial data" and allow for collaborative curation of these data. The code for *ATLMaps* is available on GitHub.[14]

Both contributing institutions have digitized historical and contemporary base layer maps. Users can then create their own projects on top of these layers, adding annotations, data points, and sound, video, or image files. *ATLMaps* also allows users to overlay contemporary and historical maps; a user might, for example, compare the historical boundaries of the city with present-day zoning (Figure 2).

ATLMaps represents a new kind of publishing initiative for ECDS: a project that invites crowdsourced contributions. While the project itself is currently being beta tested, we have had requests from institutions across

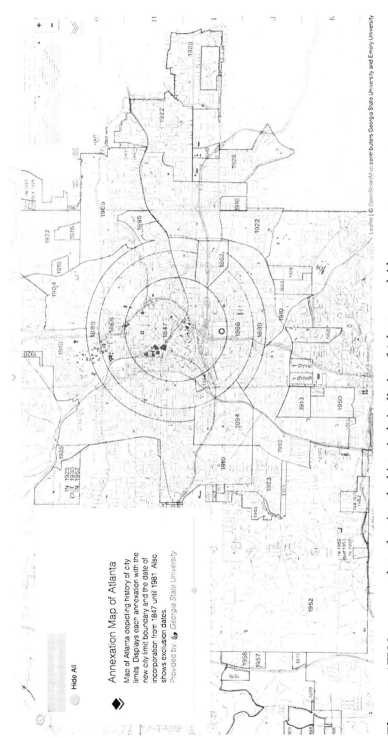

Figure 2. ATLMaps screenshot, showing the historical city limits of Atlanta overlaid on a contemporary map.

the country to help set up similar projects in other cities. By making the source code publically available, the center endeavors to provide reusable prototypes for other centers and interested individuals.

GEORGIA CIVIL RIGHTS COLD CASES

The *Georgia Civil Rights Cold Cases* project is an example of the center's work with pedagogical initiatives across the university. The project grew out of an undergraduate course on cold cases of the civil rights era, cotaught by Hank Klibanoff, a journalism professor, and Brett Gadsden, a faculty member in African-American Studies. The course explores unsolved (or unpublished) racially motivated murders in the civil rights era. As the site describes:

> By using primary evidence—including FBI records, NAACP files, personal archives, family photographs, old newspaper clippings, court transcripts and more—and by immersing themselves in the scholarship of historians, journalists and memoirists, students come to see and understand a history that is little known from the inside looking out and long forgotten from the outside looking in.[15]

The research for the project was undertaken by undergraduates in the course, under the supervision of the two faculty members. The project is open access and is hosted on a WordPress site. Representing ECDS's commitment to innovative digital publishing, the project features essays by students in the course, maps, timelines, and primary documents about the cases.

OPENTOURBUILDER

The *OpenTourBuilder* application is a content management system for building geospatial tours in a mobile environment.[16] Developed in partnership with software engineers in Emory's Library and Information Technology Services, *OpenTourBuilder* was launched in 2014 with the *Battle of Atlanta* tour app (http://battleatl.org), a comprehensive tour of battlefield sites. ECDS also piloted *OpenTourBuilder* during a 2014 Summer Institute for Digital Scholarship with librarians from historically black colleges and universities. Institute participants created tours of their own campuses and libraries. In keeping with ECDS's commitment to creating open-source tools, the code for *OpenTourBuilder* is available on GitHub.[17]

As the first tour created with *OpenTourBuilder*, the *Battle of Atlanta* tour app demonstrated the versatility of the platform. Featuring twelve stops, the app "locates multiple features on an interactive map connecting them with written text, an archive of primary documents, and historical photographs about the battle itself."[18] Each stop includes videos, primary documents, and driving, walking, biking, and transit directions (Figure 3). The app is also accompanied by an essay on *Southern Spaces* providing further historical context and additional resources.[19]

Figure 3. *OpenTourBuilder* screenshot, showing a *Battle of Atlanta* tour stop with video and text.

READUX SCHOLARLY EDITIONS

The *Readux Scholarly Editions* project builds on *Readux*, an open-source tool for reading, annotating, and publishing digitized texts. The initial phases of the *Readux* project allow users to search the content of TEI-encoded digitized books in Emory's special collections, send books to

Voyant for textual analysis, and add PDFs of the books to Zotero.[20] ECDS and library software engineers are developing the next phase of the project, which will allow for annotating and exporting of embedded annotations in web and e-book formats.

The pilot project for the annotation phase of *Readux* is the *Original Sacred Harp*, an early twentieth-century shape-note tune book. Jesse Karlsberg, a postdoctoral fellow at ECDS and a scholar of Sacred Harp singing, is providing the scholarly annotations and managing the project's current phase. Annotations include the original editors' notes about design and music notation. The *Original Sacred Harp* is an especially rich pilot project, given the unique challenges of encoding musical notations. The center has designed *Readux* so that it will be able to ingest any digitized text from Emory's repository. *Readux*'s source code is available on GitHub, and ECDS hopes that it will be a model for others working in digital publications.[21]

ATLANTA EXPLORER PROJECT

The *Atlanta Explorer* project is a suite of projects that aim to (1) make materials in Emory's Manuscript, Archives, and Rare Book Library (MARBL) more accessible, (2) create tools for GIS research about historical Atlanta, and (3) provide a model for similar projects. *Atlanta Explorer* began with the digitizing of the 1928 Atlanta Atlas, a precursor to phone books.[22] MARBL made these scanned pages publically available on their Digital Historic Maps Collection page.[23] Under the direction of geographer Michael Page, Emory graduate and undergraduate students constructed a geocoder, a "combination of software and spatial databases that can transform location data, often in the form of addresses, into geographic coordinates."[24] Students took the data from the Atlanta Atlas—including names, addresses, and racial classifications of inhabitants—and plotted them on the digitized maps. All told, the first phase of the geocoder assigned coordinates to over 70,000 buildings in the city. When completed to include the greater Atlanta area, the geocoder will map over 200,000 points.[25]

For the next phase of the project, ECDS has begun working with an Atlanta developer, nVis360, to build a platform for users to explore three-dimensional renderings of the city circa 1930. In collaboration with these engineers, ECDS has developed a prototype of a downtown city block. Using the gaming platform Unity, users can walk through the historical city as streetcars and automobiles pass. The locations of roads, streetcar lines, fire hydrants, and manhole covers are based on data from the digitized planning documents and maps.

The three-dimensional renderings also include information about each building and, when available, historical photographs. Archival sources from Emory and Georgia State University provided details about building facades. Wiki functionality is built into the *Atlanta Explorer* project, allowing users to add their own scholarship and data about places. ECDS is currently looking at funding options to expand this work and make the platform stable for beta testing.

LESSONS LEARNED AND RECOMMENDATIONS

ECDS draws on a number of preexisting Emory projects and resources. The *Readux* project, for example, repurposes code from an older project that library software engineers had developed. This "recycling" allowed us to make use of previous efforts and foster further collaboration with the software engineering team. Indeed, the center's work is only possible through collaboration with Emory subject librarians, metadata specialists, copyright and scholarly communications experts, software engineers, and exhibit designers—to say nothing of ECDS's partnerships with other institutions. Collaboration is a core part of the center's mission and ethos.

Here, I want to turn to the lessons ECDS has learned from working on these projects and the center's previous incarnations. I find Miriam Posner's work on digital humanities in libraries particularly helpful and use her arguments as a basis for further recommendations.

INFRASTRUCTURE NEEDS

Digital scholarship cannot be undertaken lightly. In her article "No Half Measures: Overcoming Common Challenges to Doing Digital Humanities in the Library," Posner argues that digital scholarship requires substantial institutional support in order to be successful. "We do not acknowledge often enough," writes Posner, "that if a library is to engage in digital humanities activity, its leaders need to give serious thought to the administrative and technical infrastructure that supports this work."[26] Drawing on Trevor Muñoz's scholarship, Posner notes that librarians (and, indeed, engineers, metadata specialists, and all others who are part of these projects) provide intellectual labor to digital scholarship, and their job responsibilities should reflect this work. Thus, Posner offers, "many of the problems we have faced 'supporting' digital humanities may stem from the fact that digital humanities projects in general do not need supporters—they need collaborators."[27] A collaborative relationship requires commitment, especially from institutions.

In forming the advisory and editorial boards for *Atlanta Studies*, for example, we encountered anxiety over long-term support for the project. Understandably, our collaborators wanted to know that the project had the necessary infrastructure for longevity. ECDS was able to provide technical support and dedicate staff time to the project. Without this commitment, it would have been difficult to launch the publication. As is often the case for editorial work, *Atlanta Studies'* board members generally do not receive much professional credit for their labor; journal editing often carries very little weight in the all-important tenure and promotion standards. The center knew that we would need to provide material support and labor to make the project successful. In the case of *Atlanta Studies*, this support included paid staff time to design the site, lay out and copyedit pieces, and provide editorial guidance.

Flexible infrastructure, Posner continues, is a key component of a successful digital humanities project in the library.[28] In its position between library and IT services, ECDS is able to draw on the resources of both when necessary. *OpenTourBuilder*, for example, required the ECDS project manager to work closely with the library software engineers and front-end designer. This work included technical components—making sure the application could support multiple kinds of media—but also content considerations. Because the app was designed for public audiences, it was important for the text to be legible and easy to understand. Having open communication between different project stakeholders was crucial.

Likewise, ECDS staff must have access to the appropriate resources. Posner notes that digital humanities projects often require resources from many different parts of an institution, including "time from a developer, time from a designer, time from a metadata specialist, time from a system administrator, project management expertise, server space, a commitment to host the project in the long term. . . ."[29] These resources are crucial for many digital scholarship projects, and it is important for staff to be able to draw on them easily.

The *ATLMaps* project involved a tremendous amount of collaboration—and resources—across institutions. We had to ensure that geoservers at Georgia State and Emory were properly working, obtain SSL certificates for user account creation, craft a terms of service agreement with the help of our scholarly communications office, secure permissions for all the media used—to say nothing of writing the code for the application and designing the user interface. It was essential for the center to be able to communicate with the project's stakeholders and obtain the support *ATLMaps* required with minimal red tape. Ultimately, these projects have required tremendous support in the form of staffing, resources for development, design, and hosting, and institutional encouragement of library publishing activities.

CONCLUSION

ECDS has embraced library publishing, an emerging subfield that places the library at the center of intellectual output. We believe that the library can be the incubator and generator of scholarship, not just the archive or final destination. By taking a broad view of publishing, the center is able to provide a home for publishing projects that might not be supported in other venues.

In particular, ECDS is interested in supporting work that is public-facing. *ATLMaps*, *OpenTourBuilder*, *Atlanta Studies*, and the *Atlanta Explorer* projects are all examples of initiatives that want to engage publics outside the academy, in addition to providing resources for scholars. These projects also take existing Emory resources—digitized maps, images, and data sets—and make them publicly available. The center's commitment to open-access publication and open-source software are not only part of this bent toward public scholarship, but are part of ECDS's sustainability plan. By sharing resources with other institutions and developers, the center is able to cultivate collaboration and garner support for its projects.

The center has learned many lessons from its own development and the work of other digital scholarship centers. Digital projects require an incredible amount of institutional support. Beyond the staff time and money required for this work, a center must be able to draw on resources across the library (and often across institutions) in a timely manner. Staff working on these projects must also have access to the help they need quickly and without having to wade through layers of bureaucracy.

We have not always been successful in our endeavors. As Posner notes, doing digital scholarship cannot be "business as usual" in a library. To be successful, she writes, "a library must do a great deal more than add 'digital scholarship' to an individual librarian's long string of subject specialties. It must provide room, support, and funding for library professionals to experiment (and maybe fail)."[30] Indeed, the center has seen projects flounder, fizzle, or fail to launch. And despite generous support from Emory, funding can still be a challenge. The *Atlanta Explorer* project, for example, will likely require external funding to build three-dimensional models of the entire cityscape of 1930s Atlanta. Providing long-term preservation plans for our projects can also be difficult. As anyone who has worked in the field of data curation knows, preserving something as seemingly straightforward as a web page raises a number of questions. (Even once-ubiquitous web technologies like Flash are no longer supported!) These are real challenges for digital publishing projects, but we have found that being part of communities like the Library Publishing Coalition connects us with others who are working on these same problems.

Despite these challenges, ECDS continues to develop its publishing program with these lessons learned in mind. At present, we have projects under way that will expand our efforts to include open monographs, open educational resources, and other formats of digital publishing. We continue to build relationships with other institutions and look forward to future collaborations.

NOTES

1   "About the Emory Center for Digital Scholarship," *Emory Center for Digital Scholarship*, http://digitalscholarship.emory.edu/about/index.html.

2   ECDS considers student training to be a crucial part of its work. In addition to employing graduate students, the center runs workshops and a semester-long series aimed at equipping students with digital scholarship skills.

3   Katherine Skinner, Sarah Lippincott, Julie Speer, and Tyler Walters, "Library-as-Publisher: Capacity Building for the Library Publishing Subfield," *Journal of Electronic Publishing* 17, No. 2 (2014), http://dx.doi.org/10.3998/3336451.0017.207.

4   "Home," *Library Publishing Coalition*, www.librarypublishing.org.

5   James L. Mullins, Catherine Murray-Rust, Joyce Ogburn, Raym Crow, October Ivins, Allyson Mower, Daureen Nesdill, Mark Newton, Julie Speer, and

Charles Watkinson, *Library Publishing Services: Strategies for Success: Final Research Report* (Washington, DC: SPARC, 2012): 6.

6   Sarah K. Lippincott and Katherine Skinner, introduction to *Library Publishing Directory 2015*, ed. Sarah Lippincott (Atlanta, GA: Library Publishing Coalition, 2015): vii.

7   Jennifer Vinopal and Monica McCormick, "Supporting Digital Scholarship in Research Libraries: Scalability and Sustainability," *Journal of Library Administration* 53, No. 1 (2013): 34.

8   Dr. Allen Tullos, the journal's senior editor, also serves as ECDS's codirector.

9   Lippincott, Skinner, and Watkinson, introduction to *Library Publishing Directory 2014*, xi.

10   "Home," *Southern Spaces*, http://southernspaces.org.

11   Allen Tullos, "'Needless to Say': Articulating Digital Publishing Practices as Strategies of Cultural Empowerment" (paper presented at the annual Digital Humanities conference, Lausanne, Switzerland, July 7–12, 2014).

12   Stanford's Jack Reed, formerly of Georgia State University, developed the prototype with colleagues at GSU. In the fall of 2014, the project moved to Emory for active development.

13   "About," *ATLMaps*, http://atlmaps.com/#/about.

14   "emory-libraries-ecds/ATLMaps-Server," *GitHub* (2015), https://github.com/emory-libraries-ecds/ATLMaps-Server.

15   "About," *The Georgia Civil Rights Cold Cases Project at Emory University*, https://scholarblogs.emory.edu/emorycoldcases/about.

16   "emory-libraries-ecds/OpenTourBuilder-Server," *GitHub*.

17   Ibid.

18   "The Battle of Atlanta Tour App," *Emory Center for Digital Scholarship*, http://digitalscholarship.emory.edu/projects/project-digital-atlanta-mapping-battle.html.

19   Daniel A. Pollock, "The Battle of Atlanta: History and Remembrance," *Southern Spaces* (May 30, 2014), http://southernspaces.org/2014/battle-atlanta-history-and-remembrance.

20   "Readux Digitized Repository Now Live," *FYI: Robert W. Woodruff Library* (August 13, 2014), https://scholarblogs.emory.edu/woodruff/fyi/readux-digitization-repository-now-live.

21   "emory-librarys/readux," *GitHub*, https://github.com/emory-libraries/readux.

22 The year 1928 provides a good snapshot of Atlanta development for several decades. Much city development halted during the Great Depression. Likewise, many building materials were requisitioned during World War II.

23 "HistoricMapCollection,"MARBL,www.digitalgallery.emory.edu/luna/servlet /EMORYUL~3~3.

24 Michael Page, "Atlanta Explorer 1930" (presentation at Southern American Studies Association, Atlanta, GA, February 19–21, 2015).

25 "Atlanta Studies Network," *Emory Center for Digital Scholarship*, http:// digitalscholarship.emory.edu/projects/project-digital-atlanta-studies.html #atl_explorer.

26 Miriam Posner, "No Half Measures: Overcoming Common Challenges to Doing Digital Humanities in the Library," *Journal of Library Administration* 53, No. 1 (2013): 44.

27 Ibid., 45.

28 Ibid., 47–48.

29 Ibid., 47.

30 Ibid., 51.

7 | Copiloting a Digital Humanities Center: A Critical Reflection on a Libraries– Academic Partnership

Brian Rosenblum and Arienne Dwyer

STARTING A DIGITAL HUMANITIES CENTER FROM SCRATCH

The University of Kansas (KU) Institute for Digital Research in the Humanities (IDRH)[1] was established in 2010 to provide resources and training in the practices and tools of the digital humanities, and to facilitate interdisciplinary academic collaborations and externally funded research. IDRH's major programs include an annual digital humanities conference featuring workshops and scholarly research presentations, digital humanities seed grants, regular hands-on workshops for faculty and graduate students, monthly digital humanities seminars, course development grants for teaching faculty, sponsorship of Humanities, Arts, Science, and Technology Alliance and Collaboratory (HASTAC) scholars, and consulting on digital humanities projects or ideas.

IDRH was a collaborative venture from the beginning. It was founded by and administered under the financial support and guidance of three campus entities: the Hall Center for the Humanities, the College of Liberal Arts and Sciences, and the KU Libraries (we refer to these in this chapter as "the stakeholders") and is led by two codirectors, one from the college and one from the Libraries. From the perspective of the Libraries, the collaborative nature of IDRH is an effective framework for connecting with faculty and students, and for the overall success of IDRH programs. The collaboration has enabled the Libraries to play a significant role in the growth of digital humanities at KU, and has helped establish new relationships between the Libraries and other campus units, faculty, and students. Via IDRH,

111

librarians play a role in teaching and training, grant proposal development and review, digital humanities consulting, course development, and student mentoring. In addition, IDRH gives the Libraries an opportunity to have a strong impact on other initiatives on campus, such as the development of proposals for external faculty hires, cosponsorship of related events, and the facilitation of other interdisciplinary conversations.

From the perspective of the KU Libraries, IDRH is a productive channel for librarian engagement with faculty and graduate students across campus and beyond that also enables librarians to develop greater expertise in digital humanities. IDRH provides the Libraries with a framework to take part in interdisciplinary conversations across campus, to learn more about faculty and graduate student research interests and needs, and to strengthen connections to relevant areas of library expertise such as data services and metadata.

This chapter will first describe IDRH's programs and the role of the stakeholders and codirectors in the partnership, and discusses some of the benefits and challenges of this collaborative model of support and leadership. We then discuss some of the specific ways in which IDRH has tried to build partnerships on campus and establish relationships between faculty and the libraries, including the formation of an advisory board and providing multiple opportunities for faculty to get involved in review committees or as instructors in workshops. This chapter will also serve as a critical review of IDRH's first four years, from its founding in fall 2010 to fall 2014, when this chapter was written.

SYNERGY WITH DIGITAL SCHOLARSHIP INITIATIVES ON CAMPUS

Prior to the launch of IDRH in the fall of 2010, KU Libraries was already engaged in a variety of digital initiatives. KU's institutional repository, KU ScholarWorks, launched in 2005 and serves as a space for faculty research output, including published articles, monographs, data sets, and other similar materials.[2] The repository continues to serve as the platform for KU's open-access policy, passed in 2008.[3] In 2007, the Libraries launched a digital publishing program to provide support to the KU community for the design, management, and distribution of online publications, including journals, conference proceedings, monographs, and other scholarly content.[4] The Libraries currently provides a digital publishing platform (via *Open Journal Systems* or *D-Space*) for seventeen scholarly publications edited or published at KU. In addition to these services, the Libraries has specialists in GIS and data services, statistical computing, and digital humanities consulting. These services have primarily been conceived of as consulting and support services rather than as mechanisms for generating new forms of digital research and teaching on campus.

In the fall of 2008, the College of Liberal Arts and Sciences, the Libraries, and the Hall Center for the Humanities formed a twenty-person Task Force on Digital Directions in the Humanities to "1) evaluate the current climate for digital scholarship at KU, 2) make recommendations for encouraging a culture of digital scholarship at KU, and 3) plan and hold KU's first Digital Scholarship Summit in 2009."[5] The task force investigated the resources in digital humanities currently available on campus, conducted a survey to measure how well faculty understood and used those resources, and sought input on the degree of faculty interest in the use of digital resources in their teaching and research. Survey results indicated that there was an imperfect awareness of currently available resources, and a large degree of interest in more opportunities and assistance for digital projects. As the task force reported, "faculty interest in using digital technologies exceeds the actual use of them." The task force also investigated efforts at peer institutions to support the digital humanities. Recognizing that digital humanities scholarship was beginning to flourish at many campuses and that there was significant interest at KU in more opportunities and assistance for digital projects, the task force recommended that KU form an institute for computing in the humanities at the university.

The task force made some very specific recommendations about the goals and structure of the proposed institute. Although not all of the task force recommendations were followed—limited resources, evolving needs, and codirector perspectives all impact the way things play out in practice—the recommendations nevertheless provided the foundation for the establishment and operation of IDRH. In the task force's vision, the institute would have the following goals:

1. To **provide ongoing educational opportunities** for faculty and graduate students in the utilization of digital technology for humanistic inquiry.
2. To **develop and support research initiatives** that use technology to pose and answer research questions about the human record.

3. To work proactively to **build a flagship project** that demonstrates the value and viability of innovative digital approaches to research.

4. To support the use of technology and web-based digital media to **publish peer-reviewed research** in new forms and to encourage all faculty and administration to recognize the valuable transformation occurring in humanities scholarship through the application of computing technologies.

Goals 1 and 2 remain a core part of IDRH's charter and activities, whereas goals 3 and 4 have not as yet been pursued, as we will discuss below.

The task force also recommended that two codirectors lead the institute, one from the College of Liberal Arts and Sciences faculty, and one from the Libraries. This codirector model was inspired by the examples of the University of Nebraska and the University of Virginia where, the task force noted, the digital humanities centers were physically located in libraries and were co-led by a librarian and an English professor (Nebraska) or a computer scientist (Virginia). In the original conception by KU's task force, the two codirectors would have highly specific roles within the institute. "One, drawn from the College faculty, would be primarily concerned with the scholarly contribution of research projects and educational programs. The other, from the Libraries, would focus on the digital realization of scholarship and the access, organization, and preservation of sustainable digital research content working with various campus partners." While the codirector model as implemented by IDRH has been one of the key factors in its success, the specific roles of the codirectors as the institute has evolved are not as strictly defined as in the task force recommendations. The benefits and challenges of the codirector model and the roles of each codirector are described at greater length in a later section.

Yet another recommendation of the task force was that the IDRH's funding would increasingly come from external granting sources. The task force suggested that a significant responsibility for the codirectors be development and grant activities to ensure incoming funding over time. Although grant development continues to remain a goal, it has not been feasible so far for the codirectors to pursue external grant funding, given their limited allocated time (25 and 50 percent for each codirector) and given the more immediate need to start a program from scratch, build a campus identity, launch and continue new events and grant programs, build a website, and create and maintain a DH community on campus.

When IDRH's activities and priorities do not entirely mesh with the task force vision—for example, we have not (yet) developed a flagship project, published new models of peer-reviewed research, or pursued external funding; and the codirectors have a more integrated set of responsibilities than outlined in the recommendations—the reasons are varied: in some cases, other units on campus are pursuing similar efforts; in other cases, staff time was limited, or other priorities have taken precedence. The section below describes the actual programs, activities, and outcomes of the institute.

BUILDING CORE PROGRAMS AND ACTIVITIES

The name of the institute was immediately modified from the suggested Institute for Computing in the Humanities to the Institute for Digital Research in the Humanities. Besides modernizing the title, the change shifted the focus to the institute's charge on *research*. In pursuit of this research objective, however, we have found that in digital humanities in particular, teaching is an inseparable component, particularly on a campus where digital technologies are novel. Many IDRH initiatives thus have a pedagogical component. Our core activities revolve around a series of research and pedagogical initiatives held throughout each academic year:

- *Digital Humanities Forum.* The DH Forum is an annual conference held every September. The forum consists of two or three days of hands-on workshops, a THATCamp self-organizing "unconference," and a day of research paper and poster presentations along with prominent keynote speakers, each year addressing a different general theme. The themes of the five conferences to date have been "Representing Knowledge," "Big Data and Uncertainty," "Return to the Material, "Nodes and Networks," and "Peripheries, Barriers, Hierarchies."[6] The forum is free and open to all, and each year attracts 80 to 120 local, national, and some international speakers and participants, including librarians, scholars, and students from a range of disciplines.

- *Digital Jumpstart Workshops.* In the spring semester we hold a two-day program of hands-on workshops. These free workshops provide faculty, staff, and graduate students with learn-by-doing introductions to digital tools and practices related to capturing and digitizing data, discovering and analyzing patterns in data, and presenting and disseminating scholarship and results. All skill levels, from beginner to seasoned digital humanist, are welcome.

- *Digital Humanities Seminar.* Cosponsored by the Hall Center for the Humanities, the DH Seminar provides a monthly forum for sharing and discussion of new digitally enabled humanities research efforts, with a specific focus on what digital humanities tools and practices can do for a range of humanistic research. The seminar is held four times per semester and features a mix of KU and external presenters. The seminar focuses not so much on DH tools, but on the research results and questions that can be answered by digital methods.
- *Seed Grants.* The IDRH digital humanities seed grants are intended to encourage KU faculty and academic staff to plan or pilot a collaborative project using digital technologies, which should in turn result in a more competitive subsequent external funding application. The grants provide up to $15,000 to create pilot projects, develop ideas via a workshop, attend workshops, support project-related travel, hold a substantial planning or brainstorming session, or similar activities.
- *Course Development Grants.* In the absence of a DH-oriented curriculum at KU, these small grants are intended to help spur the development of an interdisciplinary palette of courses in digital humanities at KU. The grants provide a $1,000 stipend to tenured and tenure-track faculty who develop a new course in the digital humanities. Priority is given to proposals that target undergraduates or undergraduates/graduate students, that will attract students from a variety of departments and disciplines, and that use open-source, nonproprietary, cross-platform tools.

In addition to the above core programs, IDRH supports some other, less time-intensive initiatives, including supporting graduate students through the HASTAC Scholars program, offering small travel grants, organizing one-off workshops as opportunities arise, and cosponsoring events with other entities on campus.[7]

We also maintain an email listserv and a website that lists events, provides profiles of DH practitioners on campus, and links to further DH resources at KU and beyond. We capture as many of our guest speakers as we can on video and make the videos available on our YouTube channel, which provides additional visibility for the institute and is a popular resource. (As of December 2014 the YouTube channel contained 64 videos, had received 8,780 views, and had 53 subscribers.)[8]

The codirectors are also extensively engaged in activities and conversations across campus in the form of project consulting, contributing to

"Foundation Professor" (targeted hire) or cluster hire proposals, attending conferences, recruiting speakers and workshop instructors, and general planning and administrative concerns.

Outcomes. The programs and activities described above have led to a range of concrete and visible outcomes during the past four years. IDRH has awarded three DH seed grants supporting faculty research on campus, and seven course development grants, strengthening the content of those courses at KU. Eleven students (five HASTAC scholars and six student assistants) have benefited from IDRH mentoring and support. We have offered over thirty workshops on a range of digital tools and practices, and our Digital Humanities Forum attracts 80 to 120 participants each year. The Digital Humanities Seminar, cosponsored by the Hall Center, has featured twenty-eight presentations since it was launched in 2011 (half of which are KU presenters, and the other half, external speakers). The codirectors also engage in regular project consultations and conversations with colleagues across campus. Significantly, IDRH has facilitated the coalescence of a digital humanities community at KU during the past four years. Thus, the institute was able to form an advisory board in late 2012 comprised largely of KU-based digital humanists (including a graduate student).

Staffing. IDRH is managed by the codirectors and student assistants, recently augmented by the assistance of a postdoctoral researcher. The institute does not have any full-time staff. Even the codirectors are part-time: the university has assigned the college codirector to only 25 percent time, and the Libraries codirector to about 50 percent time. The part-time student assistants (usually graduate students, occasionally undergraduates) work ten to twenty hours per week, helping with daily operations such as website maintenance and content development, events preparation and videography, and creating or managing documentation. For major events such as the annual conference, we have relied on volunteer teams of librarians to help serve on the planning committee.

COLLABORATIONS MAXIMIZE BENEFITS

Contributions of the Three Stakeholders

The three campus stakeholders—the Hall Center for the Humanities, the College of Liberal Arts and Sciences, and the KU Libraries—provide the financial support and guidance for the institute. Having three distinct stake-holders is beneficial for all involved: the codirectors receive useful advice from three campus entities with overlapping but quite distinct interests, and the stakeholders share the expense of the institute and also share the role of institute sounding board. Bureaucracy in triplicate is avoided with a division of labor between the three units, which we will describe below.

The core support from all three stakeholders comes in the form of base funding for the institute, shared equally by all three stakeholders. These funds provide the operating expenses and funding for seed grants, speak-ers, events, codirector travel, and other expenses. In addition, the stake-holders all take part in an annual meeting to review accomplishments of the past year and approve the budget and activities (proposed by the codi-rectors) for the coming year. Each stakeholder provides additional in-kind contributions, perspectives, and interests in supporting and guiding IDRH.

The core activities of the Hall Center for the Humanities (http://hall center.ku.edu) are bringing faculty together for seminars, providing inter-nal grant mechanism and external grant development support, along with hosting a wealth of invited speakers and panels. For IDRH, the Hall Center extends its core functions toward digital humanities in three ways. First, it cosponsors a DH seminar, which meets monthly at the Hall Center for a DH talk and discussion. The Hall Center provides some additional funding for external speakers. Inclusion in the Hall Center's seminar offerings is a highly visible way of signaling to faculty on campus that the digital humani-ties are a core humanities activity, one of many on campus.

Secondly, the Hall Center —above and beyond its one-third contribu-tion to IDRH finances—contributes to the funding of graduate research assistants and undergraduate assistants for IDRH, generally one a year. These assistantships can resemble apprenticeships, as the students need mentoring and supervision. These students tend to work in many areas: from writing tools tutorials, to conducting interviews with DH practitioners on campus, to managing the IDRH website, to helping with major events.

Finally, the Hall Center generously allows faculty with IDRH seed grant proposals to use the services of the Hall Center's Grant Development Office.

The second stakeholder, the College of Liberal Arts and Sciences (http://clas.ku.edu) is primarily engaged with two activities: it supervises the IDRH faculty codirector, who reports to the Humanities associate dean.

The college provides one course release per year for the faculty codirector; the faculty codirector's allocated time commitment is thus 25 percent.

The third stakeholder, KU Libraries (http://lib.ku.edu), provides the main administrative support for IDRH. It supervises the IDRH librarian codirector, who currently reports to an assistant dean in the Libraries, and the Libraries also does most of IDRH's accounting, including payroll and payroll reporting for student assistants, financials for events, honorariums and expenses for guest speakers, and travel for the IDRH codirectors. The librarian codirector was allocated a 50 percent time commitment for the first three years (since a Libraries reorganization, the time commitment has been less clearly defined).

The spread of commitments between the three stakeholders works well; granted, at present the Hall Center and the Libraries are contributing far more in-kind resources than the college. IDRH's activities benefit all three stakeholders in different ways. The Hall Center can show that its ongoing activities (which prominently include the monthly DH seminar held there) reflect the latest trends in the humanities, and the extramural research proposals generated by IDRH's seed grant program are submitted through the Hall Center's grants office. The KU Libraries benefit because IDRH helps provide continuing education to its staff and acts as an important outreach mechanism to faculty and students. Further, IDRH is a shiny arrow in the Libraries' quiver of digital initiatives, including open access, digital scholarship, and digital publishing services. These initiatives complement and strengthen each other, strengthening the Libraries' overall commitment to promoting and supporting new models of scholarly communication. Finally, the College of Liberal Arts and Sciences benefits from IDRH by the necessary interdisciplinarity that digital humanities research involves: Deans across the country speak of "breaking down the silos," and IDRH gives faculty concrete reasons why interdisciplinarity will help individual humanities researchers. Further, college faculty (and grad students) very much appreciate that IDRH workshops and seminars are right on campus and free, and use them to upgrade their skills. The three grant mechanisms IDRH offers (seed grants, course development grants, and travel grants) directly benefit individual faculty. Thus, the institutions and constituents of all three stakeholders reap considerable short- and longer-term benefits from a modest investment.

Roles of the Two Codirectors

When IDRH was established, the librarian codirector was appointed (by the Libraries), and the faculty codirector was hired via a competitive internal search (by the College of Liberal Arts and Sciences and the Hall Center). The Libraries appointed its librarian codirector based on his background in digital humanities. (Prior to IDRH, he had been hired based in great part on those skills.) The college and Hall Center selected their faculty codirector based on her 15 years of DH-grounded sponsored research, grant evaluation, and outreach experience. The two codirectors began their collaborative directorship in October 2010.

The task force originally envisioned a very specific division of roles between the codirectors, with the faculty codirector focusing on the scholarly contribution of faculty research projects and educational programs, and the librarian codirector focusing on the realization of digital projects. But because IDRH is not primarily a digital production unit, the codirectors' roles have been more fluid and collaborative, with both contributing to the design and realization of all major activities (variably according to skills and available time).

Coadministration offers both benefits and challenges, both of which were immediately apparent. As we set our initial goals for IDRH, built a website, and began to organize events, we noticed the considerable benefits of having two different perspectives: we could brainstorm creatively, problem-solve efficiently, fill in each other's disciplinary knowledge gaps, and alternate taking the lead on any given activity. Pinch-hitting for each other is also useful when one or the other codirector has other commitments, thus providing stability and continuity. By benefiting from each other's perspective, our programming could reach wider audiences, for it was not limited to the imagination of a single individual.

One immediate challenge was bridging the Libraries and academic department cultures that each of us represented. Canonically, librarians tend to be extremely service oriented, and humanities faculty often are driven by individual research topics. The digital humanities approach is a mashup of both, with a new twist: DH research is fundamentally collaborative (unlike canonical humanities research); it tends to focus more on methodology than traditional research; and yet, like librarians, DH research is fundamentally outward looking, often concerned with issues of access, usability, and engagement.

Melding the library-style approach with the grounded disciplinary analysis of the traditional humanist *and* with the collaborative, creating-a-resource-for-all approach of the digital humanist has been an ongoing challenge from day one.

Other challenges are more mundane and not specific to the digital humanities: any coadministrators need to work toward a compatible vision of their unit and its place within the university ecosystem. Beyond learning who our core clientele, colleagues, and interested allies were, we learned to adjust our joint vision of our institute to the needs and budget of our institution, also in discussion with our stakeholders. The codirectors experienced a prolonged mutual acculturation phase, as is inevitable with co-leadership: we needed to adjust to and negotiate each other's work and communication styles. Even though we divide up tasks, consulting each other on most all matters has been key. Speaking with a unified voice (and with "we" statements) both acknowledges the contributions of both, and presents a stable vision of the institute.

One of the likely unintended benefits of the codirectorship is that IDRH accrues double the social capital than it would with a single director. The librarian and faculty codirectors can tap two quite different academic social networks, both on campus and off; we have used these networks to recruit reviewers on campus for conference paper and grant proposals, and off campus to recruit guest speakers and workshop instructors. Our university is benefiting significantly, because many of these academic connections long predate our employment at KU.

The division of labor between the codirectors proceeds in two ways: each codirector does what is considered within one's bailiwick, and then we share the rest of the tasks. If this division results in inequities (relative to our respective 50 and 25 percent time commitments), we have learned to adjust our activities accordingly. Thus, the librarian codirector liaises with Libraries staff and administration, and represents IDRH at Libraries meetings. He also plays a central role in maintaining the IDRH website, and regularly works with our student employees. In advance of events such as our annual conference, his leadership role within the Libraries is particularly strong in that he coordinates the team of volunteers that helps with the conference.

The faculty codirector has taken the lead in drafting most of the IDRH position papers and represents IDRH at the college's Chairs and Directors' monthly meetings. She conceived the advisory board and prepares its annual agendas and drafts annual reports to stakeholders. She also established IDRH's seed grant application criteria, drafted numerous call for papers/proposals (CFPs), and facilitated many of these meetings. She sometimes supervises student employees.

Both codirectors envision the scope and content of the annual Digital Jumpstart workshops and DH Forum conference; recruit and arrange for speakers; plan and do campus logistics for events; do outreach to faculty on campus (as presentations or discussion meetings); run grant competitions; attend external DH-related conferences; strategize about new goals and initiatives for the institute; and actively participate in other initiatives on campus, including writing and reviewing proposals for cluster hires or foundation professors, or meeting with visiting lecturers or job candidates who are visiting campus.

For the current scope of IDRH, this division of labor has worked well, with each of us regularly volunteering to spell the other. Nonetheless, both codirectors are working at the upper limits of their respective time commitments, especially since the librarian codirector is effectively given much less than 50 percent time. The involvement of the codirectors in administrative minutiae (e.g., booking flights for speakers) takes precious time away from necessary planning, both short and long range. Given more resources or time, the codirectors could pursue external grant funding, develop digital projects and tools, and/or develop a DH certificate or praxis program.[9]

The next section provides a look at how IDRH has proved a fruitful channel for engagement between librarians and faculty.

BUILDING RELATIONSHIPS TO BEGET NEW COLLABORATIONS

IDRH aims to build relationships with researchers and faculty on campus through our core programs described in the section above: the DH Forum, the Hall Center seminar, our Digital Jumpstart workshops, and the course development grants. Several of these programs have a built-in "involvement multiplier." For example, the successful applicants from the previous several years' course development grants join the current year's successful applicants and exchange tips about what works in DH courses. New awardees thus find that they have an instant cohort of colleagues with whom to exchange ideas. That the previous years' awardees return voluntarily shows that they're enjoying and benefiting from the exchange as well.

Our advisory board provides another opportunity to both draw in and recognize significant campus (and off-campus) expertise in DH; at our first meeting, many KU members were surprised and thrilled to see so many colleagues present, so many of whom were new to them. The advisory board provides a sounding board for ideas brought forth by the codirectors, a source of new ideas from scholars on and off campus, input from a range of perspectives and disciplines, and a communication network to help get the word out about IDRH resources and services. Formed in late 2012 and meeting for the first time in 2013, the advisory board comprises eight faculty members from a range of disciplines, one graduate student, three external digital humanists, and several ex-officio members from the stakeholder entities.

IDRH also offers many service opportunities for faculty and academic staff to get involved, including as reviewers of grant proposals and conference abstracts, as instructors in workshops, as introducers of keynote speakers, and so on. This service, like the advisory board service, helps faculty become invested in IDRH's vision. The service commitments are not too intensive, making faculty more likely to accept invitations to serve. In addition, we do not invite only those who are already DH specialists. We also invite faculty or academic staff who have participated in a workshop in the past or attended a seminar or talk, or others from our academic networks who may not have any explicit interest in digital humanities but who we think would be good reviewers or instructors. This inclusion helps bring new scholars into the fold, and in several cases it has led to a faculty member who was new to DH eventually submitting a course development grant proposal and doing further digitally inflected research projects.

The IDRH codirectors have also led (or participated extensively in) the development of faculty hiring proposals. Developing a proposal for a university-wide cluster hire in data visualization, for example, or for a targeted hire in digital humanities, involves building consent between many units across campus. IDRH's engagement in these initiatives has led to new relationships with individuals and departments across campus, and have established IDRH as a go-to unit for collaboration on such efforts. KU Libraries has benefited from such efforts; a recent cluster hire proposal centrally includes a proposed Libraries academic staff position to support digital humanities and arts. The codirectors regularly evaluate visiting job candidates in a range of humanities fields. IDRH also cosponsors and advertises events via an extensive communication network (including a listserv of two hundred subscribers).

STRENGTHENING AND EXPANDING CORE ACTIVITIES

Our fifth year presented a number of opportunities to expand IDRH programs and to strengthen the Libraries' internal and external engagement in digital humanities. In fall 2015 we were scheduled to begin offering the DH course that is most needed on campus: a general introduction to digital humanities. This course, open to graduate students and upper-level undergraduates, will be cross-listed in several departments, attracting a truly multidisciplinary cohort of students. At other universities, such a course is typically offered through a single humanities department (e.g., English or History) and requires a significant commitment of teaching resources on the part of that host department, as well as considerable prior DH expertise. At KU, our solution has been to include the teaching of this course into the activities of the inaugural IDRH postdoctoral scholar. Teaching such a survey course (including tools, methods, and practices) gives the postdoc valuable teaching experience directly in her field of expertise, and it brings in outside DH talent without taxing any one humanities department, while benefiting all.

The postdoctoral researcher (on a two-year appointment), besides her own research, is also involved in outreach and program development. She is based in KU Libraries and formally reports to the Libraries codirector (with input from the faculty codirector). The postdoc's outreach efforts give the Libraries greater visibility and allow for the building of greater digital humanities skills and expertise among faculty and library staff. Such training occurs both through formal training sessions as well as simply by working together in proximity.

IDRH presents further opportunities to strengthen connections to other areas of library expertise. With recent staff hires (a data services librarian, metadata librarian, and digitization services coordinator), KU Libraries can now offer a suite of services intersecting with digital humanities concerns, including data management consulting, digital publishing platforms, metadata expertise, and information literacy instruction. We expect these connections to grow stronger in the immediate future.

CONCLUSION

This chapter has shown how libraries can collaborate with academic units, and librarians can collaborate with research and teaching faculty via the crucial node of digital humanities. Such an institute can reach a large cross section of the campus community via its critical skill-honing services and activities. Libraries encourage best practices, and provide an interdisciplinary space to pursue research and teaching and to bring together the campus community, free of the interests of any single department. The collaborative model for institute stakeholders spreads both the benefits and the risks of supporting a digital humanities institute, creates wider buy-in, and most importantly allows the institute to take advantage of the different perspectives and academic social networks of the codirectors and stakeholders. This collaboration has allowed IDRH to achieve much more on its limited resources than it could have if it was based in an individual unit or with a single director.

NOTES

1 University of Kansas (KU) Institute for Digital Research in the Humanities (IDRH), http://idrh.ku.edu.

2 See Holly Mercer, Brian Rosenblum, and Ada Emmett, "A Multifaceted Approach to Promote a University Repository: The University of Kansas' Experience," *OCLC Systems & Services* 23, No. 2 (2007): 190–204.

3 Ada Emmett and Town Peterson, "Achieving Consensus on the University of Kansas Open-Access Policy," *Research Library Issues: A Bimonthly Report from ARL, CNI, and SPARC*, No. 269 (April 2010): 5–7, www.arl.org/resources/pubs/rli/archive/rli269.shtml.

4 For a description of our early digital publishing pilot efforts, see Brian Rosenblum and Holly Mercer, "Supporting Campus Publications at the University of Kansas Libraries," *Brick & Click Libraries: Proceedings of an Academic Library Symposium,* ed. Connie Jo Ury, Frank Baudino, and Sarah G. Park, (Maryville: Northwest Missouri State University, 2007), 95–99, http://hdl.handle.net/1808/1783.

5 The full report of the task force is available online in KU's institutional repository at http://hdl.handle.net/1808/10340.

6 Descriptions of all the conferences, along with video presentations and other material, can be found on the IDRH website: Representing Knowledge

(https://idrh.ku.edu/dhforum2011); Big Data and Uncertainty (https://idrh.ku.edu/dhforum2012); Return to the Material (https://idrh.ku.edu/dhforum2013); Nodes and Networks (https://idrh.ku.edu/dhforum2014); Peripheries, Barriers, Hierarchies (https://idrh.ku.edu/dhforum2015).

7 Descriptions of all these programs can be found on the IDRH website: http://idrh.ku.edu.

8 University of Kansas IDRH (YouTube channel), http://youtube.com/idrhku.

9 *The Praxis Network*, http://praxis-network.org.

8 | Advancing Digital Humanities at CU-Boulder through Evidence-Based Service Design

Thea Lindquist, Holley Long, and Alexander Watkins

INTRODUCTION

In 2012, librarians at the University of Colorado Boulder became increasingly aware that interest in digital humanities was gaining ground on our campus. A growing number of graduate students, new faculty members, and established faculty members had been exposed to digital humanities tools and methodologies at disciplinary conferences and were asking questions about incorporating digital modalities into research, teaching, and learning. A handful of prominent scholars with well-publicized digital humanities-related initiatives had a history of involvement, a good example being Lori Emerson and her Media Archaeology Lab.[1] However, little centralized coordination and support for this work were available to the campus community. A previous campus Digital Humanities Initiative (DHI), which administrators in the University Libraries and Center for Humanities and Arts had spearheaded several years before, had unfortunately failed to take root.[2] The more recent interest that surfaced on campus had a different character in that it emanated from the grassroots, both from within the Libraries and from campus researchers.

The authors—the History and Germanic Studies librarian, the Digital Initiatives librarian, and the Art and Art History librarian—proposed the creation of a new initiative within the Libraries to develop expertise relevant to digital humanities in the Libraries and on campus and to partner with researchers on digital projects. To inform this initiative, Libraries administration formed the Digital Humanities Task Force in January 2013.

The task force membership was selected from volunteers who responded to an open call sent to faculty and staff in the Libraries. Three librarians and two staff, with expertise in metadata, research services, collection development, and archives and special collections, joined us on the task force. Additionally, we invited two academic technology consultants from the Office of Information Technology (OIT)—one in the humanities and one in the social sciences—and the director of the Visual Resources Center in the Department of Art and Art History to join the task force with the goal of forging partnerships with other campus technology centers from the outset.

The task force was charged with investigating and reporting on digital humanities activities and needs on campus and formulating evidenced-based recommendations for how we might partner with other campus units to support them. The initial phase involved exploratory work to reveal who, beyond the small cadre of prominent digital humanists already known to the task force, had an interest in digital humanities or were already incorporating it in their scholarship or teaching. Identifying these stakeholders was a crucial first step since we planned to take a participatory design approach to fulfilling our charge. We also aimed to evaluate current campus services and resources in order to identify service gaps that the Libraries and its partners might fill. Finally, we researched how other institutions with library-associated digital humanities initiatives structured, staffed, and funded their services to provide potential models for our own.

RESEARCH DESIGN

Taking a Mixed Methods Approach

The task force took a multimodal approach to our work, employing environmental scans, surveys, interviews, and other techniques to gather the richest possible data set on which to base our analysis. Our methodology was in line with mixed methods research (MMR), an approach by which investigators "collect and analyze data, integrate the findings, and draw inferences using both qualitative and quantitative approaches or methods in a single study."[3] MMR is particularly valuable when investigating complex questions similar to those we undertook for this study, because it results in a robust data set that can be triangulated to provide an additional consistency check.[4] Fidel Raya's 2008 study found that in a sample of five hundred library and information science articles, only 5 percent applied mixed methods. Given the significant investment in time, this figure is not surprising; however, the returns are well worth the effort. In our investigation, the multimodal study was planned out in three phases (see Figure 1) and took over nine months of intensive work to complete. Each stage of the investigation synergistically built on previous work. For example, the campus scan uncovered potential participants for the interviews and symposium that occurred in later phases.

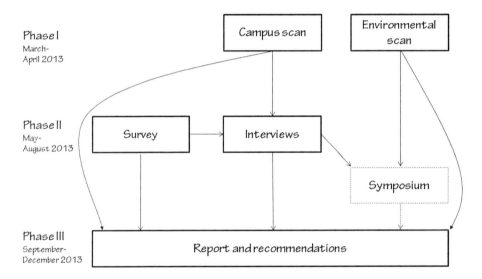

Figure 1. Phased activity of the task force as well as representations of the flow of the research studies.

Environmental Scan

In March and April 2013, one subgroup of the task force conducted an environmental scan of library-based digital humanities initiatives to draw inspiration and learn from others' approaches. The group considered initiatives worldwide ranging in scale from full-fledged digital humanities centers to more modest collaboratories. Potential sites were culled from publications and websites such as the Association of Research Libraries' (ARL) SPEC Kit 326: *Digital Humanities* and the Alliance of Digital Humanities Organizations' centerNet as well as our own knowledge.[5] We focused on digital humanities centers and services that were affiliated with libraries, since they would have the greatest affinity, and thus applicability, to any initiative we started. This criterion shortened the list considerably to thirty-eight institutions. The group reviewed these initiatives' websites and supplemented this information with statistics from sources such as ARL and LibQual+ to collect data on their services, staffing models, and representative projects, as well as staffing, budgetary figures, and collection size for the parent libraries.[6] The group identified a broad range of relatively standard services offered by library-based digital humanities initiatives, with the most common being lecture series and training. Other frequently offered services include, in order of prevalence, collaborative working space, digital collection services, project management support, consultations, equipment, web publishing, and professional networking.

Data on staffing models were not readily available on most of the websites consulted, but we were able to infer from "About" and "Contact" pages that most digital humanities centers were staffed by a mix of librarians, faculty, technologists, and students. Furthermore, a faculty advisory board guided many initiatives. Analysis of institutional statistics highlighted the fact that the CU-Boulder Libraries is below average in terms of staffing and funding, but supports a larger population and manages a larger collection compared to its peers. While this is important to take into consideration when planning services, the potential problems implied by these statistics are not insurmountable since two other institutions with similar statistical profiles offer robust digital humanities services.

Campus Scan

Working in parallel with the external scan subgroup, a second subgroup of the task force undertook an internal scan of activity at CU-Boulder, with the goal of identifying people and projects associated with the digital humanities, as well as campus resources that are currently available for digital work. We searched campus faculty profiles (powered by *VIVO* open-source software) using a variety of keywords to find individuals involved or potentially involved in digital humanities.[7] The subgroup also investigated the websites of likely departments for projects or resources of interest. We analyzed campus-wide services, such as those OIT offered, to identify which would be of potential use to digital scholars. The information we gathered was intended to serve as the foundation of a centralized knowledge base of resources and services that could later be expanded on and made available to the campus community.

Survey

After the internal and external scans were completed at the end of April 2013, we went about directly querying our study populations through a campus-wide survey and in-depth individual interviews. The survey subgroup created an instrument in *Qualtrics* that the task force distributed in June 2013 to CU-Boulder faculty, graduate students, and other researchers regarding their interest and involvement in digital humanities. In keeping with the broad swath of activities that we had set out to capture, we invited them to respond regardless of departmental or disciplinary affiliation. The survey went out to approximately eight thousand affiliates, and we received 345 responses from participants in programs, schools, institutes, departments, schools, and colleges across campus. We encountered a few challenges with the survey that should be mentioned. The first is that, due to unanticipated delays, it was not administered until June, when many faculty and particularly graduate students are not regularly monitoring campus communications. The second is that because the survey was billed as a digital humanities survey, many in the social sciences and sciences may have assumed that it did not apply to them. The last is that other campus units sent out surveys at around the same time, so survey fatigue was almost certainly a factor. Despite these challenges, the survey responses proved an extremely rich and broad data source to inform our report and recommendations.

Using the survey method, we collected a broad array of easily collatable and analyzable data directly from users, who fell into three major categories:

1. Those who were already involved in digital humanities;
2. Those who were interested but not yet involved in digital humanities; and
3. Those who were not interested in digital humanities.

The survey data showed us, among other things, in which campus departments and colleges respondents were rostered; in which digital scholarship methods they were interested; what existing internal and external services and resources they use; and which they wished were available.[8] The survey reached a key group that other methods did not—those who were interested but not yet involved in digital humanities, the largest respondent group. It also enabled us to collect data from those who said they were not interested in digital humanities. The survey proved a useful source for identifying interviewees, as the respondents had the option to volunteer at the end of the survey.

Interviews

Concurrently, a task force subgroup interviewed seventeen faculty and three graduate students who were already incorporating digital humanities in their teaching or research. We asked interviewees about the services, resources, and methodologies they have utilized. We wanted to discover their desired services and any barriers they had encountered in their digital humanities work. We also asked about how they keep up with developments in digital scholarship and about their cross and intra-institutional collaborations. Besides learning about digital scholars' habits, we enlisted their help in designing a support infrastructure by employing participatory design techniques. For example, we asked questions about the single biggest problem that they would choose to solve and what their ideal support network would look like. Interviewees completed a drawing exercise that graphically represented a recent digital project; we asked them to mark areas where support would have been useful. These participatory methods elicited more reflective responses than straightforward questions alone. Finally, to facilitate identification of themes and trends in the data, we coded and analyzed notes and audio files from the interviews in *NVIVO* qualitative data analysis software.

Symposium

In August 2013, the task force organized the "dh+CU Symposium on Future Directions," a daylong symposium for campus graduate students, faculty, librarians, information technology professionals, and other administrative and support staff interested in digital humanities. The initial goal of the symposium was to generate momentum for digital humanities by raising the profile of transformative and cross-disciplinary digital research on campus. The symposium also proved a source of anecdotal and informal focus group information about digital humanities activities, resources, and needs on campus to supplement that gathered through other methods.

The symposium featured three experts from outside institutions who delivered keynote addresses on the future of digital humanities in higher education, followed by CU-Boulder presenters showcasing their own projects.[9] Ample opportunity was built in for discussion, particularly during the birds-of-a-feather sessions at the end of the day. After the symposium, the task force held a half-day workshop that included the outside experts and a small group of administrators from campus units potentially interested in partnering in a digital humanities initiative. During the workshop, potential campus partners discussed the local context, and experts shared their candid assessment of the needs of campus researchers and suggested various models for how the Libraries and campus could support and participate in existing and future digital humanities efforts. These conversations were influential in the task force's report and recommendations.

FINDINGS AND ANALYSIS

After gathering the data, we began the task of integration and analysis. We held several meetings where we discussed the data and used these co-viewings to divide our results into six main themes:

- Current resources, services, and demographics,
- Teaching and student interest,
- Methodologies,
- Collaborations,
- Barriers, and
- Potential support networks.

Within each of the themes, we integrated the data from our various studies. In each section, we presented a synthesis of our scan, interview, and survey findings. Each data stream was able to provide information that filled in gaps in the others. The survey gave us a broad base of standardized responses. The details and nuances lacking in the survey could then be filled in by directed interview questions and follow-ups. For each theme, we were then able to present a holistic overview of the state of digital humanities at CU-Boulder.

Demographics and Interest

The task force's research suggested that there was notable interest in digital humanities on campus. The survey indicated that a significant minority of respondents, 12.5 percent (43), most of whom were faculty, were already active in digital humanities. The majority of respondents, 54.5 percent (188), were interested in digital humanities but not yet involved. One-third (114) were not interested, either because digital humanities required too much time or was not applicable to their research.

Multidisciplinary interest in digital humanities on campus came across strongly in our survey data. Figure 2 shows the number of respondents who were interested in or already involved in digital humanities across schools and colleges at CU-Boulder. While the College of Arts and Sciences, as might be expected, housed the largest number in these categories, a significant number also self-identified in the College of Engineering, College of Music, and School of Education as either involved in digital humanities or interested but not yet involved. The greatest percentages of affirmative faculty responses were in the Libraries (16.3 percent), Journalism (11.5 percent), Music (10.3 percent), and Education (9.8 percent). Among graduate students, Journalism garnered the highest percentage (12.1 percent).

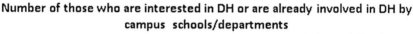

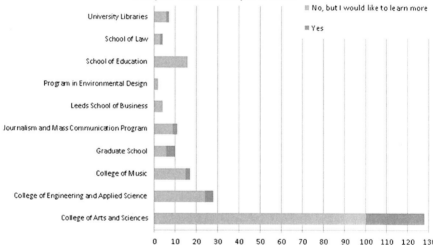

Figure 2. Number of respondents who were interested or already involved in digital humanities across schools and colleges at CU-Boulder.

Figure 3 shows that among divisions in the College of Arts and Sciences, involvement and interest in digital humanities was strongest in the division of Arts and Humanities, where 16.7 percent of faculty replied affirmatively. The greatest numbers were in the departments of History (32.4 percent), French and Italian (26.7 percent), Philosophy (24.1 percent), Asian Languages and Civilizations (19 percent), English (18.4 percent), and Germanic and Slavic Languages and Literatures (17.6 percent). However, departments across the divisions of Social Sciences and Natural Sciences were also involved or interested in investigating humanities-related digital modalities. Among faculty in the Social Sciences, the departments of Linguistics (33.3 percent) and Sociology (7.7 percent) showed notable interest. We were also pleasantly surprised by the response from faculty in the Natural Sciences, particularly in the departments of Psychology and Neurosciences (4.3 percent) and Geography (4.3 percent). Interestingly, the graduate student response was strongest in the division of Social Sciences (5 percent). Graduate student response percentages were as follows in the departments of French & Italian (13.6 percent), History (7.7 percent), Philosophy and Classics (6.3 percent), Linguistics (5.6 percent), Geography (5.2 percent), and Sociology and Psychology (4.7 percent). Disciplines that stood out overall for both faculty and students, therefore, were History, Philosophy, English and foreign languages and literatures, and Linguistics.

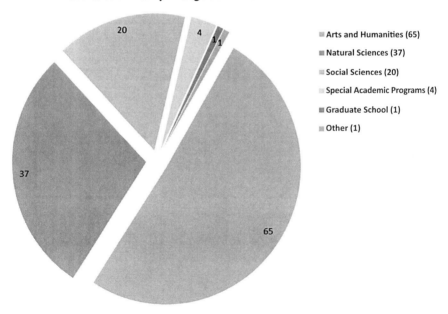

Number of those who are interested in DH or are already involved in DH by College of Arts & Sciences divisions

Arts and Humanities (65)
Natural Sciences (37)
Social Sciences (20)
Special Academic Programs (4)
Graduate School (1)
Other (1)

Figure 3. Number of respondents who were interested or already involved in digital humanities in the College of Arts and Sciences divisions.

The demographics of the survey and interview data suggest that partnerships to support digital humanities across campus departments are needed and that the siloing of support networks are likely inhibiting interdisciplinary collaboration. Community is especially vital to connect digital scholars who are rostered in disparate departments and colleges. Additionally, though interest on campus is substantial, more support and collaboration is needed to enable interested faculty and graduate students to become active digital scholars. The need is especially great among graduate students, who may need these skills as they enter challenging job markets. We are regularly contacted by graduate students to provide experiential learning opportunities in this area.

Digital Humanities Methodologies Employed in Research

Survey and interview data indicated interest or activity in a broad range of methodologies. Digital publication (66 percent) and multimedia editing (53 percent) garnered the largest percentage of responses. Respondents also noted a strong interest or activity in text mining and analysis (43 percent). The remaining top methodologies ranged from geospatial analysis to gaming to computational linguistics. Digital humanities embraces a broad range of methodologies that presents both opportunities and challenges for service design. The more methods that an initiative can support, the larger its potential user base; on the flipside, more services require more resources. Given this reality, the task force was eager to learn which methodologies were most prevalent on campus so it could make targeted recommendations that would support the areas of greatest activity.

Information on faculty research projects gathered during the interviews and internal environmental scan demonstrates the disparate nature of digital humanities research activities taking place on campus. For example, English professor Lori Emerson created the Media Archeology Lab in 2009 as "a place for cross-disciplinary experimental research and teaching using obsolete tools, hardware, software and platforms, from the past."[10] The project aims to preserve obsolete technologies and promote the creation of new products using older technology. Professor Ken Foote, formerly of the CU-Boulder Geography Department, was working on a research project to use narrative cartography techniques to map trends in racial violence across nineteenth and early twentieth-century America. In *Remix the Book,* Art and Art History professor Mark Amerika created an online platform for scholars and artists working in the realm of remix art. These initiatives illustrate the broad interest in digital humanities across disciplines as well as the many manifestations that they can take.

Digital Humanities in Teaching

Interview data suggests that faculty are interested in the potential pedagogical applications of digital humanities. Sixteen of the twenty interview respondents stated that they use these methods in the classroom. Though some respondents conflated digital humanities with educational technologies more generally (discussing, for example, clickers, Google apps, or MOOCs), there were several examples of truly transformative uses of technology in the classroom setting. One English PhD candidate interviewed incorporated the text analysis tool *Voyant* into her course discussions and assignments. Additionally, a professor of Classics and Archaeology developed an educational video game called *Project Osiris* in which students play the role of an archaeological dig director for a site in Amarna, Egypt.

Graduate students expressed strong support for digital humanities and would like to see it more fully integrated into all aspects of academics, including the classroom. Faculty perceptions of undergraduate interest in digital humanities, however, were mixed and evenly distributed between "very interested," "interested," and "not interested." Faculty also observed that new technologies require significant scaffolding to effectively incorporate into instruction and that undergraduates can be ambivalent about expending the effort to learn them. In multiple contexts, faculty and graduate students remarked that undergraduates are less likely to draw a distinction between digital humanities and traditional methods, which opens the door to incorporating digital methods into the classroom.

Needs and Barriers

One of the task force's main goals was to better understand current digital scholars' desired resources and services, as well as the barriers that they encounter in their work. For those researchers who were interested, we also wanted to discover what perceived needs were preventing them from becoming involved in digital humanities. Figures 1, 4, 5, and 6 represent the barriers as well as the desired services and resources. The aim was to formulate recommendations that would provide these desired services and mitigate or eliminate obstacles. Thus, both the interviews and survey asked respondents questions about desires and barriers.

Once the task force coded the interviews, we found 224 different instances of comments that were coded with a specific need or barrier. The most frequently cited are illustrated in Figure 4. The survey asked digital humanities-involved respondents to select from a predefined list of barriers with "lack of other resources" as a write-in option. The results are illustrated in Figure 5. Survey respondents who were interested but yet not involved with digital humanities were asked what desired services would make them more likely to begin work in the field. The most commonly requested services are represented in Figure 6. As the task force interpreted the interview and survey data, we saw that the services desired by those not yet involved correspond to the barriers faced by scholars who were already involved. These two concepts are complementary and indeed were two sides of the same coin, as illustrated in Figure 7.

Overall, respondents cited an opportunity to build relevant skills as the most important desire and need for undertaking digital humanities work. Technology training was the most desired service named in the interviews and by digital humanities-interested survey respondents. A high percentage of survey respondents, 72.9 percent (137), expressed a desire for trainings and workshops. The interview format allowed us to ask follow-up questions regarding the types of training interviewees would find useful. They asked for training on specific software and technology skills like programming. Several mentioned current technology workshops that are offered at CU-Boulder as a very useful forum for exchanging ideas with other peers.

The needs for improved technology support and infrastructure were also highly ranked issues. Fully 64.9 percent (122) of survey respondents who were interested in digital humanities expressed a desire for improved campus technology infrastructure. Most interview comments on this subject related to database design, as well as web hosting and design. We heard accounts of websites developed by students or consultants that were lost or taken down once developers were no longer available to support and maintain the sites. Interviewees also desired better software and hardware. Some of them requested more infrastructure in the form of smart classrooms and laptop carts for digital humanities-related pedagogy, while others found reliance on the campus-approved suite of tools to be limiting and preferred the latitude to use more open-source and third-party, cloud-based applications.

Unsurprisingly, digital scholars who responded to the survey identified lack of time as a significant barrier. Interviewees pointed out that becoming involved with digital scholarship requires a significant investment of

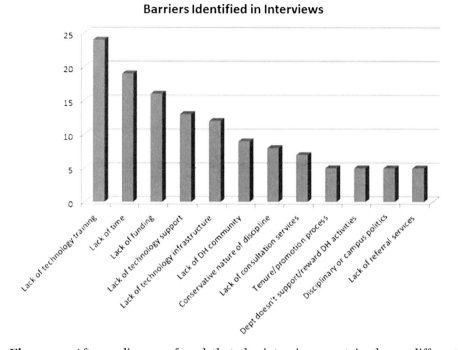

Figure 4. After coding, we found that the interviews contained 224 different instances of "gaps and barriers"-related comments. This figure illustrates the most common categories.

time to become competent in the methodologies, and then either do the research or integrate them into the classroom. Finding the time to explore digital modes of scholarship alongside traditional ones is difficult. Further, narrow expectations about what types of research outputs count in hiring, tenure, and promotion processes keep them on the back burner for many researchers. Our research suggested that scholars highly desired a framework for evaluating digital humanities activities for promotion and tenure. Indeed, of the 43 survey respondents already involved in digital humanities, 11 (26 percent) cited not knowing how digital outputs would be evaluated in the tenure and promotion process as a barrier to engaging with digital humanities in their work. A substantial minority, 37.8 percent (71), of survey respondents who were interested in digital humanities expressed a desire for institutional recognition before they were willing to dedicate the necessary time. The interviews brought nuance to these

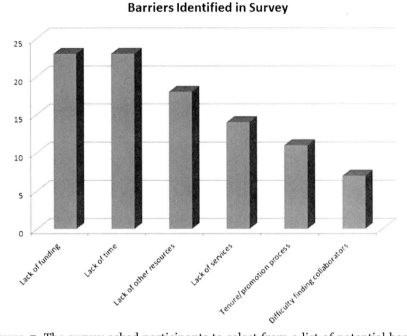

Figure 5. The survey asked participants to select from a list of potential barriers with a write-in option for "lack of other resources."

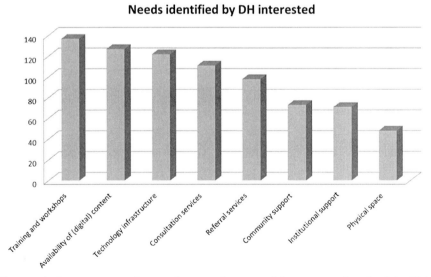

Figure 6. Survey respondents who were interested but not yet involved in digital humanities were asked about what resources and services would make them more likely to begin work in the field.

Figure 7. Barriers, desired services, and resources.

desires—interviewees cited the conservative nature of their disciplines, uncertainty about credit for digital humanities in the tenure process, and lack of support or rewards from their department for digital scholarly outputs. Given the pervasiveness of this concern, we recognized that any significant effort to promote digital humanities at CU-Boulder should also address its role in tenure and promotion.

Survey respondents pinpointed lack of funding as their major concern with 53.4 percent (23) of digital humanities-involved respondents selecting it as a barrier. The more in-depth comments from interviewees about funding proved useful for delving deeper into the issue. The most frequently mentioned theme was that they did not have access to adequate funds to initiate the many interesting ideas they had for digital research projects. Secondly, for those initiatives fortunate enough to acquire grant funding, interview respondents noted that reliance on soft money is not sustainable. Finally, many faculty expressed a desire for funding to secure more student assistants and staff support. Many initiatives are run entirely by volunteers—a model that is not particularly sustainable or equitable for students. Our research suggested that offerings such as fellowships, technology infrastructure, and other funding sources are in high demand.

One of the barriers to a full-fledged digital scholarship ecosystem at CU-Boulder is the lack of a coherent community of practitioners. In the survey, difficulty finding collaborators was cited by 16 percent of the digital humanities-involved respondents and 38.8 percent of digital humanities-interested respondents. Most digital scholars are involved in some kind of collaboration with external partners, and our interviewees desired a local community to link digital humanities researchers, especially matching those with subject knowledge to those with technological expertise. The overwhelmingly positive response to the symposium as a networking event further underscored the desire for community.

While the lack of resources and support discussed so far is certainly a valid issue, the task force noted that in many cases respondents were not aware of existing resources and services on campus that might be helpful in their work. Thus, we believe that new referral services will be a vital component of any digital humanities initiative for our campus.

RECOMMENDATIONS

After a nine-month investigation, the task force had gathered an immense amount of data on which to base our recommendations. A clear and nuanced picture of user needs and service gaps emerged from the combined findings, pointing to five high-level goals for a digital humanities initiative: foster community, develop strategic partnerships, build technical infrastructure, create support services, and develop mechanisms to evaluate alternative scholarly outputs. We came to consensus on these broad objectives relatively quickly and focused most of our discussions on which specific recommendations and strategies would best achieve them. We organized the recommendations into three phases according to what we believed could be achieved over the short, medium, and long term. Phase I represented recommended immediate actions. Phase II recommendations would create a base level of support for digital humanities, and phase III goals would result in establishment of a campus-wide center for digital humanities research. Finally, these recommendations were situated in the context of the university's strategic plan, Flagship 2030, to demonstrate how the proposed digital humanities initiative would further CU-Boulder's core mission.

Based on feedback from external experts and interviewees who believed that many resources and services on campus are siloed in individual schools, colleges, and departments, we concluded that the Libraries is a natural entity to lead these efforts and to provide a focus for digital humanities on campus. The Libraries' mission to remain a vital part of the research process motivates us to find new resources and innovative ways to support scholars and teachers in their digital endeavors. The Libraries also offers neutral space in the heart of the campus that is both welcoming and easily accessible to users in all disciplines.

The recommendations for actions by the Libraries formed a base on which our further recommendations could be accomplished by the groups and people and in the spaces recommended. They included most importantly the hiring of a digital humanities librarian in phase I who would dedicate his or her time to the work outlined in the further recommendations, and a digital humanities center, which would be planned in phase II and implemented in phase III. This center would be where the resources and support services recommended would be located. Such a center would anchor the growing digital humanities community and offer workshops and training. It would also house hires that the task force recommended: the digital humanities librarian, a programmer, and graduate assistants.

Given our users' desire for the facilitation of collaborations and intellectual exchange, the first objective the task force set from our multimodal inquiry was strengthening community. Until a more formalized infrastructure can be built, developing a community of scholars with interests in digital humanities is crucial to supporting existing practitioners in their work. Thinking further ahead, continued engagement with the digital humanities community on campus is key to building a base of support for continued investment in the digital humanities, as well as to the ongoing assessment of needs and priorities.

Another objective we identified was forging partnerships on campus and beyond. Both librarians in the early stages of establishing digital humanities centers who we interviewed and the external experts emphasized the importance of establishing strategic partnerships outside of the library. Given the sizable resources required to launch an initiative and the collaborative nature of digital humanities work itself, garnering external support is essential for success. Thus, in phase I, the task force recommended forging campus partnerships with the College of Arts and Sciences, Center for Humanities and Arts (CHA), Graduate School, OIT, and United Government of Graduate Students, among others, in order to build support for the initiative, raise its visibility, and pool partner resources for an initiative using a "stone-soup" model.[11] In phase II, the task force recommended pursuing partnerships with Boulder's thriving technology sector to forge public-private scholarly collaborations and provide students with valuable experiential learning opportunities. Furthermore, this partnership could result in injections of much-needed private funding. Since phase III of the plan focused on establishing a campus-wide center, partnership-building activities during this phase would concentrate on forming a high-level advisory committee with representatives from interested units to provide strategic direction.

The third objective focuses on building more robust technical infrastructure to support the more comprehensive digital humanities initiative the task force envisions. Furthermore, we discovered that the campus community is not sufficiently aware of existing technology services, which as a result are underutilized. To address these issues, we made several recommendations. In phase I, we suggested expanding the website for CU's digital humanities community to become the virtual nexus for the initiative during its early stages. It could serve several functions including highlighting campus digital humanities projects, a registry for campus resources, and referral services. The task force also recommended collaborating with OIT to increase awareness of existing technology services, developing new infrastructure where needed, and acquiring hardware and software for the center. Since experimentation and creation of new technologies often go hand-in-hand with digital humanities, in phases II and III our recommendations include fostering greater participation in the open-source software community and providing sandbox environments to explore new tools.

The fourth broad objective the task force identified was development of a suite of services in response to specific needs that are tailored to targeted audiences on campus. The task force made four recommendations and phased them based on ease of implementation. In phase I, we suggested promoting the Libraries' digital content, both digitized in-house and licensed, as source material for digital humanities projects. To facilitate use of licensed resources for activities such as text mining, the task force proposed negotiating for expanded licensing terms for vendor-supplied content. In phase II, the Libraries would offer consultation services on areas such as digital humanities tools and project management. In phase III, the group recommended developing a workshop series that would both empower novices to join CU's digital humanities community as well as broaden the skill sets of more advanced practitioners.

Evaluating digital humanities projects for the purposes of tenure and promotion was a key concern and therefore was the fifth objective to come out of our study. Our research indicated that a lack of recognition of alternative scholarly outputs plays a key role in inhibiting digital humanities work, which applies to faculty within as well as outside of the Libraries. We recommended that the Libraries' tenure committee develop its own standard for evaluating the digital humanities work of faculty librarians. We also recommended further conversations with appropriate campus stakeholders to start creating broader guidelines; if necessary, the Libraries' standards could serve as a model. These broader guidelines could then be promoted to encourage adoption by campus departments.

The creation of a campus center for digital humanities that would build on the partnerships and trust established with other campus units in the preceding phases was the ultimate objective that the task force highlighted. A portion of the infrastructure and personnel would already be in place in the Libraries as a result of the hiring of a digital humanities librarian and creation of a digital humanities lab and would serve as a core of critical support for the center. The task force recommended a collaborative leadership model for the center similar to that of the Maryland Institute for Technology in the Humanities at the University of Maryland and the Center for Digital Research in the Humanities at the University of Nebraska–Lincoln, which are codirected by one library and one nonlibrary faculty member.[12] The center would provide funding, assistance, training, and other opportunities for graduate students, faculty, and researchers interested in digital humanities and would integrate with the campus curriculum through seminars and credit courses. We also envisioned it as a locus for grant writing and fund-raising. Our recommendation for a center supports two goals in our current university strategic plan, namely, #5, "Transcending Traditional Academic Boundaries," in its promotion of interdisciplinary teaching, learning, research, creative work, and scholarship, and #6, "Investing in the Tools for Success," in its physical space in the Libraries that would encourage individual and collaborative learning, research, and creative work."[13]

Outcomes

The task force report laid out the research behind the recommendations in substantial detail, and our next step was to communicate the findings and recommendations to our colleagues in the Libraries and to the interested campus community to solicit feedback.[14] We shared the executive summary with links to the full report with all faculty and staff in the Libraries and asked particular colleagues with an interest in digital scholarship on our cross-functional Scholarly Communications Working Group for input. Additionally, we did a public presentation to our colleagues and to the Libraries' management team, received their feedback, and fielded their questions. Further, we shared this material with potential partner units on campus that had expressed interest in our investigations, and whose faculty and graduate students showed particular interest in digital work in the survey and interviews. In some cases, we created tailored reports, for example, on interest among graduate students for the dean of the Graduate School, among Arts and Humanities departments for the associate dean of that division and for the director of the CHA, and in particular departments like History and English for their chairs.

After publication of the report, the initiative has broadened from being more narrowly focused on digital humanities to encompassing digital scholarship. Much of this move was inspired by the data we gathered for the report, such as the demonstrated interest from many scholars outside of the humanities. This evolution also reflected conversations with our colleagues about the potential of a digital scholarship center to become a hub for the library's digital services such as data management, scholarly communications, digitization, metadata, and digital archiving. Thus, a focus on digital scholarship had more potential to break down silos and to build partnerships across the university.

The Libraries' management team was supportive of our recommendations and requested the task force assemble a panel of campus faculty to provide feedback on them for further consideration. The panel's endorsement, and that of the co-chairs of the campus Research Data Advisory

Committee, lent further weight to the recommendations. Building on the groundwork we laid, the Libraries' recent program review included a strong recommendation to invest in new positions in the area of digital scholarship, and campus partners, including the new College of Media, Communication, and Information, the CHA, the Graduate School, the Center for STEM Learning, and Research Computing in OIT, are stepping up to support the Libraries' bid with campus administration to create a research center for digital scholarship. The center is proving a unique opportunity to bring investment to the library from multiple campus partners, to engage with scholars and work as equal partners on digital projects, and to secure the library's place at the heart of a changing research landscape.

In the meantime, campus partners have not stood still. The History Department, for instance, is offering a graduate-level digital history class, which the History and Germanic Studies librarian co-teaches with a History faculty member. It has also hired an instructor whose job duties include acting as a digital liaison for the department. Together with the incoming director of our Institute for Behavioral Sciences, we organized a grant-funded digital humanities speaker and workshop series in 2015 that was also financially supported by departments, schools, and institutes across the disciplinary spectrum.

Time will tell what the final outcomes of the task force's recommendations are and how the initiative will grow. It is already clear, though, that the task force's data-driven approach to our investigation resulted in a strong foundation for the future of the initiative. Employing a variety of methodologies to collect data created a more complete and nuanced understanding of the current digital humanities landscape and made evidence-based service design possible. In addition to the obvious benefits, involving stakeholders in all aspects of the investigation instilled a shared sense of purpose, and perhaps even co-ownership, in any resulting initiatives that will only serve to strengthen support for our efforts.

NOTES

1   See: http://mediaarchaeologylab.com.

2   DHI members participated in Project Bamboo, which shared a similar fate. See Quinn Dombrowski, "What Ever Happened to Project Bamboo?," *Literary and Linguistic Computing* 29, No. 4 (December 2014): 4014. doi:10.1093/llc/fqu026.

3   Abbas Tashakkori and John W. Creswell, "Editorial: The New Era of Mixed Methods," *Journal of Mixed Methods Research* 1, No. 1 (2007): 4.

4   Raya Fidel, "Are We There Yet?: Mixed Methods Research in Library and Information Science," *Library & Information Science Research* 30 (2008): 266–67.

5   Tim Bryson et al., comps., *Digital Humanities*, SPEC Kit 326 (Washington, DC: Association of Research Libraries, 2011) and Alliance of Digital Humanities Organizations, "centerNet: An International Network of Digital Humanities Centers," www.dhcenternet.org.

6   Association of Research Libraries, "ARL Statistics: Annual Library Statistics," www.arlstatistics.org/analytics, and "LibQUAL+: Charting Library Service Quality," www.libqual.org/home.

7   See http://vivo.colorado.edu.

8   The questions regarding needs were phrased differently for the group that was already involved in digital humanities and the group that was interested but not yet involved. The former group's questions were presented in terms of barriers to achieving their digital humanities goals, since they could be expected to have concrete thoughts on the subject, while questions for the latter group were phrased in terms of desires, that is, what they thought might enable them to become involved in the digital humanities community. Despite this disconnect, wants and needs can be viewed as two sides of the same coin, so we were fortunately able to categorize this data to include the feedback of both groups as necessary.

9   More information about the presenters and links to their presentations are available at http://ucblibraries.colorado.edu/research/subjectguides/Digital Humanities/digitalhumanities-symposium-people.htm.

10   See: http://mediaarchaeologylab.com/about/why.

11   This phrase refers to a folk tale in which hungry travelers persuade townspeople to contribute different food items to create a stew.

12   See http://mith.umd.edu and http://cdrh.unl.edu.

13   University of Colorado Boulder, "Flagship 2030 Serving Colorado Engaged in the World: A Strategic Plan for the University of Colorado at Boulder."

14   The report is openly available at Thea Lindquist, Holley Long, Alexander Watkins, Leo Arellano, Michael Dulock, Eric Harbeson, Erika Kleinova, Viktoriya Oliynynk, Elaine Paul, and Esta Tovstiadi, "dh+CU: Future Directions for Digital Humanities at CU Boulder" (2013), http://scholar.colorado.edu /libr_facpapers/32.

Part 4

PEDAGOGY AND INSTRUCTION

9 | A Collaborative Approach to Urban Cultural Studies and Digital Humanities

Benjamin Fraser and Jolanda-Pieta van Arnhem

INTRODUCTION

This chapter will respond simultaneously to three different forces that are influencing the development of humanities research: (1) urban cultural studies, (2) the digital humanities, and (3) collaborative research and practice. Because of the interdisciplinary nature of each of these forces—and because of the need to work both at the theoretical and the practical levels here—each is introduced concisely as a way of preparing the road for what is to follow. This will be necessary to understand both the disciplinary misperceptions as well as the interdisciplinary potential inherent in the implemented project: namely, a graduate class conducted during the spring semester of 2014 at the College of Charleston.

The course, titled "SPAN 630: Digital Humanities Project: Madrid's Gran Vía through Visual Culture," was supplemented by the strategic use of collaboration between a librarian and language and literature faculty interested in exploring best practices and practical applications for implementing digital humanities methods for research and teaching in the classroom. This effort anticipated the Association of College and Research Libraries' (ACRL's) call for broader collaborations between library and information professionals with the wider academic community to "redesign assignments and curricula to create more coherent information literacy programs."[1] It also enabled the library's Digital Scholarship and Services Department's first real effort to affect program development alongside campus faculty and use library instructional materials in the classroom in a way that is more deeply and directly interwoven into the curriculum and to the faculty instructor's approach to objectives and competencies.

A number of pedagogical and ethical considerations required research prior to selecting the content management system (CMS) and designing course assignments, instructional activities, and final exhibit requirements, including best practices for permission, fair use, copyright, and Family Educational Rights and Privacy Act (FERPA) requirements. Student and faculty technological skill sets and familiarity with digital humanities scholarship also required evaluation in order to determine the types of library instruction that were required to facilitate the project. Stanford University Library provides ample resources dedicated to issues of copyright and fair use. The "Proposed Educational Guidelines on Fair Use" provided helpful information on creating multimedia projects and were used to craft a syllabus statement to inform project authors of their responsibilities when finding media for digital projects. The statement outlines student expectations to research and determine the copyright status of materials prior to uploading assignments in the class exhibit or to provide signed permission or consent forms if required.[2]

Based on Cathy Davidson's valuable post on legalities and practicalities in "Public Blogs and Video in the Classroom and FERPA Compliance," on the Humanities, Arts, Science, and Technology Alliance and Collaboratory (HASTAC) blog, a sample "Release of Course Materials for Public Availability and Faculty Use of Student Work" form was developed.[3] Further discussions were held with the college's institutional review board (IRB) to seek guidance on college research policies, procedures, and best practices related to the public distribution of student work. As a result, the following best practices guidelines were developed for faculty and library collaborative digital humanities projects:

1. Students may opt out of publishing their work.
2. Students may elect to publish using an alias (pseudonym).
3. Students maintain ownership of the work created in the course.
4. Assignments (items) included in the class exhibit are licensed under a Creative Commons license (specifically CC BY-NC 4.0/attribution-noncommercial 4.0 International).
5. Students are informed and consent to exhibit curation.

This means that the final appearance of assignments on the student exhibition site is subject to approval by the professor and that individual items or entire exhibits may be taken down for reasons related to quality and appropriateness as well as the future direction of the project as a whole. Additionally, exhibits become part of the library digital collections at the college and these exhibits are collectively licensed under a Creative Commons Attribution-NonCommercial-NoDerivatives 4.0 International License to guard against inadvertent derivatives of student work by third parties. The syllabus statement, permissions template, and best practices were created in an effort to inform students and guide faculty considerations when working with students on digital projects published on the web. To ensure student materials are exhibited by permission, participating students are required to complete and turn in to their instructor a "Release of Course Materials for Public Availability and Faculty Use of Student Work" form customized to include specific course information, assignments, and exhibit information for the course. The instructor must deliver a copy of the signed consent forms from all students to the library before the exhibit will be made public.

To proceed with the project, it was important to identify the appropriate content management system for the project. WordPress and Omeka are both open-source CMS platforms commonly used in digital humanities projects. Both platforms offer self-hosted and hosted options. WordPress provides a blogging environment with information presented in reverse chronological order and static pages that can be used to create an online exhibit. Omeka, developed by the Center for History and New Media (CHNM) at George Mason University, is a CMS and web publishing platform designed for scholarly digital collections and exhibits that uses Dublin Core metadata standards to catalog, organize, curate, and display digital exhibits and collections.[4] Anthony Bushong and David Kim discuss the importance of the use of Dublin Core metadata and compare Omeka to WordPress noting that "this additional layer helps to establish proper source attribution, standards for description and organization of digital resources—all important aspects of scholarly work in classroom settings but often overlooked in general blogging platforms."[5] Since one of the goals of the course was to introduce students to the field of digital humanities and creating digital scholarly online exhibits, Omeka was selected as the CMS for the project.

Once the platform had been selected, the library installed a locally hosted instance of Omeka 2.0 with the Neatline plug-in. The self-hosted, Omeka.org version of the software was selected over the hosted, Omeka.net version in order to allow the library to expand Omeka's capabilities and customize the Omeka installation by adding additional themes and plug-ins. The self-hosted installation of Omeka shown in Figure 1 also allowed the library to have more control over space limitations and overall functionality, which is more limited when using the hosted version from Omeka.net. Neatline was also installed in order to facilitate, as described by Iman Salehian, a space-based counternarrative to the more static, gallery-style online exhibit of class assignments.[6]

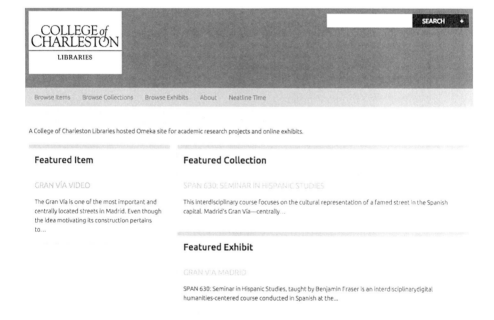

A College of Charleston Libraries hosted Omeka site for academic research projects and online exhibits.

Featured Item

GRAN VÍA VIDEO

The Gran Vía is one of the most important and centrally located streets in Madrid. Even though the idea motivating its construction pertains to...

Featured Collection

SPAN 630: SEMINAR IN HISPANIC STUDIES

This interdisciplinary course focuses on the cultural representation of a famed street in the Spanish capital, Madrid's Gran Vía—centrally...

Featured Exhibit

GRAN VÍA MADRID

SPAN 630: Seminar in Hispanic Studies, taught by Benjamin Fraser is an interdisciplinarydigital humanities-centered course conducted in Spanish at the...

Figure 1. College of Charleston Libraries–hosted Omeka site for academic research projects and online exhibits.

The overall goal of the collaborative partnership between librarian and language and literature faculty was to pilot a semester-long digital humanities project with assignments tailored to a specific discipline in order to thread discipline-specific content with information literacy skills development. This skills development was based on the ACRL Information Literacy Competency Standards for Higher Education Task Force recommendations in order to help students "be successful academically and in the workplace of the future."[7] A second goal of the collaboration was to expose students to digital humanities methods and research and provide hands-on project experience in an effort to help students better understand the emerging interdisciplinary field. A third goal of the project was to develop a better understanding of how to scaffold course assignments and library instruction that could be adapted in other language contexts as well as other interdisciplinary undergraduate and graduate courses in order to promote independent student learning. The fourth goal of the project was to provide an *in situ* experience for library faculty to develop, assess, and evaluate the pilot in order to create educational materials for online exhibit building and interactive mapping projects to add to the library's Digital Scholarship and Services Department's growing list of digital humanities tools and instructional services offered to faculty and students at the College of Charleston. (The implication throughout is that this type of endeavor can be adapted to other language contexts as well as undergraduate classes in which students become the producers of digital content while preserving the cultural critique that has long been the hallmark of humanities disciplines.)

During the course, library instruction was created and course assignments were revised as needed in order to facilitate student learning as each step of the process unfolded. To introduce students to digital humanities, an instructional guide was created using Springshare's LibGuide platform. In the spirit of the digital humanities collaborative process, much of this instruction was adapted from Creative Commons sources and delivered via a Library Digital Humanities Research Guide shown in Figure 2, largely adapted from "A Guide to Digital Humanities," from the Center for Scholarly Communication and Digital Curation at Northwestern University Library[8] and *The CUNY Digital Humanities Resource Guide* from CUNY Academic Commons.[9] The guide included numerous resources for getting started with digital humanities; introduced relevant vocabulary; discussed pedagogical implications for teaching, research, and publication; provided additional resources on finding books and journal articles at the library as well via open-access repositories; noted prominent centers; included additional resources for digital humanities tools and tutorials; and advised students of methods and tools for keeping up with digital humanities news and events and continuing their professional development in the interdisciplinary field.

Figure 2. College of Charleston Libraries Digital Humanities Research Guide created using the Springshare LibGuide content management system.

In addition to the introductory guide on digital humanities, an additional instructional guide and related educational materials on using Omeka and Neatline were created for students. Figure 3 illustrates the course guide, which provided an overview of Omeka, discussed hosted and self-hosted options, and introduced students to interactive mapping. The guide also facilitated discussion about copyright, fair use, and permission considerations in regards to publicly accessible digital humanities projects. Students were provided information on how to log in to the library-hosted Omeka site, an introduction to permissions associated with their accounts, and step-by-step tutorials on how to upload items, add metadata, associate items with the class collection, and add pages to the class exhibit. To support the multimedia requirements required for course assignments, a third instructional guide was created to assist students with video and audio production techniques and introduce them to using video and audio production tools. All of these guides were licensed under a Creative Commons license.

Figure 3. The College of Charleston Libraries Omeka Instructional Guide provides tips, tutorials, and recommendations for using Omeka to publish online multimedia exhibits, digital heritage collections, and research projects.

In the remainder of this chapter, we will first trace the methodological background that figured into the course design and content of SPAN 630 (the "Approaching the Urban, Digitally" section). The emphasis here is on introducing the general reader to disciplinary shifts that have unfolded at a broad scale in recent decades, but which are not necessarily tied to library and information science. Next, in the "Practical Scale: Students as DH Producers in the Language Classroom" section, we consider the practical considerations that required the course to meet a divergent set of pedagogical and instructional goals. As part of this discussion, attention is given to the issue of language of instruction, which is often perceived as a barrier to DH collaboration across language areas—but which need not be so perceived. In the final section, "Interdisciplinarity, Urban Cultural Studies, and the Digital Environment," we return to the interest in Lefebvre among faculty in Library and Information Science[10] in order show

how his understanding of interdisciplinarity can reinvigorate an urban approach to digital humanities work.

APPROACHING THE URBAN, DIGITALLY

Because readers may not be familiar with what goes by the name of "urban cultural studies," it makes sense to begin there. We use the term here to invoke a particular fusion of the concerns of both (1) urban studies and (2) cultural studies. It is necessary to point out that although interest crossing each of these areas is on the rise in certain circles, generally speaking such interest is still very much in the margins of disciplinary conversations that continue to dominate the scholarly landscape. Urban studies as a discipline has traditionally leaned away from the humanities and toward the social sciences and the sciences: urban planning, economics, political economy, sociology, geography, anthropology, architecture, and so on. As an example we take to be representative, consider a paper published as recently as 2010. In "What Is 'Urban Studies': Context, Internal Structure and Content," an article from the *Journal of Urban Affairs*, the authors name seven constitutive subfields: (1) urban sociology, (2) urban geography, (3) urban economics, (4) housing and neighborhood development, (5) environmental studies, (6) urban governance, politics and administration, and finally (7) urban planning, design, and architecture.[11] One should note that culture is not specifically mentioned in this list. Moreover, it is necessary to point out that even within the subfields of urban sociology and urban geography that are indeed mentioned, there is still a pervasive and continuing split between qualitative (human, cultural) approaches and quantitative (statistical, economic) approaches, an "internal" disciplinary division that recapitulates the wider marginalization of humanities-centered cultural paradigms within interdisciplinary work crossing the humanities and the social sciences.

Of course, over a number of decades, a vocal minority of urban studies theorists have turned increasingly toward culture as a way of understanding the urban phenomenon. Chief among them, perhaps, is David Harvey, who has consistently articulated a view of the urban that prioritizes the dialectical interaction between culture and space. Harvey's work has drawn meaningfully from that of urban philosopher Henri Lefebvre, whose name also enjoys recognition in certain academic circles.[12] Furthermore, in the relatively newly articulated urban cultural studies paradigm expressed through the recent creation of the *Journal of Urban Cultural Studies*,[13] this urban cultural studies tradition is blended with an emphasis on humanities-centered definitions of culture—definitions that privilege "texts" such as literature, film, music, and other cultural products. Directly appropriating the cultural studies method as defined by pioneering scholar Raymond Williams, an urban cultural studies method gives equal weight to the project (art) and the formation (society) while considering such humanities texts to be crucial.[14] This move is a corrective for the disciplinary tensions that have continued to inform both the cultural studies paradigm as a whole and also the way in which the social sciences have most often preferred to tackle the notion of urban culture at a scale that excludes humanities texts themselves.[15]

Meanwhile, it should come as no surprise that there has been a sea change in the humanities that concerns technological shifts, methodological consequences, and the rise of innovative digital research and teaching.[16] The issue here, as above, has been that digital humanities work that crosses the humanities and the social sciences divide, specifically, has tended to privilege the humanities discourse of history over the artistic questions of textual representation and representational structure that have generally informed literary studies—even in its nontraditional formulations (we would include here incursions into film, graphic novels, popular music, and so on). One need only look at three relatively recent volumes merging geography and the humanities in a digital paradigm to gain a sense of this continuing marginalization of artistic and broadly "literary" matters.[17]

It is significant that interdisciplinary collaboration figures into both urban cultural studies and the digital humanities. Our judgment is that although urban cultural studies collaboration is in its inception (that is, at present, collaboration is implicit in the increased fusion of disciplinary concerns if not also explicit through the creation of unique projects such as "hypercities" that call for collaboration between programmers and cultural critics), in the digital humanities, on the other hand, collaborative work has rapidly become the norm. Kathleen Fitzpatrick's landmark study *Planned Obsolescence*[18] has undoubtedly celebrated the death of the individual author somewhat prematurely if not unnecessarily, but the fact remains that collaborative work is gaining ground. Along with this new foothold in the academy comes a degree of respect that collaboration has not enjoyed in humanities disciplines for some time. All this despite the unique circumstances present over the years in a number of scholarly digital labs, for example, from the University of Virginia's Speclab to the CulturePlex Lab, headed by Juan Luis Suárez at the University of Western Ontario. We believe that what makes the present chapter so timely and relatively unique is that it investigates how a collaborative effort can unfold at a smaller scale, outside of the designated (and often quite large) budgets that—whether from grant funding, institutional funding, or some combination of both— sustain such large-scale laboratories and creative digital workshops.[19] With this in mind, we assert the value of how a small-scale partnership between a humanities faculty member and a librarian can speak at once to the inter-disciplinary push and the collaborative spirit of both urban cultural studies and digital humanities, while grounded in an institutional context that is often left out of both of these discussions—the language classroom.

THE PRACTICAL SCALE: STUDENTS AS
DH PRODUCERS IN THE LANGUAGE CLASSROOM

The class "SPAN 630: Digital Humanities Project: Madrid's Gran Vía through Visual Culture" was conceived through discussions that brought a faculty member from Hispanic Studies together with library faculty. Because it boasts a diverse set of goals, the initial planning for SPAN 630 required some troubleshooting and some compromise if the digital compo-nent was to be realized in the course—goals that deserve our attention here.

First among them was meeting the expectations of the MEd program in which the class was offered. Some explanation is in order. The typical graduate student enrolled in College of Charleston's master's in education degree program tends to be a full-time K–12 teacher at a public or private school in one of the surrounding counties. The majority of the program's students are currently pursuing a concentration in Spanish—although an undergraduate degree in Spanish is itself not required for entrance into the program—and the program has historically focused also on attracting and producing instructors of French and German. Although these students take core courses taught in English on topics devoted to pedagogy and instruc-tion, they simultaneously enroll in elective courses taught in the language of their content area—the Spanish language, in the present case—and devoted to a range of literary, filmic, and/or cultural topics. That is, faculty mem-bers from the Hispanic Studies Department who teach this class have the flexibility to develop course content to align with their own research interests. While there is currently no requirement to do so, it can be beneficial for the students if the faculty member builds opportunities into the class for students to continue to engage with issues of pedagogy and instruction. This is due to the fact that, as noted above, these students tend to be practicing K–12 teachers who will likely continue in that profession after graduation from the MEd program.

Second among the goals of the course—and following from the description above—was the need to expose students to a given set of literary, filmic, and/or cultural topics and evaluate their engagement with those topics, dependent on the expertise of the individual faculty member teaching SPAN 630. In the case study presented here, students were exposed to visual texts and works of art (a number of fiction films, a documentary, a painting, a digital video installation) that focused on a single street in central Madrid, Spain. The creation of this street—named the Gran Vía—was a major urban construction project of the early twentieth century that sought to put the city of Madrid on par with other European capitals as emblematic of modernity. Although construction of the Gran Vía began in 1907, the idea for the project itself dates to the nineteenth century and followed up on other urban projects carried out in the center of Madrid, particularly the renovation of the Puerta del Sol area to the south from the 1860s onward. As with the nineteenth-century urban reconstruction projects of central Paris (Georges-Eugène Haussmann) and central Barcelona (Ildefons Cerdà), existing roads and buildings in the central area of the city were demolished to make room for a wide urban artery that would symbolize the city's (and thus also the nation's) entrance into European modernity. Drawing on a robust area of urban cultural studies criticism, this iteration of SPAN 630 thus requires students to synthesize various disciplines through readings, class presentations, and course assignments (including architecture, built environment, film, geography, literature, painting, philosophy, and urban planning).[20] Figure 4 illustrates the results of student efforts in the form of an interactive map using Neatline, created to complement the Gran Vía Madrid digital humanities Omeka exhibit.

Along with this second goal, several other factors demanded consideration. While expectations are clearly different for each group of students, it must be stated from the outset that classes taught at the graduate level in

GRANVIAMADRID

Figure 4. The Gran Vía Madrid digital humanities interactive map created by students in SPAN 630: Seminar in Hispanic Studies to complement the class Omeka exhibit.

Spanish are fundamentally similar to classes taught at the undergraduate level in Spanish in one important respect. This is to say that the acquisition of a second language may begin during a student's undergraduate years, but it necessarily continues at the graduate level. Students at the master's level need to continue to develop their skills in speaking, listening, and writing in a second language at the same time that they engage in a higher level of critical thinking and place more focus on their analytical abilities.

The third goal of the class in reality folds each of the above goals together. This goal involves the digital humanities, and as such, may be more carefully defined via mention of two related subgoals. Students must first be introduced to the digital humanities as a concept. Although digital humanities is increasingly a component of higher education in general, and although it does enjoy a significant presence in traditional language and literature fields (Spanish, French, German, Russian, Arabic, Japanese, etc.), Departments of Spanish (and perhaps also of Modern and Classical

Languages in general) have more work to do to adapt to this changing academic landscape. Depending on whether faculty doing DH work have been integrated into existing departmental structures in the language fields (their presence seems to be more frequent in departments of English than in Foreign Language departments), it is not very likely that graduate and undergraduate students in the languages have been exposed to digital humanities as a concept. In practice, this means that even at the graduate level, this introduction to DH must be explicitly incorporated into SPAN 630 in order to give students a more global understanding of digital work on which the course can then build.

In our approach to SPAN 630, we thought the best solution was to devote one class period early in the semester entirely to understanding digital humanities in the most general sense. Because of language students' relative lack of familiarity with digital methods, it was important that this lesson be carried out in English. As part of the library instruction, students were provided with an introduction to the field of digital humanities scholarship and its key concepts, scholars, methodologies, and tools. Students were also introduced to resources for getting started with digital humanities, relevant vocabulary was explained, and pedagogical implications for teaching, research, and publication were discussed. Since the course was largely composed of K–12 educators, it was also relevant to discuss how these students could continue their professional development in this interdisciplinary field. Students were instructed in copyright law and also introduced to the Creative Commons, learning to perform Creative Commons searches in order to find shared and safely usable media for their projects, as illustrated in Figure 5. The team also introduced students to the fair use advocacy video hosting site Critical Commons, which supports the "transformative reuse of media in scholarly and creative contexts."[21] As part of this initial library instruction session, students searched for Creative Commons images related to Gran Vía, noted the license agreement, and downloaded a project-related image.

The students were then instructed on how to log in to the College of Charleston–hosted Omeka installation shown in Figure 6, where each created an item in the class collection. At this point the students had their first hands-on experience with descriptive metadata. The students were also shown how to add a page to the class exhibit. Students were encouraged to make individual appointments or contact the librarian with specific

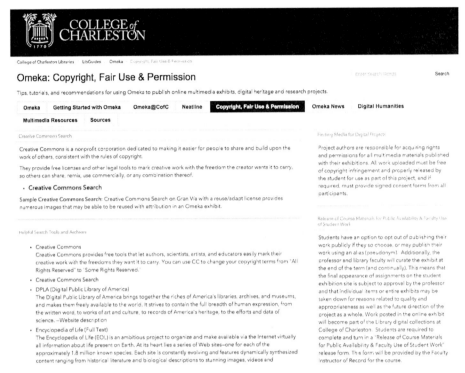

Figure 5. The College of Charleston Libraries Omeka Instructional Guide provides resources on copyright, fair use, and permission, and information on searching the Creative Commons site to locate images and media for use in digital projects.

questions related to their own unique projects for one-on-one help, in an effort to provide scaffolding for course assignments. These activities provided students with individual support as well as a theoretical, "big picture" view of a digital humanities project and detailed, sequential experience in beginning one. The importance of metadata is underscored by introducing the importance of media licensing and intellectual property law as a piece of metadata that cannot be separated from the media.

Building on the general introduction to DH work, students must next be exposed to the specific way in which the digital has been incorporated into the class. One way to express the central premise of DH work is to say that students become active creators of content instead of passively digesting the research of others. This is not to say that previous work is unimportant, only that the expectations for students must shift somewhat. It may

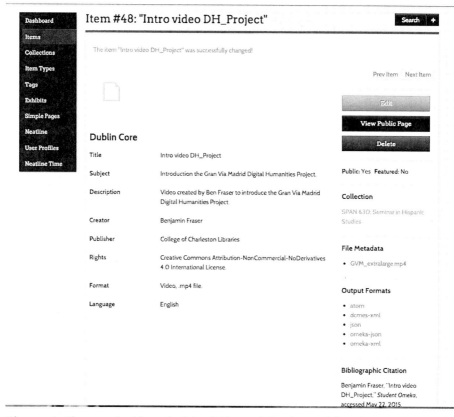

Figure 6. The user dashboard of the College of Charleston Libraries Omeka installation illustrates descriptive metadata for uploaded items.

even be said that, in a way, it is more demanding to ask students to create a digital product that incorporates previous research than merely to ask that they apply their received knowledge through traditional exams or papers. In the case of SPAN 630, students were asked to create a series of written papers, audio files, lesson plans featuring film clips, and even an original narrated video, all in Spanish (with the exception of one product in English, to be discussed below). Dependent on student permission to post these products online, the end goal was to use Omeka with a Neatline plug-in to map the locations associated with these projects to an interactive digital representation of the Gran Vía in Madrid, with linked and embedded audio, video, and written content produced by the students in the class. The final class exhibit with interactive timeline is shown in Figure 7.

Figure 7. Students in SPAN 630: Seminar in Hispanic Studies reviewed a variety of visual texts and collaborated with Professor Benjamin Fraser and library faculty Jolanda-Pieta van Arnhem to create the Gran Vía Madrid digital humanities exhibit and interactive map using Omeka and Neatline during spring 2014.

Readers may perceive that there are two (related) types of friction involved in the work carried out as part of SPAN 630. One difficulty comes from the issue of language: Spanish vs. English. This difficulty is notable at two distinct levels. First, because this is a class that provides credit in a language area, students are expected to read, speak, write, and analyze texts in Spanish. Because of the relative lack of materials published in Spanish and focusing on digital humanities and motivated by the need to dialogue with the digital humanities in a broadly institutional (i.e., necessarily Anglophone) context (discussed next), a certain friction exists between exposing the class to materials in English and ensuring a focus on the development of Spanish proficiency. Second, it is clear that—with very few exceptions—digital humanities have been institutionalized within the North American university as a largely Anglophone area. This is perhaps due to two causes that are similarly related: (1) the relative lack of faculty trained in both language and literature fields and also in DH projects, and (2) the fact that DH work is being positioned to capture the attention of constituencies whose primary language is English (university administrations, university students as a whole, the public surrounding North American universities, etc.). At this moment in time, these dynamics will (and perhaps should) necessarily have an effect on any course that attempts to engage with digital humanities in the broadest sense. The second difficulty involved stems from the addition of further competencies into a class that already has multiple and somewhat competing goals (second language proficiency and development of analytical skills/knowledge of content area). Under a banking-education model of learning that is widespread but also widely critiqued,[22] it would be inauthentic to think that the number of competencies involved in the present iteration of SPAN 630 would not cause issues for the assimilation of content. Our belief, however—one that is grounded in the educational paradigm shift that supports DH work and the "culture of makers" that accompanies it—is that, while seemingly challenging, the multiple competencies of and interdisciplinarity of SPAN 630 as detailed here are advantages for students, for teachers, and for the learning process as a whole. A similar approach is supported by the ACRL framework, which encourages faculty to "[h]elp students view themselves as information producers, individually and collaboratively" by considering how students "interact with, evaluate, produce, and share information in various formats and modes."[23] In addition, there is a close connection here between the multiple competencies involved in SPAN 630 and the urban content of the class, in that the urban phenomenon as an object of study is itself unavoidably interdisciplinary, multifaceted, and complex.

INTERDISCIPLINARITY, URBAN CULTURAL STUDIES, AND THE DIGITAL ENVIRONMENT

The methodological foundation of SPAN 630 draws on the interdisciplinary understanding of the urban phenomenon as advanced by Henri Lefebvre specifically. It is significant that Lefebvre is not unknown among librarians, as is evident in the chapter by Gloria J. Leckie and Lisa M. Given titled "Henri Lefebvre and Spatial Dialectics," published in the edited volume *Critical Theory for Library and Information Science: Exploring the Social from Across the Disciplines*. There, the authors cogently present Lefebvre's theory of spatial production and conclude by pointing out that "[t]here are a number of scholars working in information-related fields (such as education, sociology, and other disciplines) who have drawn on Lefebvre's ideas to explore virtual spaces—an area of study that holds a great deal of promise for future investigations within library and information science proper."[24] Here, rather than repeating Leckie and Given's valuable and still relevant presentation of Lefebvre as a spatial theorist, we focus on the interdisciplinarity of his thought.

For Lefebvre, the compartmentalization and fragmentation of differing areas of knowledge were ideologically suspect.[25] They were also dependent on a way of thinking that became institutionalized during the nineteenth century at the same time that practices of urban planning and city environments were themselves being linked to capitalist exchange value.[26] Connecting the urban phenomenon to his discussion of knowledge formation more generally, Lefebvre writes that

> [e]very specialized science cuts from the global phenomenon a "field," or "domain", which it illuminates in its own way. There is no point in choosing between segmentation and illumination. Moreover, each individual science is further fragmented into specialized subdisciplines. Sociology is divided up into political sociology, economic sociology, rural and urban sociology, and so forth. The fragmented and specialized sciences operate analytically: they are the result of an analysis and perform analyses of their own. In terms of the urban phenomenon considered as a whole, geography, demography, history, psychology, and sociology supply the results of an analytical procedure. Nor should we overlook the contributions of the biologist, doctor or psychiatrist, or those of the novelist or poet. . . . Without the progressive and regressive movements (in time and space) of analysis, without the multiple divisions and fragmentations, it would be impossible to conceive of a science of the urban phenomenon. But such fragments do not constitute knowledge.[27]

This extremely important and revealing quotation must be understood at two levels simultaneously. As indicated above, here there is an "urban" meaning that coexists with a larger critique of disciplinary knowledge in general. To understand these two levels as separate from one another would be to disarm Lefebvre's thought of its main strength, which is to "urbanize" our understanding of the totality of contemporary political, economic, cultural, and social life. In this context, the following two statements can be made. First, the "urban" meaning of this excerpt holds that the urban phenomenon cannot be understood through purely disciplinary approaches. It is in this sense that Lefebvre writes elsewhere that the urban is neither a system, nor semiology,[28] nor merely "a collection of objects."[29] Instead, it is a point of departure for analyzing the interconnection of seemingly distinct areas of knowledge.[30] Second, Lefebvre also mentioned education specifically in other works. One example is *The Explosion*, published in the wake of the events of 1968, where he noted that "[a]n educator is not a mere conveyer, nor is the institution called 'university' a warehouse"[31] and that learning itself is not reducible to being a mere product enmeshed in the laws of the capitalist logic of exchange.[32] For the French urban theorist, the urban is not a specialized disciplinary concern, but rather a way of relating different disciplinary specializations to one another.

A Lefebvrian approach asserts that the complexity of the urban phenomenon "makes interdisciplinary cooperation essential. [It] cannot be grasped by any specialized science"[33] Once the primacy of the disciplinary understanding of knowledge begins to wane, new connections can be forged between areas of thought that have traditionally been relatively isolated from one another within university structures. One key aspect of this traditional isolation of disciplines from one another involves the humanities and the social sciences in particular.

The rise of the digital humanities paradigm in particular provides momentum for making connections across these two areas, defined broadly.[34] In Patrik Svensson's "Envisioning the Digital Humanities" the author writes "the university and the humanities need to change to accommodate this type of work."[35] This is undoubtedly true. There is still more work to be done, but questions remain—questions that SPAN 630 attempts to address. For example, the precise relationship between the humanities and the social sciences established in digital humanities work tends to emphasize the social sciences at the expense of the humanities. In an article published in *Digital Humanities Quarterly*, Paul Rosenbloom makes the somewhat simplistic assertion that "the humanities naturally fit within the sciences as part of an expanded social domain."[36] In "New Media in the Academy: Labor and the Production of Knowledge in Scholarly Multimedia," for example, Helen J. Burgess and Jeanne Hamming affirm the notion that the biggest obstacle to the digital humanities is the fact that humanities scholars don't understand the "kinds of 'work' that go into producing scholarship in multimedia form."[37] Although a certain complex truth is hidden by the simplicity of such statements, these need to be understood in their enduring academic context—one in which, as Alvin Kernan wrote in the introduction to *What's Happened to the Humanities?*, "shifts in higher education have not, I think it is fair to say, been kind to the liberal arts in general, and to the humanities in particular."[38]

As regards SPAN 630 specifically, the course benefits from reflecting a Lefebvrian approach to the urban as an interdisciplinary topic and from a precise mixture of disciplinary knowledge that draws from both the humanities and social sciences. To see how this is so—and to avoid engaging in discussions that are too disciplinarily focused—it is best to trace the influence of the humanities and social sciences in broad strokes through the specific urban-themed written, audio, and video "products" required by the students in their roles as DH practitioners.[39]

The written work produced by the class (for potential publication on the web) was centered on two complementary and interdisciplinary axes, one historical and one related to cultural critique. Some written assignments were devoted specifically to historical narratives in Spanish that require students to synthesize the discourses of history, architecture, urban culture, and urban planning in relation to a specific building situated on the Gran Vía. Other written components were designated as papers that required students to employ the technical vocabulary of filmic criticism (shots, takes, camera angles and movements, mise-en-scène, sets, props, lighting, editing, etc.) in an original analysis of the role of a space associated with the Gran Vía in a Spanish film. Ultimately, of course, both kinds of papers speak to similar sets of interdisciplinary connections as demonstrated by the Gran Vía Madrid digital humanities interactive map shown in Figure 8. The latter papers on film analysis, of course, follow the robust tradition of film scholarship dovetailing with the urban question and from a series of film theorists concerned with the iconicity and indexicality of the filmic sign.[40]

Figure 8. The Gran Vía Madrid digital humanities interactive map incorporates course assignments, which are designed to speak to similar sets of interdisciplinary connections.

The audio work for the class (also produced by the students for potential publication on the web) follows and builds on the written work described above, with the additional step that students must record their voice in an audio file. Using the program *GarageBand* on Apple's Mac OS computers, students must simultaneously develop a technical (if relatively basic) computer skill, ideally engaging with the concept of metadata associated with digital media and learning to manage and edit sound input. Advanced students are able to work with inserting sound clips, music, and even a sophisticated intro or outro into their audio file (provided copyright restrictions are respected), while students less familiar with such processes may concentrate on the more basic aspects of creating digital audio media.

The video work for the class (also produced by the students for potential publication on the web) similarly follows and builds on the written work described above, as shown in Figure 9. Adapting a piece of written work to a video format requires the addition of visual media (provided copyright restrictions are respected) and a series of much more complex technical skills involved with editing and the synchronization of audio and video content together (here the program used was *iMovie*). Moreover, the significance of this component is that it reaffirms the course conversations surrounding the structure and composition of visual media that students have practiced in class discussions, but which they now have to actually employ in the creation of a video project.

Figure 9. Gran Vía Madrid DH digital exhibit pages build on the written work, lead to the creation of audio and video products, and provide opportunities for students to learn a series of much more complex technical skills.

Looking back at our initial goals, the goal of collaborating to create an instructional project that could serve as a model for future collaborations between faculty and digital scholarship and services librarians in the classroom was achieved. The second goal of exposing students to digital humanities in a hands-on project was also achieved. For the third goal of understanding how to best structure instruction, the importance of scaffolding and building assignments toward the final project was underscored. The faculty librarian was available to provide individual support online and in one-on-one sessions. This alleviated some student confusion with media assignments that were not connected to the overall project, an approach that the team is now unanimous in feeling should be avoided. All assignments should build toward the final project to alleviate confusion and aid in student engagement and retention of learning. As for the fourth goal of providing library faculty with experience in developing tools to tie digital humanities into instructional services, the three guides and included lesson plans and tutorials are reusable in other courses and provide a firm basis for future instruction. The library is currently taking and reviewing proposals from campus faculty for future collaborations in tightly integrating instruction.

APPENDIX

A. Gran Vía Madrid Project (including introductory video, syllabus, map interface)

[http://libguides.library.cofc.edu/omeka]
[http://studentomeka.library.cofc.edu/exhibits/show/granviamadrid]
[http://studentomeka.library.cofc.edu/neatline/show/granviamadrid]

B. DH, Multimedia Production, and Omeka How To Guides

[http://libguides.library.cofc.edu/Omeka]
[http://libguides.library.cofc.edu/dh]
[http://libguides.library.cofc.edu/movies]

NOTES

1   Trudi Jacobson and Craig Gibson, "Info. Lit Competency Standards Revision Task Force Interim Report (June 2014)," *ALA Connect,* p. 3, Association of College and Research Libraries, http://connect.ala.org/node/223580.

2   Rich Stim, "Proposed Educational Guidelines on Fair Use," *Copyright & Fair Use,* Stanford University Libraries, http://fairuse.stanford.edu/overview.

3   Cathy Davidson, "Public Blogs and Video in the Classroom and FERPA Compliance," *Cathy Davidson's Blog, Humanities, Arts, Science, and Technology Alliance and Collaboratory* (HASTAC), www.hastac.org/blogs/cathy-davidson.

4   Omeka, "Omeka: Serious Web Publishing," *Omeka,* Roy Rosenzweig Center for History and New Media (CHMN), http://omeka.org/about.

5   Anthony Bushong and David Kim, "Omeka," *Intro to Digital Humanities: DH 101*, UCLA Center for Digital Humanities, par. 1, http://dh101.humanities.ucla.edu.

6   Iman Salehian, "Neatline," *Intro to Digital Humanities: DH 101*, UCLA Center for Digital Humanities, par. 3, http://dh101.humanities.ucla.edu.

7   Jacobson and Gibson, "Info. Lit Competency Standards," 3.

8   Josh Honn, "Introduction," *A Guide to Digital Humanities,* Center for Scholarly Communication and Digital Curation, Northwestern University, http://sites.northwestern.edu/guidetodh.

9   Charlie Edwards and Matthew K. Gold, "Welcome to the Academic Commons Wiki," *The CUNY Digital Humanities Resource Guide*, CUNY Academic Commons, http://commons.gc.cuny.edu/wiki.

10   Gloria J. Leckie and Lisa M. Given, "Henri Lefebvre and Spatial Dialectics," in *Critical Theory for Library and Information Science: Exploring the Social from Across the Disciplines*, ed. G. J. Leckie, L. M. Given, and J. Buschman (Oxford: Libraries Unlimited, 2010): 221–36.

11   William M. Bowen, Ronnie A. Dunn, and David O. Kasdan, "What Is 'Urban Studies': Context, Internal Structure, and Content," *Journal of Urban Affairs* 32, No. 2 (2010): 200.

12   See David Harvey, *Rebel Cities* (London; New York: Verso, 2012); Neil Smith, *Uneven Development: Nature, Capital and the Production of Space* (Oxford: Basil Blackwell, 1984); Henri Lefebvre, *The Urban Revolution, 1970*, trans. Robert Bononno (Minneapolis: University Minnesota Press, 2003); Henri Lefebvre, "The Right to the City," in *Writings on Cities*, ed. and trans. E. Kofman and E. Lebas (Oxford: Blackwell, 1996): 63–181; Benjamin Fraser, *Henri Lefebvre and the Spanish Urban Experience: Reading the Mobile City* (Lewisburg, PA: Bucknell University Press, 2011); Benjamin Fraser, "Toward a Philosophy of the Urban: Henri Lefebvre's Uncomfortable Application of Bergsonism," *Environment and Planning D: Society and Space* 26, No. 2 (2008): 338–58; Marc James Léger, "Henri Lefebvre and the Moment of the Aesthetic," in *Marxism and the History of Art: From William Morris to the New Left*, ed. Andrew Hemingway (London: Pluto Press, 2006): 143–60; Lukasz Stanek, *Henri Lefebvre on Space: Architecture, Urban Research, and the Production of Theory* (Minneapolis; London: University of Minnesota Press, 2011).

13   Benjamin Fraser, "Inaugural Editorial: Urban Cultural Studies—A Manifesto [Part One]," *Journal of Urban Cultural Studies* 1, No. 1 (2014): 3–17.

14 Raymond Williams, "The Future of Cultural Studies," *Politics of Modernism: Against the New Conformists* (London; New York: Verso, 2007): 151–62.

15 On important studies of urban culture that nonetheless largely avoid entanglements with the humanities despite their engagement with culture, see Ash Amin and Nigel Thrift, *Cities: Reimagining the Urban* (Cambridge: Polity Press, 2002); Ben Highmore, *Cityscapes: Cultural Readings in the Material and Symbolic City* (New York: Palgrave Macmillan, 2005); Christophe Lindner, *Globalization, Violence, and the Visual Culture of Cities* (London; New York: Routledge, 2009); Lewis Mumford, "What Is a City?" (1937), *The City Reader*, ed. Richard T. LeGates and Frederic Stout, 3rd ed. (London: Routledge, 2005): 92–96; Richard Sennett, *The Craftsman* (New Haven, CT: Yale University Press, 2008); Rob Shields, *Spatial Questions: Cultural Topologies and Social Spatialisation* (Thousand Oaks, CA: Sage, 2013); Sharon Zukin, *The Cultures of Cities* (Malden, MA; Oxford: Blackwell, 1995).

16 For example, see Johanna Drucker, *SPECLAB: Digital Aesthetics and Projects in Speculative Computing* (Chicago; London: University of Chicago Press, 2009); Kathleen Fitzpatrick, *Planned Obsolescence* (New York; London: New York University Press, 2011); Jerome McGann, *Radiant Textuality: Literature after the World Wide Web* (New York: Palgrave Macmillan, 2001).

17 See, for example, David J. Bodenhamer, John Corrigan, and Trevor M. Harris, eds., *The Spatial Humanities: GIS and the Future of Scholarship* (Bloomington; Indianapolis: Indiana University Press, 2010); Stephen Daniels, Dydia DeLyser, J. Nicholas Entrikin, and Douglas Richardson, eds., *Envisioning Landscapes, Making Worlds: Geography and the Humanities* (London; New York: Routledge, 2011); Michael Dear, Jim Ketchum, Sarah Luria, and Doug Richardson, eds., *GeoHumanities: Art, History, Text at the Edge of Place* (Abingdon, UK; New York: Routledge, 2011); specifically Edward L. Ayers, "Turning Toward Place, Space, and Time," in *The Spatial Humanities*, 1–13; Denis Cosgrove, "Prologue: Geography within the Humanities," in *Envisioning Landscapes, Making Worlds*, xxii–xxv; Ian Gregory, "Exploiting Time and Space: A Challenge for GIS in the Digital Humanities," in *The Spatial Humanities*, 58–75; Gary Lock, "Representations of Space and Place in the Humanities," in *The Spatial Humanities*, 89–108; Sarah Luria, "Geotexts," in *GeoHumanities*, 67–70; Sarah Luria, "Thoreau's Geopoetics," in *GeoHumanities*, 67–70; Douglas Richardson, "Converging Worlds: Geography and the Humanities," in *Envisioning Landscapes, Making Worlds*, xix–xxi; May Yuan, "Mapping Text," in *The Spatial Humanities*, 109–23.

18 Fitzpatrick, *Planned Obsolescence.*

19 For an example of interdisciplinary collaboration that required larger-scale funding and planning, see Jolanda-Pieta van Arnhem, E. Moore Quinn, and Jerry Spiller, "Teaching Multimodal Ethnography with 'New' Media Technologies," in *Proc. of the 14th World Multi-Conference on Systemics, Cybernetics, and Informatics,* ed. N. Callaos, K. Eshraghian, M. Imai, W. Lesso, and C. D. Zinn (Orlando, FL: International Institute of Informatics and Systemics, 2010): 242–47, www.iiis.org/CDs2010/CD2010SCI/SCI_2010/PapersPdf/SA627MP.pdf.

20 See Edward Baker, *Madrid Cosmopolita: La Gran Vía 1910–1936* (Madrid: Marcial Pons, 2009); Edward Baker and Malcolm Alan Compitello, eds., *Madrid. de Fortunata a la M–40: Un Siglo de Cultura Urbana* (Madrid: Alianza, 2003); Malcolm Alan Compitello, "Del plan al diseño: *El Día de la Bestia* de Álex de la Iglesia y la Cultura de la Acumulación Flexible en el Madrid del Postcambio," in *Madrid. de Fortunana a la M–40*, 327–52; Susan Larson, *Constructing and Resisting Modernity: Madrid 1900–1936* (Madrid: Vervuert/Iberoamericana, 2011).

21 "About," *Critical Commons*, University of Southern California (USC) Institute for Multimedia Literacy, www.criticalcommons.org/about-us.

22 Paolo Freire, *Teachers as Cultural Workers: Letters to Those Who Dare to Teach,* trans. D. Macedo, D. Koike, and A. Oliveira (Boulder, CO: Westview, 1998); Paolo Freire, *Pedagogy of the Oppressed,* trans. M. B. Ramos (New York: Continuum, 1970); bell hooks, *Teaching to Transgress. Education as the Practice of Freedom* (New York; London: Routledge, 1994); Hywel Rowland Dix, "The Pedagogy of Cultural Materialism: Paolo Freire and Raymond Williams," in *About Raymond Williams*, ed. Monika Seidl, Roman Horak, and Lawrence Grossberg (London; New York: Routledge, 2010): 81–93.

23 "Framework for Information Literacy Appendices," *Association of College and Research Libraries*, American Library Association, par. 11, www.ala.org /acrl/standards/ilframework.

24 Leckie and Given, 234.

25 See Henri Lefebvre, "*The Sociology of Marx*," trans. N. Guterman (New York: Columbia University Press, 1982): 22–23; also Andy Merrifield, *Metromarxism: A Marxist Tale of the City* (London; New York: Routledge, 2002); Andy Merrifield, *Henri Lefebvre: A Critical Introduction* (London; New York: Routledge, 2006), xxxiii; and Fraser, *Henri Lefebvre and the Spanish Urban Experience.*

26 See Lefebvre, "The Right to the City," 95–96; and Julie Thompson Klein, *Humanities, Culture and Interdisciplinarity* (Albany: State University of New York, 2005): 24.

27 See Lefebvre, *The Urban Revolution, 1970*, 48–49, and particularly 53–55; and Henri Lefebvre, *The Explosion: Marxism and the French Upheaval* (New York; London: The Monthly Review Press, 1969), 41.

28 Lefebvre, *The Urban Revolution, 1970*, 50.

29 Ibid., 57. See also "Nor is it reasonable to assume that our understanding of the urban phenomenon, or urban space, could consist in a collection of objects— economy, sociology, history, demography, psychology, or earth sciences, such as geology. The concept of a scientific object, although convenient and easy, is deliberately simplistic and may conceal another intention: a strategy of fragmentation designed to promote a unitary and synthetic, and therefore authoritarian, model. An object is isolating, even if conceived as a system of relations and even if those relations are connected to other systems." Ibid., 57.

30 Lefebvre, *The Urban Revolution, 1970*, 50. In this publication Lefebvre refuses to reduce the urban phenomenon to being merely a system or a semiology. In Lefebvre, *The Urban Revolution, 1970*, 46, he likewise states that the urban is indivisible into subfields due to its "enormity and complexity."

31 Lefebvre, *The Explosion*, 156.

32 Ibid., 141.

33 Lefebvre, *The Urban Revolution, 1970*, 53; Lawrence Barth, "Revisited: Henri Lefebvre and the Urban Condition," *Daidalos* 75 (2000): 23. As critic Lawrence Barth has underscored, "the return to Lefebvre is not in pursuit of specific answers, but of his acute awareness of the complexity of problems." The quotation continues: "One had looked to Lefebvre for a way of handling questions, that is, for a method rather than an answer. In this way, the return to Lefebvre works like a test for the hypothesis that we are now subject to a new urban condition [. . .] How we read Lefebvre will shape the urban condition."

34 See McGann, *Radiant Textuality*; Drucker, *SPECLAB*; Fitzpatrick, *Planned Obsolescence*; Bodenhamer, Corrigan, and Harris, *The Spatial Humanities*; Daniels et al., *Envisioning Landscapes*; and Dear et al., *GeoHumanities*.

35 Patrik Svensson, "Envisioning the Digital Humanities," *Digital Humanities Quarterly* 6, No. 1 (2012), www.digitalhumanities.org/dhq/vol/6/1 /000112/000112.html. See also Anne Balsamo, "The Digital Humanities and Technocultural Innovation," in *Digital Media: Technological and Social Challenges of the Interactive World* (Lanham, MD; Toronto; Plymouth, UK: The Scarecrow Press, 2011): 213–25; David Perry, "The MLA, @ briancroxall, and the Non-Rise of the Digital Humanities," *AcademHack*,

http://academhack.outsidethetext.com/home/2010/the-mla-briancroxall
-and-the-non-rise-of-the-digital-humanities.

36   Paul S. Rosenbloom, "Towards a Conceptual Framework for the Digital
Humanities," *Digital Humanities Quarterly* 6 No. 2 (2012), www.digital
humanities.org/dhq/vol/6/2/000127/000127.html.

37   Helen J. Burgess and Jeanne Hamming, "New Media in the Academy: Labor
and the Production of Knowledge in Scholarly Multimedia." *Digital Humanities
Quarterly* 5, No. 3 (2011), www.digitalhumanities.org/dhq/vol/5/3/000102
/000102.html.

38   Alvin Kernan, "Introduction," *What's Happened to the Humanities?* (Princeton, NJ: Princeton University Press, 1997): 3–13.

39   For the sake of simplicity and in order to appeal to a more generally readable
audience, we will not discuss here the other (no-less) significant aspects of the
class, those relating more specifically to language acquisition, such as classroom
activities and student individual and group presentations. As with the other
course components, however, such course components also express the unique
fusion of multiple competencies (linguistic, cultural, analytical, and digital).

40   Regarding the former, see, for example, Stuart Aitken and Leo Zonn, eds.,
Place, Power, Situation, and Spectacle: A Geography of Film (Lanham, MD:
Rowman and Littlefield, 1994); David B. Clarke, ed., *The Cinematic City* (New
York: Routledge, 1997); Tim Cresswell and Deborah Dixon, eds., *Engaging
Film: Geographies of Mobility and Identity* (Lanham, MD: Rowman and Littlefield, 2002); and Andrew Webber and Emma Wilson, *Cities in Transition:
The Moving Image and the Modern Metropolis* (New York; London: Wallflower Press, 2008).

10 | Fostering Assessment Strategies for Digital Pedagogy through Faculty–Librarian Collaborations: An Analysis of Student-Generated Multimodal Digital Scholarship

Harriett E. Green

INTRODUCTION

What kind of learning occurs when a student creates a digital video log ("vlog") of interviews and integrates digital footage into their project narrative? How can we assess learning outcomes when a student tells a historical narrative via a website featuring content in five different media formats as well as text?

These are some of the questions being asked by instructors of courses across humanities disciplines, as they increasingly incorporate digital humanities tools and methodologies into their curricula. This transformation in higher education in the humanities reveals a rising emphasis on competencies in digital literacies and has critical implications for librarians in not only the methods of teaching of information literacy, but on a larger scale, the role of librarians in teaching and learning for the humanities. This chapter examines how collaborations that teach digital humanities tools and methodologies facilitate the practice of digital pedagogy and digital literacy outcomes in the classroom for undergraduate and graduate humanities courses. This chapter presents analysis of librarian–faculty collaborations in digital pedagogy through a series of case studies on collaborations between the author and faculty members, and content analysis of a sample of student websites from these case studies. From this analysis, the author considers potential learning outcomes and active assessment tools from these digital pedagogy practices and assessments that promote digital literacy and information literacy integrally with curricular outcomes.

BACKGROUND

There are multiple definitions of digital literacy, but the operating definition for this study is drawn from a 2010 *Digital Literacies* report published by the London Knowledge Lab:

> The awareness, attitude and ability of individuals to appropriately use digital tools and facilities to identify, access, manage, integrate, evaluate, analyze and synthesize digital resources, construct new knowledge, create media expressions, and communicate with others, in the context of specific life situations, in order to enable constructive social action; and to reflect upon this process.[1]

As increasingly more materials for humanities are digitized and electronic resources become embedded in humanities research and teaching, it is imperative for students to learn the tools and methodologies for navigating and manipulating digital data for scholarly investigation. The teaching initiatives, learning objects, and analytic tools for digital humanities profiled in this chapter, as well as many other digital tools adapted for educational purposes, all empower students and faculty to build digital literacy skills in creating, analyzing, and preserving digital manifestations of the textual and visual materials they study in their research. As Jones-Kavalier and Flannigan articulate, "Using the same skills used for centuries—analysis, synthesis and evaluation—we must look at digital literacy as another realm within which to apply elements of critical thinking."[2] This formulation of digital literacies corresponds with "metaliteracy," a concept that reshapes information literacy in light of the transformation in teaching and learning with digital resources, tools, and associated competencies.

As defined by Thomas Mackey and Trudi Jacobson, metaliteracy is an overarching framework for integrating information literacy with other literacies such as media literacy, digital literacy, and visual literacy. In a learning environment guided by principles of metaliteracy, the framework provides "an integrated and all-inclusive core for engaging with individuals and ideas in digital information environments."[3] Metaliteracy and digital literacies thus integrate together and provide a convergence where librarians and instructors in digital humanities can critically collaborate on learning outcomes and pedagogical strategies.

Digital pedagogy offers an innovative path to cultivate this suite of competencies for digital literacies in humanities students and scholars. It provides an experiential, discovery-oriented learning environment that uses "electronic elements to enhance or to change to [sic] experience of education."[4] Jesse Stommel also notes that "[s]tudents and learners should be central in mapping the terrain of digital pedagogy. Educational institutions should dedicate themselves to supporting this work. . . . Digital pedagogy is less about knowing and more a rampant process of unlearning, play, and rediscovery."[5]

Digital humanities in the classroom is a rapidly growing area for pedagogical innovations in the humanities, and it has taken diverse forms: in the past two decades, pioneering projects such as the *Walt Whitman Archive, Documenting the American South*, and *American Studies Crossroads* served as DH learning environments for graduate assistants as well as large research projects.[6] Today, a host of studies and teaching initiatives provides diverse models for teaching digital humanities methods and tools to graduate students and undergraduates, such as the Praxis Program at the University of Virginia for graduate students, NITLE seminars on teaching digital humanities in liberal arts colleges, UCLA Digital Humanities Center, the University of Victoria's Maker Lab in the Humanities, as well as many experimental teaching methods using Zotero, WordPress, Google Earth, or video game software.[7] The theoretical aspects and implications of digital tools in the humanities classroom have been considered by a number of scholars as well, but few studies have looked at the role of librarians in the teaching and learning for digital humanities.[8]

A number of scholars, such as Posner, Muñoz, and Sula, have considered the role of libraries in digital research workflows.[9] The role of librarian in collaborating with faculty on digital pedagogy strategies is multifaceted. With the advent of digital humanities centers, media commons, and other library-based initiatives to support digital scholarship—such as the University of Virginia Libraries' Scholars' Lab, Emory University Libraries' Center for Digital Scholarship, University of Illinois at Urbana–Champaign's Scholarly Commons, Indiana University Libraries' Scholars Commons, and University of Kansas's Institute for Digital Research in the Humanities—librarians are explicitly pursuing collaborations. There is a rich and growing foundation of teaching collaborations between librarians and faculty to integrate DH tools and concepts into the undergraduate and graduate classrooms.

DIGITAL PUBLISHING: PLATFORMS YESTERDAY AND TODAY

Digital humanities research pioneered new modes of publication for the humanities, as a notable percentage of this research was primarily published through online platforms. Numerous works of digital scholarship have been mounted on websites, but with the explosion of Internet use in the past two decades and the exponential growth in online publishing and writing, digital scholars now have a host of options for publishing their works of digital scholarship.

WordPress and Drupal are among the most prominent general-use online publishing platforms used for digital humanities research and teaching. In recent years, however, researchers have developed several other platforms specifically for digital scholarship. While these platforms were developed with professional research publication and scholarship in mind, curricular instruction and digital pedagogy have swiftly emerged as a largely unforeseen adaptation of these tools. Two of the most prominent digital scholarship tools today that were used in these case studies are Omeka and Scalar.

Omeka is a digital publishing software package (http://omeka.org) developed by digital humanities researchers at George Mason University's Center for History and New Media. Originating from a Swahili word meaning "to lay out wares," Omeka enables scholars and students to build interactive online exhibitions that display digital content (videos, audio, images, and digitized documents) along with ancillary text. It has been widely used by museums, libraries, archives, and scholars across disciplines for creating digital exhibitions, showcasing scholarly research, augmenting library collections and catalogs, and complementary content for special projects. Omeka has a lightweight web-hosted version (www.omeka.net) that is better suited for classroom use and was used for the case studies in this chapter.

Scalar (http://scalar.usc.edu) is an online publishing tool originally developed by the Alliance for Visual Culture at the University of Southern California for the electronic journal *Vectors*.[10] Scalar supports embedded video, audio, and other types of multimedia, along with functionalities for visualizations, annotations, extensive metadata tagging, and direct importation of content from partner media archives such as the Internet Archive, Vevo, YouTube, and Critical Commons, a media archive of fair use content. An on-campus workshop for Scalar with the University of Southern

California's Professor Tara McPherson as the visiting instructor served as the catalyst for the author's collaborations with faculty on employing this tool in the classroom.

WordPress (http://wordpress.org) is a widely used open commercial publishing tool that, according to a 2014 W3 Techs web technology survey report, serves as the content management system for approximately 61 percent of the websites on the Internet.[11] The web-hosted version of WordPress (www.wordpress.com) has been increasingly used in pedagogical settings as well.[12]

Together, these platforms constitute a thought-provoking approach to building learning infrastructures that critically integrate real-world applications with multimodal, complex methods of teaching and learning.

METHODS

This analysis begins with four case studies of the author collaborating with faculty and instructors to teach digital humanities tools in undergraduate and graduate courses. These courses include a graduate seminar in Library and Information Science, a two-course collaboration with a Media and Cinema Studies faculty member, an undergraduate History seminar, and a three-section undergraduate English and Rhetoric course. Then a content analysis of a selected sample of student projects from these courses is presented to explore the development of digital literacies through the faculty–librarian collaborations to teach digital humanities tools and methodologies.

The content analysis examines a sample of twenty-eight student-generated digital projects and reflective essays drawn both from these courses as well as a History undergraduate seminar's Omeka website for which the author advised. Via content analysis of the student-generated digital content and an analysis of the case studies, this study argues that the documentation and artifacts of student digital scholarship, drawn from a range of disciplines and education levels, offer unprecedented insights into how students develop digital literacies.

CASE STUDIES

To establish the context of these student-generated digital publications, the following brief case studies explain how the process of building sites occurred in each class.

LIBRARY AND INFORMATION SCIENCE

Context

The author collaborated with a Graduate of Library and Information Science instructor who sought to incorporate the digital publishing platform of Omeka into her Public History course. The seminar course was offered online with an on-campus component, and the goals of the course were to teach students how to create research projects from the viewpoint of public historians and information professionals. Omeka.net offered a platform through which these students could share their research with a larger audience.

Process

The online learning environment necessitated that the LIS graduate students be primarily self-directed in the cultivation of their skills with the digital platform: The author gave a course lecture on digital curation and introduced the students to various methods and tools for digital scholarship and publishing. Then the students engaged with the author and other University of Illinois librarians in a daylong in-person workshop that covered various issues in archival research, digital publishing, and how to use Omeka.net.

The author provided research and tool assistance to the graduate students via the online forums in the Moodle LMS used for the course, telephone reference, and email. The most significant challenge emerged in translating graduate student research into a multimodal digital artifact. The students were familiar and expert in presenting their research in an essay, but digital publication was entirely different in terms of orientation and structure. The students gradually built Omeka.net sites that brought together the archival materials gathered from the University of Illinois Archives, libraries and archives in their home locations, and online materials from digital collections.

MEDIA AND CINEMA STUDIES

Context

The author collaborated with a faculty member on two media and cinema studies courses to teach Scalar to the students as a platform for final research projects. For each course, the students built Scalar sites that displayed their research on their chosen topic in the area of media ethics and information networks. The initial introduction to the tools was in the form of two-hour workshops for each course that incorporated active and hands-on learning objects such as worksheets that asked the students to think through the search and evaluation process of gathering digital media and how to conceptualize the structure of Scalar. The guiding conceptual framework throughout the sessions was the practice of digital curation and publication.

Process

The assignments that guided the students in building the sites were sharply proscribed. The undergraduates were only slightly constrained by a familiarity with the structure of a standard essay (especially compared to the author's experiences with graduate students in other case studies as well as other courses), but the process of building out the website had to be simplified. To introduce the students to Scalar, the assignments specified how many pages, items, and annotations they had to create to build minimally effective Scalar sites. This framework enabled the students to focus on the research and on finding the best digital content for their research topic.

ENGLISH

Context

A graduate student approached the author as they were seeking to try new teaching styles and methods that engaged digital tools. This student was one of three teaching assistants (TAs) for an introductory composition course focused on the theme of documentary films. The author and TA collaborated to adapt the extremely standardized composition syllabus to incorporate Omeka as a writing platform. This graduate student then spoke with the other two TAs for the course, who also agreed to try using Omeka for the final project assignment in their sections as well.

Process

The TAs collaborated with the author in varying levels of support and engagement with Omeka. The TA who initiated the collaboration with the author arranged multiple workshops for each of the three assignments to guide students through the process of building an Omeka site. The Omeka workshop structure employed the scaffolding method to build different aspects of Omeka into the required essays. The first essay included uploading items into Omeka, the second essay required students to create a collection from the items they uploaded into Omeka.net, and the third essay incorporated the process of building a page in Omeka that displayed at least one of the items they uploaded. The other two TAs, however, requested that the instruction on Omeka for their sections be condensed into two brief workshops of approximately 30 minutes each.

This incorporation of Omeka into an introductory composition course critically ties into multimodal writing theory and how digital writing tools can enhance students' learning of core composition principles and engagement with writing practices. The reframing of writing as a synthesis between visual evidence and text helped the students build and sustain arguments about their topics. It also allowed students to experience what it means to be researchers, scholars, and digital curators.

CONTENT ANALYSIS

The final projects produced by the students evidenced how they were able to juxtapose digital media with the text (often pulled from their research papers) to reach an effective synthesis of media and text in an online exhibition. A content analysis of the student sites reveals patterns in the creation, structure, and approach to student-generated publications and the key factors that are core to an effectively built digital project.

METHODOLOGY

The author employed a purposeful sample by working with course instructors to compile a list of students from six courses who participated in collaborations between the author and the course instructors to construct final projects on a digital platform. These courses include a graduate course in library and information science, undergraduate English course, three Media and Cinema Studies courses, and an undergraduate seminar in History. The author contacted 155 students for permission to analyze their completed digital projects. Forty-nine students consented to participate. A number of the students' project sites were created by groups. A total of twenty-eight student project sites qualified as objects of analysis for this study. The project sites were built on the web-based digital platforms of Omeka.net, WordPress, and Scalar.

The author conducted a content analysis that examined particular facets of the sites to determine how well the students adapted the digital platform for scholarly use. Recorded indicators included numerical calculations of pages and sections, the numbers of different formats of media, the extent to which various multimedia formats were incorporated, and the number of metadata records, captions, references, and annotations as markers of how effectively the students positioned their work as a scholarly product compared to a simple website.

ANALYSIS

Of the twenty-eight student project sites analyzed, sixteen were created with Omeka.net, three sites were built in WordPress, and eight sites were created with the Scalar platform. In examination of the digital objects incorporated into the sites, an average of 22.61 digital objects were utilized on the student sites (Figure 1). The websites were analyzed for number of still images, videos, audio recordings, scanned documents, and other types of media (e.g., PowerPoint slides, statistical graphs, and Word documents containing students' written essays). The most frequently used type of digital media were still images, at an average of 17.45 images per site. Next most used were scanned documents and articles, with an average of 9.5 per site.

The topics on the student sites ranged widely and included the history of television broadcasting, the Anonymous movement, an analysis of the documentary *Bowling for Columbine*, the antibullying movement, and the history of the Champaign music scene. The success to which they synthesized the media and text into a coherent narrative was dependent, of course, on the course instructor's evaluation of the content. But several indicators and patterns reveal a potential way to measure the extent of coherency.

One prominent indicator was the existence of an opening introduction that explained the topic of the website project: in the sample of student sites analyzed for this study, 73 percent of the sites had opening introductions. The introductions established a core thesis for the website project and the strong statements, such as those shown in Figure 2 of an Omeka.net site.

Another indicator was the number of pages in the site: the average number of pages was 9.25, with the highest number of pages on a site being 33. The author also counted the text blocks written for the sites, and the average number was 15.9 text blocks, with a range across all sites from 5

AVERAGE NO. OF MULTI MEDIA OBJECTS ACROSS STUDENT SITES

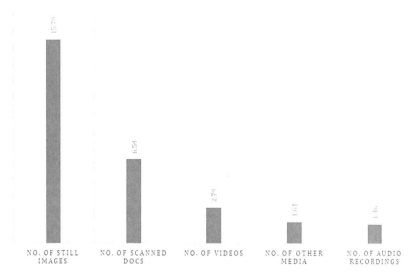

Figure 1. Average number of multimedia objects per type across all student sites.

Browse Items   **Browse Collections**   **Browse Exhibits**

Black Power at Illinois

In the fall of 1968, the University of Illinois launched the Special Education Opportunities Program which brought 568 "poor and disadvantaged" freshman to Champaign-Urbana. The SEOP, also known as Project 500, tripled the number of African American students on campus and triggered changes that reverberate to the present day. Why did such a dramatic event occur? How did it affect what had been a nearly "lily-white" university? What legacies did it leave? This exhibit will explore all of these questions, as well as others.

SEPTEMBER, 1968: CHAOS ON CAMPUS

WHAT WERE THEY THINKING?

BEFORE 1968: A WHITE CAMPUS

WHOSE CAMPUS IS THIS?

LEGACIES: WHOSE UNIVERSITY?

ENTER EXHIBIT HERE

Inside the collections, click on any picture of an exhibited item for details. Browse through groups of items by using the menu on the right or the "Next Page" and "Previous Page" buttons at the bottom of each item description.

For more on this topic, see a collection of oral history interviews at the University of Illinois Archives

Credits

Created by Students in History 386, Public History, at the University of Illinois at Urbana-

Figure 2. Omeka site for History 386: Public History, spring 2014 semester.

to 43 paragraphs of text. While numbers are not indicative in and of themselves, the depth and detail of a student's work on the website is partially evidenced through the extensiveness of the pages and text.

Another set of critical factors in determining the rigor and intellectual depth of students' sites as artifacts of scholarship was found in the completeness of metadata, references, and citations, as well as the inclusion of annotations. Of the sampled student sites, 27 percent of the student sites included metadata for their digital objects, while 55 percent had extremely sparse to no metadata at all. Metadata is a critical element of digital collections and projects, and the Scalar and Omeka platforms provide easy forms for completing metadata records for each uploaded digital object. In this case, however, while the author provided basic introduction to all students on the concept and need for metadata as a form of "citation" for their scholarly work, the assignment instructions often deemphasized metadata in favor of ensuring that the students simply posted content correctly. The students who took the time to provide complete metadata arguably demonstrated a commitment to building an intellectually rigorous digital project.

Traditionally formatted citations and references as well as hyperlinks were the other form of sourcing, yet only 27 percent of the sites listed even partial citations throughout the site or in a reference list. Annotations that augmented digital media embedded on the site were a less frequent form of sourcing and enhancement on the sites and 23 percent utilized annotations. The most frequent use was in Scalar, which includes functionality for applying annotations to videos, and this was required as part of the students' assignments.

These chronicled characteristics of the websites are individual elements that only begin to formulate the value of the site as a coherent synthesis of media and text, but the ways in which the students handle these elements reveals key clues into their learning processes.

DISCUSSION

Learning Environments and Outcomes of Digital Pedagogy

This analysis of student scholarship leads us to consider potential learning outcomes for digital literacies that can be promoted through the infusion of digital humanities tools in the course work of humanities courses. The student-generated digital projects in this sample used for the study varied in disciplines, course requirements, and topical depths, and yet they exhibit key characteristics for the ways in which students construct and collaborate on digital projects. A useful framing of this learning process and the new types of agency that students gain in this course environment is viewing students as what Jentery Sayers characterizes as "context-providers."[13] As "context-providers," the students build digital sites that articulate new syntheses of knowledge and provide new ways of viewing topics and subject areas. The report of the Visible Knowledge Project, a recent multi-institutional study "on collaborative investigation of learning, inquiry, and new technology," argues that students engage in three types of learning when building work with new media technologies:

- *Adaptive* learning includes the acquisition of "skills and dispositions . . . which enable them to be flexible and innovative in their knowledge."
- *Embodied* learning emerges in how the students engage emotional and social aspects in addition to cognitive learning in ways that highlighted the "sensual and emotional dimensions of working with multimedia representations of history and culture."
- *Socially situated* learning reveals how working with new media technologies pushes students "beyond mere knowledge acquisition to a way of thinking, acting, and a sense of identity."[14]

In light of these findings, we begin to see that students are invested with more agency in their learning environment, and achieve learning outcomes for digital literacies that are oriented toward playfulness, "tinkering," and experimental learning.[15]

The ways in which students exhibit their skills and knowledge via their digital projects necessitates a method of analyzing and assessing their work for competencies in not only subject content, but also digital literacies. As noted earlier, digital literacies are marked by the competencies of people to utilize digital tools and resources to "construct new knowledge, create media expressions, and communicate with others"; as such, this is a process that excavates "the constantly changing practices through which people make traceable meanings using digital technologies."[16] Building on this definition, Julia Gillen and David Barton suggest four pathways for developing digital literacies:

- Enhancing cognitive development and assessment practices through curriculum interventions that make use of new affordances of digital technologies;
- Supporting learning communities to work collaboratively in problem solving and the coconstruction of knowledge;
- Working collaboratively in a multidisciplinary team to create useful, practical tools; and
- Increasing authenticity and overcoming access issues.[17]

This framework of digital literacies development complements metaliteracy objectives. It places "an emphasis on active production and sharing of new knowledge through technology" and provides an "an integrated and all-inclusive core for engaging with individuals and ideas in digital information environments."[18] The digital pedagogy practices pursued in the case studies presented in this chapter sought to develop and promote these literacies through instructional design that incorporated experimentation and a newly collaborative approach in instruction. Four potential outcomes correlate to development of metaliteracy and digital literacies through these collaborative teaching practices:

- *Discover and evaluate digital content for information and interactive usage.*
  Students learned how to research effectively and gather a variety of digital content that they imported into the digital platform for analysis and/or publishing. A media and cinema studies student from China noted that he/she discovered unanticipated information sources during the research process on Tiananmen Square protests, saying "I found huge amounts of information that I do not know when doing the research, for example, like the contemporary periodicals like Youth Forum and The World Economic Herald." The students incorporated information literacy skills that enabled them to then take the next step of building critical digital projects.

- *Develop scholarly critique skills via synthesis of visual and textual content.*
  On all of these platforms, students wove together multimedia content in such a way as to build rich scholarly explications of their topic. Whether doing digital writing in Omeka or for the class scholarly journal in WordPress, the students developed skills in creating multilayered scholarly documents that drew on multiple sources and merged them together into a coherent whole.

- *Engage in a collaborative learning environment.*
  The students worked in WordPress, Omeka, and Scalar in collaborative environments and were able to engage in their peers' work from our initial teaching workshops to the end products with required peer review.
- *Build authentic transferrable skills and digital tool competencies through experiential learning.*
  The creation of Omeka, WordPress, and Scalar sites opened students' eyes to the possibilities for the reach of their scholarship and emboldened students to take their research beyond the classroom and realize the potential for the skills and digital literacies they attained. As one student stated, "After learning these skills, I have been able to transfer them to my other classes and other activities. They frustrated me a lot at times and have a need for a little improvement, but overall they taught me a lot and helped tie in with other themes of media literacy in my other classes."

These outcomes reveal how the experimental ethos of digital pedagogy translates into an innovative learning environment that enables the students to engage in different modes of learning. Assessment of the students' progress toward these outcomes is then the next critical step in digital pedagogy.

Assessment Strategies for Student Projects on Digital Literacies

Assessment of digital literacies in the humanities must take into account the influences of technology on the students' research and writing practices as they create digital projects. Kathleen Yancey notes:

> Technology isn't the villain; but as a tool, technology is not innocent. It is both shaping and assessing the writers whose work we want to assess—and not only in word-processing software. . . . Online, assessment is ubiquitous, and yet we do not often observe its effects.[19]

This quote encapsulates how assessment is essential to the use of digital tools in course work and, as such, how digital literacy outcomes frequently intersect and/or align with information literacy and disciplinary outcomes in a various ways.

When evaluating student work for learning outcomes oriented toward digital literacies, there are a range of pedagogical approaches and assignment formats. For the courses and assignments examined in this study, we employed the "scaffolding" method—a constructivist approach to instruction "designed to provide a scaffolding or support for initial learning" via a sequence of assignments that "build gradually toward a more refined and complex understanding of the concept."[20] The series of assignments developed around Scalar and Omeka guided the students in building their projects on the digital platforms.

In carrying out these assignments, the students built a type of portfolio on the digital platforms as they displayed their work on the courses' group websites before building their own websites. Portfolio assessment theory thus can, in part, reveal some insights into strategies for assessment of student-generated digital projects as composites of their work toward building digital literacies.

Within the significant amount of literature on portfolio assessment, scholars consider how to evaluate web-based portfolio work, frequently termed e-portfolios. Bret Eynon argues for the power of e-portfolios in college curriculum and learning, noting that e-portfolios enable a scaffolding approach to teaching and "support embedded pedagogy and situated learning, using multimedia authoring tools to build student engagement in learning."[21] Chris Trevitt and Claire Stocks note that a portfolio can also provide authenticity to assess student learning and progress that other types of assignments do not.[22] E-portfolios also provide a strong conduit for assessment; Yancey argues that e-portfolios "provide opportunity for formative assessment in deep and extended ways," as students display in e-portfolios how "they use multiple systems of representation to map learning in new ways . . . students also help faculty learn about how learning actually works such that we all understand learning in new ways."[23] In many studies, rubrics are a critical piece of assessment for portfolios: Chi-Cheng Chang and colleagues examine the viability of rubrics for student self-assessment of electronic portfolios, and studies of web-based portfolios for arts also examine the use of rubrics as a way to assess student work by instructors and the students themselves.[24] Portfolio assessment critically employs rubrics as a way of evaluating how well the work meets the desired standards.

Megan Oakleaf explains that the value of rubrics lies in how they "allow students to understand the expectations of their instructors," and how they "provide direct feedback to students about what they have learned and what they have yet to learn."[25] The clarity of rubrics also enables students to engage in qualitative self-evaluation, as the rubrics emphasize "understanding rather than memorization, 'deep' learning rather than 'surface' learning."[26] This sustained learning process promoted by rubrics ties directly into the ways in which digital literacies focus on the holistic and continual skill building that students engage in with each new iterative experience.

For assessment of digital projects, a number of approaches are emerging in how to approach digital or "multimodal" texts and this is especially evident in the area of rhetoric and composition studies. Yancey notes that the composition of multimedia projects is marked by diverse types of "coherence":

> Digital compositions weave words and context and images: They are exercises in ordered complexity—and complex in some different ways than print precisely because they include more kinds of threads. As important, because the context for digital compositions is still so new and ever emerging, these texts tend to live inside the gaps, such that the reader/reviewer/responder is a more active weaver, creating arrangement and meaning both, and, I think, participating in a Bakhtinian creation of textual prototypes. In other words, we don't have a final definition of many of these texts—and perhaps we never will.[27]

Yancey proposes an assessment approach that focuses on the arrangement of the multimodal content within the work and how well it conveys the coherence of the work:

1. What arrangements are possible?
2. Who arranges?
3. What is the intent?
4. What is the fit between the intent and the effect?[28]

In this vein, Cheryl Ball argues that the ways in which the modes of a multimedia text—defined as "the semiotic elements such as video, graphics, written text, audio, and so on that a designer uses to compose multimodal or new media texts"—work together are critical to the readability and meaning-making of a new media work.[29] Madeleine Sorapure argues for an assessment approach that involves examining the relations between the different modes used in a digital project, noting "the narrow question of the relations between modes is, I believe, essential in understanding not only how a multimedia text coheres but also how it creates meaning."³⁰ Jody Shipka establishes that students should also be critically engaged in the assessment process through the process of creating reflective documents called "Statements of Goals and Choices" that require students to "attend to the impact of their writerly choices as well as to the visual, material, and technological aspects of their texts and practices."³¹ These strategies all have the aim of extracting the meaning and complexity of the multifaceted nature of digital works. But rubrics can reveal insights into the digital scholarship produced by students by breaking down and atomizing the various stages and aspects of the learning and development process.

For an instruction environment oriented around digital literacies as "the constantly changing practices through which people make traceable meanings using digital technologies," an ideal assessment rubric enables both instructors and librarians to evaluate various competencies aligned with digital literacies as they are facilitated by the use of digital humanities tools and platforms.³² Rubrics for digital scholarship can measure the students' work and progress in a complex, holistic fashion, as Rina Benmayor demonstrates in her rubric that evaluates students' digital writing projects by three defined modes of "narrative or embedded theorizing," "applied theorizing," and "critical theorizing." Benmayor notes:

> In most Scholarship of Teaching and Learning rubrics, there is an implied linear progression from novice to expert learner. However, my evidence leads me to resist that progression and to posit instead a more complex usage of theorizing strategies. . . . The rubric calls my attention to the unruliness of theorizing and the need for a quantum approach to the evidence, looking at different medium-specific instances of theorizing rather than using a single linear measure of achievement.³³

This complexity and holistic approach is also evident in Ball's accounting of her development of rubric criteria for assessing students' multimedia web texts, as she worked with her students to synthesize a series of previously created multimedia assessment rubrics developed by Kuhn et al., Warner, and Dewitt and Ball into six criteria for their course.³⁴ Ball notes that in this process of rubric development, she learned that assessment of multimedia scholarship is wholly contextual and fluid:

> As my understanding improves regarding how webtexts move
> through authors' and editors' and publishers' processes and as
> I expand my theoretical understanding of multimodal composi-
> tion (i.e., writing) teaching, my pedagogy changes and so must
> my assessment criteria. This is why my values system for assess-
> ing webtexts may not, cannot, will not necessarily be yours.[35]

In light of the growing body of research literature that contemplates how we might evaluate student-generated digital projects, rubrics hold rich potential as tools for evaluation, particularly in how rubrics stretch beyond simple criteria and express the values and outcomes of a scholarly community.

Daniel Callison argues, "Rubrics are texts that are visible signs of agreed upon values. They cannot contain all the nuances of the evaluation community's values, but they do contain the central expressions of those values."[36] In this light, a rubric can be a valuable contribution to the scholarly communities that are implementing digital pedagogy, because rubrics are a step toward the coherence and normalizing of shared expectations for student scholarship produced on digital platforms.

In the case studies presented in this study, the author engaged with faculty and instructors throughout in discussions of student work and, for select courses, contributed to the initial assessment. This experience builds on a growing strategy of librarians and faculty collaborating to build course- or discipline-specific assessment rubrics for information literacy through analysis of student assignments and the curricula.[37] From the analysis presented in this study, Table 1 displays a potential rubric for assessing digital literacies via student-generated websites.

The preliminary rubric displayed in Table 1 is based on the types of projects that the students generated and the characteristics exhibited across the projects. The four levels of competencies range from the "Needs Improvement" criteria, which indicate that the site shows little to no effort was expended in the desired areas, to the "Excellence" level, which indicates a high mastery of the digital resources and demonstrated intellectual rigor in synthesizing digital media and text into a scholarly project. The five areas of focus—use of visual media, written content, use of sources, structure and organization of site, and coherence of online presentation—are the critical areas that can be evaluated both quantitatively and qualitatively by the instructors for outcomes in digital literacies. This preliminary rubric uses a linear form of assessment, but other aspects can be incorporated to explore the coherence and complexity of the students' digital work.

CONCLUSION

As more and more humanities courses incorporate digital tools into their curriculum, librarians have numerous opportunities to become engaged in digital pedagogy and collaborate with faculty in diverse ways. The growth in digital humanities as a field of study and research approach means that humanities students will need to be taught and trained in the many available diverse digital tools, methodologies, and resources. As such, there are manifold ways in which librarians and instructors can collaborate around digital pedagogy. As these collaborations grow, we move toward promoting experiential, creative modes of learning in our students that must engage all of us in the pedagogical practices. As Howard Rheingold writes:

> We must develop a participative pedagogy, assisted by digital media and networked publics, that focuses on catalyzing, inspiring, nourishing, facilitating, and guiding literacies essential to individual and collective life in the 21st century.[38]

Digital scholarship in the classroom is becoming increasingly prominent and, together, librarians and instructors can collaborate on pedagogical strategies and assessments to achieve learning outcomes for the new literacies needed for this digital age.

NOTES

1   Julia Gillen and David Barton, *Digital Literacies: A Research Briefing by the Technology Enhanced Learning Phase of the Teaching and Learning Research Programme* (London: London Knowledge Lab, Institute of Education, University of London, January 2010): 3.

2   Barbara R. Jones-Kavalier and Suzanne L. Flannigan, "Connecting the Dots: Literacy of the 21st Century," *Educause Quarterly*, No. 2 (January 2010): 8–10.

3   Thomas P. Mackey and Trudi E. Jacobson, "Reframing Information Literacy as a Metaliteracy," *College & Research Libraries* (January 2011): 70, http://crl.acrl.org/content/72/1/62.full.pdf.

Table 1. Rubric for digital literacies.

	Needs Improvement	Acceptable	Good	Excellent
Use of Visual Media	Uses too few objects (less than one per page) or too many objects. Relates to the topic only superficially or not at all. Has no citations or captions.	Meets requirements of at least one media object per page. Relates to the topic of the site. Provides basic captions and/or citations.	Uses media objects on each page. Selects multiple types of media objects. Media objects are closely related to the topic and enhance the text.	Selection of media objects is diverse. Presents the media objects in a critical context: displays the media in an innovative layout with thoughtful juxtapositions. Connects media to each other and critical ideas. Integrates annotations and advanced features.
Written Content	Provides minimal to no information about the site and/or displayed media. Material is not original—text copied wholesale from another resource. Contains erroneous spellings and grammar.	Writes basic descriptions to provide information and context for visual media. Spelling and grammar are moderately clean.	Writes longer sections of text that provide detailed descriptions, explanations, and/or context. Spelling and grammar are mostly clean.	Writes multiple paragraphs that provide in-depth information and/or context for the media objects and site topic. Critically evaluates and contextualizes the media objects in light of the topic.

Use of Sources	No sources are cited in any way. Has been copied and pasted without attribution.	Uses only the number of sources required for assignment. Mentions the author and work in-text or includes basic citations of authors and works.	Uses multiple types of resources. Provides sourcing for media objects as well as textual sources. Provides citations for all sources used.	Integrates sources throughout the text and media for the site. Provides full citations for all media objects as well as textual sources. Provides detailed citation information and links to all sources used.
Structure and Organization of Site	Has no structure in the form of paths, exhibition, or collections.	Uses basic structure of one book with multiple pages.	Connects all book pages into a path.	Builds a complex, critical structure for book with multiple paths. AND/OR Connects media and annotations to pages and paths.
Coherence of Online Presentation	Provides no clear connections between media objects and text, and/or between pages of site.	Can follow basic structure of site; all elements connect to the topic.	Focuses on topic of site; all pages and media elements connect to topic. Pages and paths flow well narratively.	Provides a critical and tightly written narrative on a topic that is easy to follow. Media objects and text are closely integrated to advance site's narrative. Site is structured with multiple paths and sections to present differing facets of the topic.

4   Adeline Koh and Brian Croxall, "Digital Pedagogy?," *A Digital Pedagogy Uncon-ference*, www.briancroxall.net/digitalpedagogy/what-is-digital-pedagogy.

5   Jesse Stommel, "Decoding Digital Pedagogy, Pt. 2," *Hybrid Pedagogy*, www.hybridpedagogy.com/journal/decoding-digital-pedagogy-pt-2-unmapping-the-terrain.

6   Kenneth Price, interview by the Crossroads Project, 1998, *The Walt Whitman Archive,* www.whitmanarchive.org/about/articles/anc.00005.html; Lisa Norberg et al., "Sustainable Design for Multiple Audiences: The Usability Study and Iterative Redesign of the Documenting the American South Digital Library," *OCLC Systems & Services* 21, No. 4 (2005): 285–99; *Documenting the American South*, http://docsouth.unc.edu; Matthias Oppermann, *American Studies in Dialogue: Radical Reconstructions Between Curriculum and Cultural Critique* (Frankfurt: Campus Verlag): 167–69; *American Studies Crossroads*, http://crossroads.georgetown.edu.

7   Bethany Nowviskie, "A Digital Boot Camp for Grad Students in the Humanities," *Chronicle of Higher Education* (April 2012), http://chronicle.com/article/A-Digital-Boot-Camp-for-Grad/131665/; Bethany Nowviskie, "It Starts on Day One," *Bethany Nowviskie* (November 12, 2011), http://nowviskie.org/2011/it-starts-on-day-one; UVa Praxis Program, http://praxis-network.org/praxis-program.html; Alyssa Arbuckle et al., "Teaching and Learning Multimodal Communications," *International Journal of Learning and Media* 4, No. 1 (2013), http://ijlm.net/knowingdoing/teaching-and-learning-multimodal-communications; Ruth Mostern and Elana Gainor, "Traveling the Silk Road on a Virtual Globe: Pedagogy, Technology, and Evaluation for Spatial History," *Digital Humanities Quarterly* 7, No. 2 (2013), http://digitalhumanities.org/dhq/vol/7/2/000116/000116.html; Jeff Howard, "Interpretative Quests in Theory and Pedagogy," *Digital Humanities Quarterly* 1, No. 1 (2007), www.digitalhumanities.org/dhq/vol/1/1/000002/000002.html; Ryan Cordell, "New Technologies to Get Your Students Engaged," *Chronicle of Higher Education* (May 2011), http://chronicle.com/article/New-Technologies-to-Get-Your/127394.

8   Paul Fyfe, "Digital Humanities Unplugged," *Digital Humanities Quarterly* 5, No. 3 (2011), www.digitalhumanities.org/dhq/vol/5/3/000106/000106.html; Craig Bellamy, "The Sounds of Many Hands Clapping," *Digital Humanities Quarterly* 6, No. 2 (2012), www.digitalhumanities.org/dhq/vol/6/2/000119/000119.html.

9   Angela Courtney and Michelle Dalmau, "Victorian Women Writers Project Revived: A Case Study in Sustainability," *Digital Humanities 2011* (June 19–22, 2011): 114–15; Vinopal and McCormick, "Supporting Digital Scholarship in Research Libraries," *Journal of Library Administration* 53, No. 1 (January 2013): 27–42; Miriam Posner, "No Half Measures: Overcoming Common Challenges to Doing Digital Humanities in the Library," *Journal of Library Administration* 53, No. 1 (January 2013): 43–52; Trevor Muñoz, "In Service? A Further Provocation on Digital Humanities Research in Libraries," *DH+LIB: Where the Digital Humanities and Librarianship Meet* (June 19, 2013), http://acrl.ala .org/dh/2013/06/19/in-service-a-further-provocation-on-digital-humanities -research-in-libraries; Chris Alen Sula, "Digital Humanities and Libraries: A Conceptual Model," *Journal of Library Administration* 53, No. 1 (January 2013): 10–26.

10   Tara McPherson, "Introduction: Media Studies and Digital Humanities," *Cinema Journal* 48, No. 2 (Winter 2009): 119–23.

11   "Usage of Content Management Systems for Websites," *W3 Techs: Web Technology Surveys* (2014), http://w3techs.com/technologies/overview/content _management/all.

12   Anastasia Salter, "Revisiting Your Learning Management System," *Chronicle of Higher Education* (April 2013), http://chronicle.com/blogs/profhacker /revisiting-your-lms/48441.

13   Jentery Sayers, "Tinker-Centric Pedagogy in Literature and Language Classrooms," in *Collaborative Approaches to the Digital in English Studies* (Logan, UT: Computers and Composition Digital Press/Utah State University Press, 2013): 279–300, http://ccdigitalpress.org/ebooks-and-projects/cad.

14   Randy Bass and Bret Eynon, "Capturing the Visible Evidence of Invisible Learning," *Academic Commons* (October 2014): 10–11.

15   Anita Say Chan and Harriet Green, "Practicing Collaborative Digital Pedagogy to Foster Digital Literacies in Humanities Classrooms," *Educause Review* (October 2014), www.educause.edu/ero/article/practicing-collaborative-digital -pedagogy-foster-digital-literacies-humanities-classrooms.

16   Jones-Kavalier and Finnegan, "Connecting the Digital Dots," 9; Gillen and Barton, *Digital Literacies*, 9.

17   Gillen and Barton, *Digital Literacies*, 11.

18   Thomas P. Mackey and Trudi E. Jacobson, "Reframing Information Literacy as a Metaliteracy," *College & Research Libraries* (January 2011): 71, http:// crl.acrl.org/content/72/1/62.full.pdf.

19   Kathleen B. Yancey, "Looking for Sources of Coherence in a Fragmented World," *Computers and Composition* 21 (2004): 93, http://rhetcomp.gsu.edu/~bgu/8121/Reading-Yancey.pdf.

20   Marilla D. Svinicki, *Learning and Motivation in the Postsecondary Classroom* (New York: Wiley, 2004): 21.

21   Bret Eynon, "'It Helped Me See a New Me': ePortfolio, Learning, and Change at LaGuardia Community College," *Academic Commons* (2009): 5.

22   Chris Trevitt and Claire Stocks, "Signifying Authenticity in Academic Practice," *Assessment & Evaluation in Higher Education* 37, No. 2 (2012): 248.

23   K. Yancey and D. Cambridge, "Making Common Cause: Electronic Portfolios, Learning, and the Power of Community," *Academic Commons* (2009): 7.

24   Chi-Cheng Chang, Chaoyun Liang, and Yi-Hui Chen, "Is Learner Self-Assessment Reliable and Valid in a Web-Based Portfolio Environment for High School Students?," *Computers & Education* 60, No. 1 (January 2013): 325–34; Chi-Cheng Chang and Kuo-Hung Tseng, "Use and Performances of Web-Based Portfolio Assessment," *British Journal of Educational Technology* 40, No. 2 (March 2009): 358–70; Heidi J. Davis-Soylu, Kylie A. Peppler, and Daniel T. Hickey, "Assessment Assemblage: Advancing Portfolio Practice through the Assessment Staging Theory," *Studies in Art Education* 52, No. 3 (2011): 213–24.

25   Megan Oakleaf, "Using Rubrics to Assess Information Literacy: An Examination of Methodology and Interrater Reliability," *Journal of the American Society for Information Science and Technology* 60, No. 5 (May 2009): 969–70.

26   Ibid., 970.

27   Yancey, "Looking for Sources of Coherence," 95.

28   Ibid., 96.

29   Cheryl E. Ball, "Show, Not Tell: The Value of New Media Scholarship," *Computers & Composition* 21, No. 4 (2004): 403–25.

30   Madeleine Sorapure, "Between Modes: Assessing Student New Media Compositions," *Kairos* 10, No. 2 (2005): 4, 14.

31   Jody Shipka, "Negotiating Rhetorical, Material, Methodological, and Technological Difference: Evaluating Multimodal Designs," *College Composition and Communication* 61, No. 1 (September 2009): W355.

32   Gillen and Barton, *Digital Literacies*, 9.

33   Rina Benmayor, "Theorizing through Digital Stories: The Art of 'Writing Back' and 'Writing For,'" in *The Difference that Inquiry Makes: The Impact of*

Learning on Teaching and Innovation in Higher Education, ed. R. Bass and B. Eynon, *Academic Commons* (2009): 8.

34 Cheryl E. Ball, "Assessing Scholarly Multimedia: A Rhetorical Genre Studies Approach," *Technical Communication Quarterly* 21, No. 1 (2012): 64–8.

35 Ibid., 68.

36 Daniel Callison, "Rubrics," *Scholarly Library Media Activities Monthly* 17, No. 2 (October 2000): 34.

37 Debra Gilchrist and Megan Oakleaf, "An Essential Partner: The Librarian's Role in Student Learning Assessment," *National Institute for Learning Outcomes Assessment* (April 2012): 9–11, 13.

38 Howard Rheingold, "Participatory Pedagogy for a Literacy of Literacies," http://freesouls.cc/essays/03-howard-rheingold-participative-pedagogy-for -a-literacy-of-literacies.html.

11 | Library Instruction for Digital Humanities Pedagogy in Undergraduate Classes

Stewart Varner

INTRODUCTION

The term "digital humanities" describes a wide variety of scholarly activities. So wide, in fact, that it is increasingly difficult to use the term with any sort of precision. It is helpful, therefore, to think about digital humanities in terms of several subcategories.

- Online social networking,
- Text mining/data analysis,
- Data visualization,
- Digital mapping,
- Digital libraries and repositories,
- Digital publishing, and
- Digital pedagogy.

To a greater or lesser extent, libraries have been crucial partners in several of these subcategories. Many libraries—and many more librarians—have been actively engaged with each other and with the wider academic community through social media. They have worked with researchers to create digital corpora for use in text mining and data analysis projects. GIS and data librarians are becoming common and some libraries have even built impressive spaces where researchers can explore this data visually. Digital libraries and repositories are no longer anything new but they do continue to evolve and have occasionally served as the inspiration—and even the foundation—for exciting open-access publications based in the library.

Libraries and librarians have also been part of the increasing popularity of digital humanities or digital humanities–inflected pedagogy. However, these efforts have not generated the same level of interest as some of the others. Perhaps this is because course-based projects are not as flashy as large-scale, showcase projects. The lack of attention could also be due to a general lack of certainty about what "digital pedagogy" actually refers to. Like "digital humanities" itself, it seems as if the term could apply to any number of things and, as this chapter demonstrates, routinely touches on or incorporates each of the subcategories listed above. Furthermore, at a time when the bulk of library instruction sessions consists of teaching students how to thoughtfully navigate online catalogs, course pages, and online databases, isn't nearly all of our pedagogy digital?

Possibly; but this chapter will explore a dimension of digital pedagogy that is in some ways an extension of traditional library instruction but is, in other ways, an entirely new pursuit. It will focus on practices that bring faculty and librarians into very close collaboration and create an opportunity for increased student engagement with a range of library resources beyond the catalogs and databases.

This chapter begins with an overview of what professors talk about when they talk about digital pedagogy and a series of arguments for why librarians should be a part of that conversation. This is followed by a close look at four kinds of class projects that are particularly well suited to librarian involvement: digital mapping, text analysis, multimedia websites/online exhibits, and Wikipedia editing. Before concluding, the chapter addresses some of the staffing, infrastructure, and workflow questions that will undoubtedly arise when librarians become collaborators in digital humanities pedagogy. Because this chapter is necessarily an overview of a sprawling set of questions, concerns, and possibilities, there are frequent pointers to more in-depth sources and examples.

WHAT IS DIGITAL HUMANITIES PEDAGOGY?

Technology has, of course, been an important part of higher education for a very long time. Usually, though not always, falling under the purview of "classroom technology," digital pedagogy is often seen in terms of smart classrooms, learning management systems, and enterprise-level software solutions. These tools are often valued for their potential to make some routine tasks easier or more efficient. However, there is a parallel, not necessarily connected conversation happening within the disciplines and among faculty about how to creatively and critically incorporate technology into assignments in ways that truly enhance student engagement and encourage them to confront how technology impacts the work they do. Faculty are developing assignments that grow out of online culture, embrace multimodal communication, and create opportunities for students to approach course topics and materials from a variety of perspectives often using lightweight, easy-to-use digital tools.

In addition to a growing presence in more traditional outlets, this grassroots approach to integrating digital humanities into course work is championed in journals like *Hybrid Pedagogy*[1] and *The Journal of Interactive Teaching and Pedagogy (JiTP)*.[2] Both of these publications are peer reviewed and freely available online. They tend to focus on concrete examples and practical explanations of assignments that use technology to truly enhance student work. *JiTP* has separate sections for sample assignments, tool tips, and what it calls "teaching fails." The refreshing humility of the pieces and their focus on practicality reflect the fact that all of this is very new to many professors who need concrete, step-by-step instructions for how to make the most of emerging technology. It also points toward an opportunity for librarians to partner with faculty who are interested in digital humanities pedagogy; not just because librarians excel at instruction but also because the library can provide access to the collections and tools that form the foundation of some of the most innovative assignments.

WHY SHOULD LIBRARIANS GET INVOLVED?

Most research librarians are engaged in some form of instruction. At its most basic, this includes explaining to students how to use the library's various discovery systems and how to properly cite the resources they find. The Association of College and Research Libraries (ACRL), in its *Guidelines for Instruction Programs in Academic Libraries*, suggests that instruction is central to the mission of the library and "should be planned in concert with overall strategic library planning."[3] These guidelines highlight "information literacy" as the goal of library instruction, defining it as "the abilities involved in identifying an information need, accessing needed information, evaluating, managing and applying information, and understanding the legal, social and ethical aspects of information use."[4] However, Cheryl LaGuardia has challenged the use of this term. In her article "Library Instruction in the Digital Age," LaGuardia suggests that "[o]ur profession's continued devotion to 'information literacy' just shows how far behind the times our national organizations are in acknowledging current realities."[5] For LaGuardia, students do not need help with information skills but with research skills and so she prefers the term "research literacy."[6] LaGuardia specifically mentions research skills like finding scholarly information and evaluating its quality. While her description of "research literacy" does not seem to depart very dramatically from the ACRL's definition of "information literacy," it does indicate an intriguing shift in emphasis toward something more holistic. "Research literacy" signals that the library is not only a storehouse for information but a connection point for all the parts of the research process.

As digital humanities pedagogy becomes more common, librarians would do well to expand their concept of instruction to include the ability to find, evaluate, and learn to use new tools for exploring, sharing, reusing, and remixing research materials. Librarians have already taken steps in this direction by providing instruction for citation management tools such as Zotero, End Note, and Ref Works. Although in some ways innovations, these tools reflect the traditional focus of the library: the collection. However, many libraries are expanding their mission beyond the collection to embrace their role as *productive* spaces on campus. This is perhaps most clear in the rise of library-based makerspaces that are outfitted with 3D printers, boxes of Arduinos, and stacks of Raspberry Pi. Facilitating creativity in digital humanities need not be quite so hardware intensive, but the makerspace movement is an indication that there are new tools and new skills to be added to the librarian's repertoire. As the following section will explain, this should include tools and skills for performing digital mapping and text analysis as well as those for building both multimedia websites and online exhibits.

This is not simply an attempt to jump on a bandwagon in the hopes of keeping libraries relevant for their own sake. Becoming active partners in digital humanities pedagogy is clearly an extension of research instruction—the established domain of expertise for librarians within the academy. Doing so will also encourage greater use of library collections.

Libraries have spent millions of dollars during the past three decades to purchase digital collections and digitize their own analog collections. In the hopes of encouraging creative uses of those collections, librarians have advocated for fair use and open access and generally put significant effort into making digital collections flexible. It should follow that librarians would also work with faculty and students to identify and utilize tools that will facilitate this work.

Furthermore, librarians may find that getting involved with digital humanities pedagogy projects is an effective and low-risk way to explore digital humanities more generally. Many librarians look back on a history of multiyear, grant-funded projects as the primary way they have collaborated with faculty who are interested in digital humanities. These projects have often placed significant demands on the library's IT staff and have raised challenging questions about maintenance and long-term preservation. This is, in large part, why the very mention of digital humanities can cause anxiety for some library administrators. However, digital humanities pedagogy projects are almost always small scale because they tend to be limited to what can be done in one semester. They are also potentially ephemeral and may not require long-term maintenance or preservation. As such, these projects could present convenient opportunities for a library to experiment with digital humanities without signing up for an unsustainable commitment.

WHAT ARE SOME EXAMPLES OF DIGITAL HUMANITIES PEDAGOGY PROJECTS?

The Digital Research Tools Directory (DiRT Directory)[7] indexes hundreds of tools that can be used for digital humanities projects and continues to add more. While the number of tools and techniques may seem unmanageable, certain genres of digital humanities pedagogy assignment are consistently popular. In her article for *Hybrid Pedagogy,* "Introducing Digital Humanities Work to Undergraduates: An Overview," Adeline Koh describes four general types of projects that are both common and ripe for library collaboration; digital mapping, text analysis, multimedia websites/online exhibits, and Wikipedia editing. This section uses Koh's outline as a jumping off point to explore each of these types of projects and suggest ways that librarians can become crucial collaborators.[8] New tools and techniques are constantly emerging, so it is pointless to try to explain how specific tools work in this chapter. However, the goals and methods of particular assignments need not be dependent on a single technology. In fact, because the tools change so frequently, it is vital for librarians to be prepared to evaluate new ones as they emerge in order to determine whether or not they are suitable for undergraduate assignments. To help with that, this section concludes with a discussion of some qualities users need to look for when deciding what tool to adopt. This points to the crucial consulting role that librarians can play in digital humanities pedagogy. Some professors may look to the library for examples of potential projects and advice on how to choose tools and design assignments. Just as librarians instruct users on the best ways to find resources in the collection, they can also show users how to use those resources in digital humanities projects.

Mapping Projects

Digital mapping software has revolutionized disciplines like geography, city and regional planning, and archaeology. Software like Esri's ArcGIS allows users to georeference maps and add layers of information to those maps, making it possible to explore the social, environmental, economic, and political life of a place. However, ArcGIS is a very powerful tool with a very steep learning curve. As a result, it may be overkill for many digital humanities projects, especially those that are part of class assignments. Fortunately, several lightweight digital mapping tools are available that can be incorporated relatively easily into class assignments. For example, Koh's article points toward a project created by Gerry Carlin and Mair Evan that marks important places in James Joyce's *Ulysses* using Google Maps.[9] This free tool allows users to label places on a map and add information about those places. Giving students an assignment to map a novel could encourage them to dig deeper into a text as they seek out geographic details. It can also help students understand the importance of the city and its spatial relationships to the text.

In addition to literature assignments, Google Maps can be useful for history classes by making it simple to place historical events on top of contemporary geography. Another tool that can easily be incorporated into history and cultural studies classes is History Pin.[10] This free tool allows users to digitally "pin" images onto a map and organize those images into tours that can be made available publicly. Several museums and archives have made images available for use on History Pin and users can augment these with their own collections.

For both Google Maps and History Pin (as well as other mapping tools like CartoDB[11] and TimeMapper[12]), no special technology is required. They are all web applications and users interact with them through their Internet browsers. Furthermore, none of these tools require programing skills—or even deep geography skills—and thorough documentation is freely available online. While the tools themselves do not require any particular technology or especially in-depth instruction to be used in classes, they provide an opportunity for librarians to suggest digitized collections that could be used to create unique projects. For example, digitized images of letters from special collections could be mapped using Google Maps, or images from university archives could be used to create campus tours with History Pin.

Text Analysis

Text analysis is a general term that encompasses a variety of techniques that aim to identify broad patterns or characteristics in a collection of digitized texts. For some scholars, this kind of work is the original DH and it traces its roots to the Text Encoding Initiative (TEI) and what was known as "humanities computing."[13] An important moment in the history of this particular field came in 2000 when Stanford literature scholar Franco Moretti used the term "distant reading" in an article in the *New Left Review* titled "Conjectures on World Literature."[14] The term is a play on "close reading," a standard method in literature studies that focuses sustained attention on specific chapters, passages, and sentences in single texts. Moretti argues that this method is not adequate for studying entire national literatures as it requires scholars to focus on just a few, typically canonical, texts. In his article, Moretti states that distant reading "allows you to focus on units that are much smaller or much larger than the text: devices, themes, tropes—or genres and systems."[15] Using computers, Moretti found he was able to study hundreds of texts at once and gain insights that he would have been physically unable to recognize using traditional methods.

Several techniques go under the names "text analysis" or "distant reading." Sometimes, the research is relatively straightforward and relies on simple word counts and frequency comparisons. For example, in his book

Reading Machines: Toward an Algorithmic Criticism, Stephen Ramsay describes how he used simple scripting to identify which words are distinctive to certain characters in Virginia Woolf's "The Waves."[16] More elaborate processes such as topic modeling, named-entity recognition, or sentiment analysis have also become more common. The Civil War historian Rob Nelson used topic modeling, a process that identifies groups of words that often appear together, to look for differences in the way the *New York Times* and the *Richmond Dispatch* reported on the war for his project called "Mining the Dispatch."[17]

Text analysis is often difficult for nonprogrammers, but tools are beginning to emerge that significantly lower the barrier to entry. For example, Voyant[18] performs very basic word counts and produces simple visualizations (word clouds, frequency comparisons) through a very easy-to-use interface. Though more demanding that Voyant, Mallet[19] is a software toolkit that facilitates topic modeling. Neither tool requires much beyond a computer and a reliable connection to the Internet. Depending on the size of the digital corpus being studied, larger computers may be necessary. However, it is typically the technical know-how (including the ability to interpret results) rather than limits of the hardware that presents the biggest challenges for scholars getting started with text analysis.[20]

While these tools and techniques are becoming common as a research method, they are also being recognized for their pedagogical value. For example, Paul Fyfe has written about an assignment he developed called "How to Not Read a Victorian Novel."[21] He asks his students to identify a novel they have not read, use a variety of text analysis tools to study it, and then write a paper on what they discover. He encouraged the students "to scrutinize any moment of frustration as . . . an opportunity to change the kinds of questions they were asking."[22] Clearly they were not able to answer the same questions they would if they had simply read the book so the exercise succeeded in getting the students to look at literature from a new perspective.

Exercises like this make excellent opportunities for collaboration between faculty and librarians. In addition to working with professors to identify appropriate tools for different assignments, librarians are well positioned to coordinate the development of digital corpora that are ready for study. For example, the University of North Carolina has made available the plain text files that run behind some of its most popular digital collections in order to encourage text analysis.[23] This may at first seem simplistic but the effectiveness of digital text analysis depends on the quality of the data the researcher uses. Digital corpora often need to be preprocessed before they can be properly analyzed. Librarians know what digital collections are available and can work with their partners to get them ready for study.

Multimedia Websites and Online Exhibits

Since the beginning of the World Wide Web, there has been excitement about the ease with which people can share information with the rest of the world. Whether or not the web has always lived up to its democratizing hype is up for debate, but it is true that professors and students now have some very exciting ways to share the work they do that differ in both degree and kind from the eight-page term paper. This section describes some ideas for using the web to present student work but also points to some special concerns with this type of assignment, including FERPA compliance and copyright issues.

Some professors incorporate blogs into their courses to encourage discussion among students outside of the classroom. For example, as part of his Introduction to Digital Studies class at Davidson College, Mark Sample asks his students to take turns taking on different roles in the class's WordPress blog each week.[24] One group, "The Readers," is assigned to write responses to the assigned readings and post them to the class blog. "The Responders" are responsible for commenting on those posts, and "The Historians" are asked to find some other resource online and connect it to that week's topic or conversation.

Other classes have utilized websites as a kind of digital publication for showcasing student work. This can be as simple as asking students to post their research papers on a publicly accessible website. However, one of the benefits of asking students to post their work online is giving them the opportunity to take advantage of all of the affordances of the web. For example, they can easily link to other resources and incorporate images as well as embedded video and audio files into their work. Students in Brian Croxall's Introduction to Digital Humanities class at Emory University post the results of their final projects—including multimedia content—to the public course website, which, like Sample's blog, is built using WordPress.[25]

A third kind of course-based website assignment is the online exhibit. Usually connected to history or cultural studies classes, these projects are about getting students into archives, working with primary sources and then using them to tell a story. Many online exhibit assignments use a tool called Omeka, an open-source content management system (CMS) specifically designed with libraries, museums, and archives in mind.[26] What separates Omeka from other CMSs is that it is built around the digitized item—rather than the web page or the blog post—so it is very good for organizing collections and highlighting individual items within them. The tool asks users to describe each digital item using Dublin Core and then allows them to assign those items to collections. Once organized into collections, items can be used in exhibits and contextualized with content written by students. For example, Professor Cathy Moran Hajo worked with students at New York University to build a collection of 1,830 images related to Greenwich Village history and then organized those images into seventy-five student-curated exhibits.[27]

Thanks to the emergence of CMSs like WordPress and Omeka, it is very easy for students and faculty to build these blogs and websites. Although simplified versions of these platforms are usually available free of charge and hosted externally, many colleges and universities have officially adopted at least one for the purpose of allowing members of their community to make work public while maintaining their institutional affiliation. Whereas using the technology is relatively simple, hosting a local installation is no small undertaking. Managing updates and establishing processes for creating user accounts can be very tricky depending on the tool.

Because these projects can include many moving parts, librarians can guide faculty through planning the entire life cycle. From the very beginning, librarians can work with instructors to make sure assignments follow Family Educational Rights and Privacy Act (FERPA) regulations. According to Kevin Smith, dean of libraries at the University of Kansas, students need to be informed about an assignment early in the semester, given the option of using a pseudonym, encouraged to be very careful about posting private information, and, possibly, given the choice of completing an alternative assignment in order to protect their privacy.[28] Even if hosting local instances is not possible, librarians can still work with faculty to incorporate free and externally hosted versions of these tools into course work. One role is to simply act as consultant and explain what each tool does and why one might be better than another for a particular assignment. Once a class adopts a tool, librarians can be valuable partners in instructing students how to use the tool. This can include both technical instruction and also guidance on intellectual property rights and fair use. If the project is going to use images from special collections, the librarian can help the professors think strategically (and realistically) about digitization and also instruct students on proper metadata practices. This is particularly important in Omeka projects that depend on good metadata for organizing and searching collections.

Wikipedia Editing

Scholars and librarians have a complex relationship with Wikipedia. The crowdsourced digital encyclopedia seems to circumvent traditional means of establishing authoritative information. On the other hand, its size, ubiquity, and frequently surprising level of trustworthiness have made it difficult to ignore.[29] This anxiety over Wikipedia is particularly obvious in the classroom. Some professors flatly refuse to allow students to cite it as a source. Others have taken more of an "if you can't beat them, join them" attitude and have encouraged students to become Wikipedia editors, at least temporarily, in the context of a Wikipedia Edit-a-thon. A Wikipedia Edit-a-thon is an event where people meet for the express purpose of improving Wikipedia. These events are usually tightly focused on improving a specific aspect of the resource such as adding more women scientists or African American artists. While an edit-a-thon requires more time than a typical class session, planning and participating in one could be developed as a class project.

Contrary to popular fears, there are actually several mechanisms in place to combat unverifiable information and "vandalism" in Wikipedia. For example, there are limits to how many new users can request editor accounts at once and a sudden flurry of unexpected activity can set off moderator alarms. Therefore, Wikipedia advises groups planning to host edit-a-thons to plan ahead by creating an official project page on the Wikipedia:Meetup site and inviting several experienced editors to advise new users. Detailed instructions of planning and hosting an edit-a-thon can be found at Wikipedia.[30]

Libraries and librarians can be involved in Wikipedia edit-a-thons in several ways. For example, the library could be the perfect venue for such an event, particularly if it is happening on the weekend and/or involves participants from more than just one class. Also, there is a good chance some librarians are also active Wikipedia editors and could help show those who are unfamiliar with the process how it works. In the case of a targeted event, librarians could prepare in advance by developing lists of suggestions for work the participants might do. These could be suggestions for subjects that need to be added as well as existing subjects that need further development or additional citations. Most importantly, librarians can be there for the editors and work with them to find the kinds of verifiable information Wikipedia requires. To this end, they may want to identify and organize appropriate resources for the participants in advance.

EVALUATING DIGITAL TOOLS

One of the real benefits of digital humanities pedagogy projects is that they encourage experimentation. However, there are still pros and cons for each tool and it is important to ask some questions before investing time and effort even if the stakes are relatively low. While every tool will raise its own specific questions, below are a few general questions users need to ask about any tool.

Exports

Many digital tools are used to create some kind of image, chart, map or table. When evaluating a tool it is important to consider what the tool actually allows you to do with what it creates. For example, Voyant allows users to download image files of the visualizations it creates that are easily embedded in websites. Other programs don't offer this functionality and force users to resort to relatively low-quality screenshots if they want to use the images elsewhere. When building entire websites or exhibits, this question can be even more important. Both WordPress and Omeka allow users to export entire sites. This can be useful if a scholar moves to another institution or if the original institution decides it can no longer maintain the site. Note that individual Omeka exhibits cannot be separated from their collections. This means that if students individually build exhibits as part of a class project, they cannot simply download their part and take it with them after the class is over.

Data Storage and Intellectual Property

Digital humanities pedagogy projects that are entirely or in part public may require special considerations about privacy. In addition to confirming that tools and assignments comply with FERPA regulations, librarians will need to be vigilant about intellectual property rights and make sure students and faculty understand what kinds of content can and cannot be incorporated into public projects. In addition to copyright concerns, librarians should also pay attention to restrictions that may be part of donor agreements for items in special collections. Additionally, it is important to become familiar with the terms and conditions that govern the use of the tools they choose. This is particularly important with free tools that may claim certain rights over user-generated content stored in the application.

Documentation

Documentation refers to the instructions and notes that are available to help users understand how to use a tool. Some tools are extremely well documented with user manuals and how-to videos. Other tools, usually boutique projects developed for specific purposes, have virtually no documentation. For open-source and/or free tools, documentation is particularly crucial because no customer service representatives are available to troubleshoot the project. In addition to (or, if none exists, as a substitute for) documentation, look for detailed, user-created tutorials and instructional videos. Tools with large user communities often have online forums that can be very helpful but check to see if they are currently active.

Stability

The legitimate concern that libraries and archives have for stability is often at odds with the rapid pace of technological change. It is unreasonable to ask for a tool to be available and stable for even five years, but there are strategies for identifying tools that will at least get a class through to the end of the semester. When evaluating potential tools, look for a track record and a large user community. For example, WordPress has been around since 2003 and, as of June 2015, was being used by 23.9 percent of the top one million websites on the Internet.[31] With so many people depending on the tool, there are better odds that it will persist and that a forward migration plan will emerge, which is important if a project needs to live for at least a couple of years. However, if a project is more ephemeral, that could be an opportunity to experiment with something that is interesting but less stable. Regardless of how stable a tool seems to be, it is important to ask the questions and manage expectations appropriately. If something goes wrong, collaborators are likely to be more understanding if everyone understood the technological limitations from the beginning.

Usefulness

The bottom line for any pedagogical tool is whether or not it is useful. Usefulness can be subjective but, in general, useful tools have at least two qualities: they add a new dimension to the way students engage with course material and they are not so distracting that they keep students from learning. For example, students working on an Omeka exhibit will have to describe each item in their collection with Dublin Core. This can be a powerful way for students to wrestle with primary sources. Furthermore, the knowledge that their exhibits will be public adds an additional opportunity for students to demonstrate what Virginia Kuhn and Vicki Callahan call "critical intentionality."[32] They suggest in "Nomadic Archives: Remix and the Drift to Praxis" that, while students may be more engaged because their work is public, "part of being digital deeply means being discriminating about how, when and where one places one's work and information online."[33] Thinking through these issues in the classroom can be a very valuable experience for students who will almost certainly spend a significant amount of their professional life online.

The other end of that spectrum is when the technology gets in the way. For example, students who attempt an overly ambitious text analysis project may find that they spend so much time trying to make the technology work that they only superficially deal with the course material. Technology can also be distracting when there is simply too much of it. In his article "Tired of Tech: Avoiding Tool Fatigue in the Classroom," Brian Croxall found that his urge to create opportunities for his students to experiment with digital tools resulted in underwhelming work and student frustration.[34] When technology is meant to enhance a class rather than define it, tools must be chosen with care and purpose. "Letting our students know what we hope they will learn . . . by using a new tool helps them understand that they are being set a new and unfamiliar task not out of sheer caprice but rather with a pedagogical goal in mind."[35]

HOW CAN A LIBRARY GET READY TO COLLABORATE ON DIGITAL HUMANITIES PEDAGOGY PROJECTS?

By focusing on free, easy-to-use tools and restricting development to the confines of a course, digital humanities pedagogy projects usually require less investment from the library than other types of projects. However, less investment does not mean no investment, and libraries that want to get involved will need to take steps to be ready. This includes looking at staff, infrastructure, and workflows to see if this new work can be managed or if any changes need to be made.

Staff

Where the responsibility for providing digital humanities pedagogy instruction should fall will depend on how a library is organized as well as its institutional culture. Some libraries may have dedicated instructional staff who would be able to add these tools to their set of skills with relative ease. For other libraries, it may be the subject liaisons who should take on this role. Whoever winds up doing the instruction, it is a good opportunity for cross training. This not only increases the number of people who are able to collaborate with classes, but also helps raise awareness about what kinds of projects users are interested in and what tools are being used.

Infrastructure

Most of the examples presented in this chapter require no special infrastructure beyond what is typically found in a research library. The exception to this would be CMSs like WordPress and Omeka that can be installed locally though free, externally hosted versions of each exist. Regardless of whether or not a library wanted officially to offer a tool that requires local hosting, some dedicated "sandbox space" can be extremely useful for testing and evaluating emerging tools. Of course, the presence of a sandbox implies that someone is responsible for managing it and providing assistance when a tool or technique needs to be tested.

Workflows

The decision to collaborate with faculty and students on digital humanities projects will likely lead to many other decisions. If a library is going to offer Omeka for class projects, who will be responsible for managing user accounts and how long will projects remain live? If a project requires digitization of items from special collections, how will those items be added to the queue and how will they be delivered to the class? Regardless of the project, who in the library will be responsible for instruction and how will that be reflected in their job descriptions? If a project is to result in a public-facing product hosted and maintained by the library, what guidelines for scholarly integrity and quality should it meet? There are many ways of dealing with each of these scenarios that will depend on local circumstances and goals. Time can be saved and frustration avoided if paths through these decisions can be established early and projects can be guided along with relative consistency.

CONCLUSION

Digital humanities pedagogy has an experimental, DIY sensibility and uses technology to help students engage with course material. There is an ongoing conversation among faculty who share assignments and tools with one another and it is important for librarians to be a part of that. By partnering with professors who are teaching digital humanities techniques, librarians can build on their role as instructors and reflect the emerging identity of the library as an active and productive space on campus and not only a warehouse of primary and secondary sources. Furthermore, connecting the library to digital humanities work will create new ways for users to work with library collections and give the library a low-stakes way to experiment with emerging tools.

Some common ways for libraries to collaborate with classes include creating digital maps, performing text analysis, and building multimedia websites and online exhibits. As interest in these kinds of projects grows, more tools and techniques for building them will emerge. By remaining current on developments and trends in the field, librarians can be important collaborators in digital humanities. However, to support librarians in this capacity, libraries need to establish effective training opportunities for staff, ensure proper infrastructure is available, and create workflows that will facilitate innovative work.

NOTES

1   See www.hybridpedagogy.com.
2   See http://jitp.commons.gc.cuny.edu.

3   ACRL Board of Directors, *Guidelines for Instruction Programs in Academic Libraries*, (October 2011), www.ala.org/acrl/standards/guidelinesinstruction.

4   Ibid.

5   Cheryl LaGuardia, "Library Instruction in the Digital Age," *Journal of Library Administration* 51, No. 3 (2011): 304.

6   Ibid.

7   See http://dirtdirectory.org.

8   Adeline Koh, "Introducing Digital Humanities Work to Undergraduates: An Overview," *Hybrid Pedagogy* (August 14, 2014), www.hybridpedagogy.com /journal/introducing-digital-humanities-work-undergraduates-overview.

9   Notes on James Joyce's *Ulysses*: https://sites.google.com/site/notesonjamesjoyce.

10   See www.historypin.org.

11   See http://cartodb.com.

12   See http://timemapper.okfnlabs.org.

13   Susan Schreibman, Ray Siemens, and John Unsworth, "The Digital Humanities and Humanities Computing: An Introduction," in *A Companion to Digital Humanities,* ed. Susan Schreibman, Ray Siemens, and John Unsworth (Oxford: Blackwell, 2004), www.digitalhumanities.org/companion.

14   Franco Moretti, "Conjectures on World Literature," *New Left Review* 1 (January–February 2000): 56.

15   Ibid., 57.

16   Stephen Ramsay, *Reading Machines: Toward an Algorithmic Criticism* (Champaign: University of Illinois Press, 2011), 11–17.

17   See http://dsl.richmond.edu/dispatch/pages/home.

18   See http://voyant-tools.org.

19   See http://mallet.cs.umass.edu/topics.php.

20   For an introduction to text analysis for humanists, see Ted Underwood's blog post, "Seven Ways Humanists are Using Computers to Understand Text," *The Stone and the Shell*, http://tedunderwood.com/2015/06/04/seven-ways -humanists-are-using-computers-to-understand-text/.

21   Paul Fyfe, "How to Not Read a Victorian Novel," *Journal of Victorian Culture* 16, No. 1 (2011): 102–06.

22   Ibid., 103.

23   DocSouth Data, http://docsouth.unc.edu/docsouthdata.

24   See http://sites.davidson.edu/dig101/course-guidelines/blogging-guidelines.

25   See www.briancroxall.net/s14dh.

26   See http://omeka.org.

27   See http://gvh.aphdigital.org.

28   Kevin Smith, "Guidelines for Public, Student Class Blogs: Ethics, Legalities, FERPA and More," *HASTAC* (blog), (November 30, 2012, 6:57 pm), www.hastac.org/blogs/superadmin/2012/11/30/guidelines-public-student -class-blogs-ethics-legalities-ferpa-and-more.

29   For an overview of research on Wikipedia, see Mostafa Mesgari et al., "'The Sum of All Human Knowledge': A Systematic Review of Scholarly Research on the Content of Wikipedia," *Journal of the Association for Information Science and Technology* 66, No. 2 (February 2015): 219–45. For guidance on the effective use of Wikipedia in college research, see Stefanie Hilles, "To Use or Not to Use? The Credibility of Wikipedia," *Public Services Quarterly* 10 (July 2014): 245–51.

30   See http://en.wikipedia.org/wiki/Wikipedia:How_to_run_an_edit-a-thon.

31   "Usage of Content Management Systems for Websites," *W3Techs: Web Technology Surveys*, http://w3techs.com/technologies/overview/content _management/all.

32   Virginia Kuhn and Vicki Callahan, "Nomadic Archives: Remix and the Drift to Praxis," in *Digital Humanities Pedagogy: Practices, Principles and Politics*, ed. Brett Hirsch (London: Open Book Publisher, 2012): 306.

33   Ibid.

34   Brian Croxall, "Tired of Tech: Avoiding Tool Fatigue in the Classroom," *Writing and Pedagogy* 5, No. 2 (2013): 249–68.

35   Ibid., 253.

Index